About the Author

NITIN PANDEY works as a Consultant with NIIT. In his two years of work experience at NIIT, he has authored several books, which include *Commerce Server 2000 Configuration and Administration, Visual Studio .NET for Dummies*, and *C# Professional Projects*.

At NIIT, Nitin has been a SME (*Subject Matter Expert*) for seminars and WBTs developed for Microsoft. He has also actively worked on all languages of the .NET Framework, Visual Studio .NET, and .NET Enterprise Servers.

When he is not at work, Nitin enjoys reading and playing volleyball.

Contents at a Glance

Contents

Introduction

ASP (*Active Server Pages*) has long been used as a Web programming language for creating dynamic Web sites. ASP.NET is the next version of ASP 3.0, and it simplifies the development of ASP applications for the Internet. ASP.NET forms an important component of Microsoft's .NET initiative.

With the release of Visual Studio .NET, creating ASP.NET applications has become very simple. Visual Studio .NET provides all of the necessary tools and support for creating ASP.NET applications. The easy-to-use interface of Visual Studio .NET coupled with the power of ASP.NET makes programming Web applications an easy and interesting experience.

ASP.NET Fast & Easy Web Development equips you with the necessary skills to create ASP.NET applications. The characteristic visual emphasis of the book introduces ASP, Visual Basic .NET, and ADO.NET concepts to novice developers. These concepts help you get started with ASP.NET. Thereafter, the book delves into the advanced features of ASP.NET, which include validating user input; developing user controls and composite controls; reading XML data; creating XML Web services; managing, retrieving, formatting, and displaying data using ADO.NET data objects; and creating and implementing Web services.

Who Should Read This Book

Readers who are proficient in HTML and have some experience in Web programming can best utilize this book. You will probably benefit more from the book if you have worked on a scripting language before. After reading this book, you will be proficient in ASP.NET and able to create high-performance dynamic Web sites. If this is your expectation, then this book is certainly for you!

Although the book builds from very elementary concepts, it delves into fairly advanced topics that provide valuable information to both novice and expert developers. If you have already programmed in one or more of the .NET languages, you might want to skip the first five chapters of the book, which lay the foundation for novice developers.

Added Advice to Make You a Pro

To benefit as much as possible from this book, you should download the code for the sample application that is available at http://www.premierpressbooks.com/downloads.asp. The sample application runs through all of the important chapters of the book, with each chapter building on the application in some way. Therefore, as you read the book, you will have a professional application ready to use.

After you read this book, your next objective should be to create an application that is similar to (or even more advanced than) the application developed in this book. This will give you adequate hands-on practice in creating ASP.NET applications. You should also regularly visit some of the useful Web sites on ASP.NET that I have listed in Appendix D, "Online Resources for ASP.NET." These Web sites provide the latest information on the developments in ASP.NET.

Conventions Used in This Book

In the book, you will find several special elements that will make using this book easier.

- Tips give you helpful information or shortcuts to accomplish a goal more quickly or easily.

- Notes provide you with additional information or background about a given topic.

- Cautions warn you of potential pitfalls or glitches in an application or procedure.

1

Introducing the .NET Initiative

ASP.NET is the follow-up to ASP 3.0. It is a key component of the .NET initiative. The .NET initiative was launched by Microsoft to enable application providers to deliver customer-oriented solutions. The foremost advantage of this initiative is the ability to provide a customized solution that enables an application provider to deploy applications that match the exact requirements of customers.

This chapter provides an introduction to the .NET initiative and the products and technologies included in the initiative. Next, the chapter discusses the components of the .NET Framework, which is a key enabler of the .NET initiative. Finally, the chapter covers the types of applications that you can develop with ASP.NET and the role of Visual Studio. NET in application development. Put briefly, in this chapter you'll learn about:

- Products and technologies associated with the .NET initiative
- Applications created using ASP.NET

Products and Technologies in the .NET Initiative

The .NET initiative was introduced in response to the shift in focus from desktop computing to distributed computing. In distributed computing, a number of applications are integrated to provide a solution. For example, if you need to display a list of the latest books published by a number of publishers, you might implement a Web site that retrieves details of new books from publishers.

With the focus on distributed computing, it became imperative to devise a mechanism by which resources at remote locations could be integrated with the existing line-of-business applications. The .NET initiative is the outcome of this necessity.

With the implementation of the .NET initiative, you can integrate your business processes or automate your business transactions with business partners to enhance customer experiences and improve business productivity.

The .NET initiative is being implemented by more than just one product. A number of products and technologies that make up .NET enterprise servers, the .NET Framework, and Visual Studio. NET implement the .NET initiative. In this section, you will learn about the components of the .NET initiative and how ASP.NET fits into the initiative.

.NET Enterprise Servers

.NET enterprise servers are sets of servers that are used to build, host, and maintain .NET applications. The .NET enterprise servers include Application Center 2000, BizTalk Server 2002, Commerce Server 2002, Content Management Server 2001, Exchange Server 2000, Host Integration Server 2000, Internet Security and Acceleration (ISA) Server 2000, SharePoint Portal Server 2000, SQL Server 2000, and Windows 2000 Server.

Although all .NET enterprise servers are equally important in their domain, I will describe only those servers that are related to ASP.NET applications or their deployment.

Commerce Server 2002

Commerce Server 2002 is a .NET enterprise server that is used to create scalable business-to-business and business-to-consumer Web sites. With Commerce Server 2002, you can create highly personalized Web sites that can support personalized advertisement targeting, a million user profiles, and an elaborate set of catalogs.

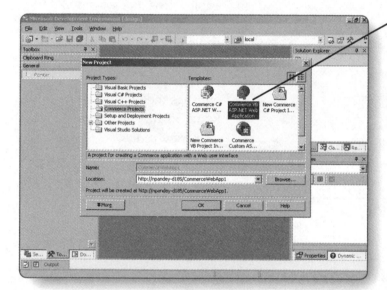

You can create Web sites for Commerce Server 2002 using either ASP.NET or ASP 3.0. When you use ASP.NET to create Commerce Server 2002 Web sites, you can use Visual Studio .NET as the development platform because Commerce Server 2002 is directly integrated with Visual Studio .NET. When you install Commerce Server 2002 on your computer, enterprise templates for creating Commerce Server 2002 Web sites are automatically added to Visual Studio .NET. The enterprise templates for Commerce Server 2002 enable you to create a new Commerce Server 2002/ASP.NET Web site. These templates use Visual Basic .NET and Visual C# as the scripting languages. See Chapter 4, "Visual Basic .NET Basics," for more information about enterprise templates.

TIP

You can use two languages for server-side scripting in ASP.NET—Visual Basic .NET and Visual C#. You can even use a combination of the two languages for the same application. For example, you can create the default page of a Web site, Default.aspx, in Visual Basic .NET and the menu of the Web site, Menu.aspx, in Visual C#. See Chapter 4 for more information.

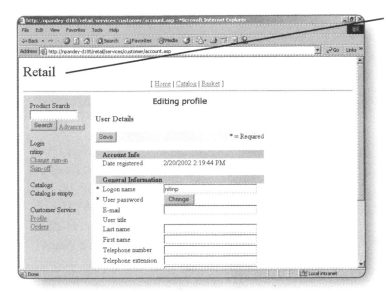

Commerce Server 2002 also includes sample sites known as Solution Sites, which can be used out of the box to create business-to-business and business-to-consumer applications. For example, the Retail Solution Site provides complete functionality for you to create a business-to-consumer Web site. You can enhance the functionality of the Retail Solution Site or customize it for your business requirements.

NOTE

When this book was written, Commerce Server 2002 was in the Beta 1 stage. The Retail Solution Site in the Beta 1 version is built on ASP 3.0. However, this Solution Site might be built on ASP.NET by the time the final version of Commerce Server 2002 is shipped.

BizTalk Server 2002

BizTalk Server 2002 offers a complete business-to-business solution for enterprises to integrate their internal applications and securely connect to business partners on the Internet. It includes extensive support for industry standards, such as XML (*Extensible Markup Language*), SOAP (*Simple Object Access Protocol*), and PKI (*Public Key Infrastructure*). By including support for these standards, BizTalk Server 2002 enables you to exchange data with business partners in a platform-independent manner.

After you install BizTalk Server 2002, you can use the Microsoft BizTalk Server 2002 Toolkit for Microsoft .NET to develop BizTalk Server 2002 solutions using Visual Studio .NET. The toolkit also includes comprehensive documentation about integrating Visual Studio .NET with BizTalk Server 2002.

ISA Server 2000

Internet Security and Acceleration Server 2000, commonly referred to as ISA Server 2000, can be used by organizations to enable Internet access for their employees. ISA Server 2000 includes several advanced features that enable you to block access to restricted Web sites and monitor Internet usage.

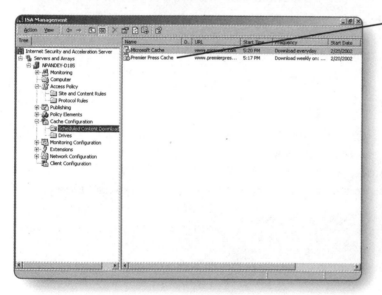

You can also deploy ISA Server 2000 as a *cache server*. As a cache server, the server stores a copy of the data that it has retrieved from one or more data sources. The stored data is referred to as a cache.

By caching data, you can speed up data retrieval, because you don't need to connect to the main data source every time the request for data is made. By caching content of frequently visited Web sites, a cache server can speed up Internet access.

For example, if the employees of an organization access http://www.microsoft.com frequently, ISA Server can cache this Web site and retrieve site data from the cache when a user requests it. Such a feature improves the response time for a request and optimizes Internet usage.

Application Center 2000

Application Center 2000 is used to ensure high availability of Web sites. Availability of a Web site is defined as the percentage of time that the site remains operational. Application Center 2000 ensures high availability of Web sites by implementing NLB (*Network Load Balancing*). In NLB, a cluster is created and a number of computers are added to it. Each computer has an identical directory structure and is connected to a network. A Web site is installed on each computer in the cluster, and the cluster is exposed to the Internet by a single IP address.

When a user requests a resource, Application Center 2000 identifies which computer on the network is least busy and directs the request to that computer. Similarly, if a computer in the cluster stops responding, it is dynamically removed from the cluster, and other computers in the cluster start processing the requests for the non-responding computer.

SQL Server 2000

SQL Server 2000 is an RDBMS (*Relational Database Management System*) that can be used for large-scale enterprise transactions. SQL Server 2000 includes built-in support for XML. Therefore, you can exchange data between databases in XML format or construct XML documents from the results of SQL (*Structured Query Language*) statements that are run in SQL Server databases.

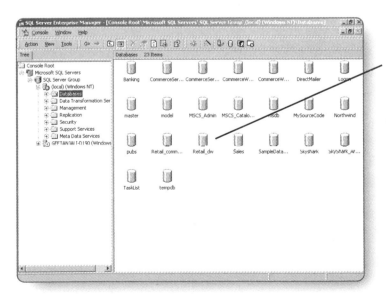

SQL Server includes the Enterprise Manager, which can be used to perform all the tasks that were conventionally performed using SQL statements. Enterprise Manager has a GUI (*Graphical User Interface*) that enables you to easily perform common tasks, such as creating databases and tables and managing relationships between tables.

I will use SQL Server 2000 to create databases, tables, and stored procedures for explaining the data management capabilities of Visual Studio .NET. For more information about using SQL Server, see Chapter 4, "Visual Basic .NET Basics."

.NET Framework

The .NET Framework provides the necessary classes and namespaces to create .NET applications. The .NET Framework is made up of three components—the CLR (*Common Language Runtime*), the class library, and ASP.NET. In this section, you will learn about each of the three components of the .NET Framework.

Common Language Runtime

One of the foremost objectives in developing .NET languages is addressing the need for cross-language interoperability. Therefore, a developer should be able to extend an application that is developed in Visual C# (a .NET language) by using Visual Basic .NET. To ensure interoperability between applications, Microsoft introduced the CLR. The CLR, which is the common run-time across all .NET languages, is responsible for:

• Efficient execution of code

• Memory and thread management

• Exception handling

The CLR includes several features that help to accomplish these tasks. For example, to ensure that code is optimized, the .NET Framework compiles it as MSIL (*Microsoft Intermediate Language*) code. The MSIL code can be readily interpreted when it is executed. In addition to MSIL interpretation of code, I'll cover the other two important features of CLR—garbage collection and exception handling.

GARBAGE COLLECTION

The CLR uses a garbage-collection mechanism to implement memory management. When you declare objects in a program, these objects occupy memory space. When an application is running, a number of objects might collect and occupy an inordinate amount of memory space, and some of these objects might no longer be needed by the application. In the earlier versions of programming languages, you had to explicitly remove these objects from memory. However, in .NET the garbage collector automatically removes objects that are no longer needed from the memory. This ensures that your application executes optimally.

EXCEPTION HANDLING

In .NET, you can create an application in one language and debug it in another. Consider an example. You have created one component of your application in Visual C# and you are using it in another application that was developed using Visual Basic .NET. If the component that you have developed in Visual C# throws an exception, you don't need to debug it in Visual C#; you can debug it in Visual Basic .NET.

Similarly, when an application throws an exception during execution, you can attach a debugger to the application to debug it, irrespective of the language in which the application was originally developed. See Chapter 20, "Debugging ASP.NET Applications," for more information about debugging and exception-handling techniques.

TIP

To develop mobile applications in Visual Studio .NET, you need to download and install the Mobile Internet Toolkit. I'll describe the procedure for creating mobile applications in Chapter 16, "Building Mobile Web Applications."

Class Library

The .NET Framework includes a comprehensive class library that provides the necessary classes and interfaces to access system resources. By using the .NET Framework class library, you can develop applications ranging from ones that run on a stand-alone computer to ones that are deployed for access on the Internet and mobile phones.

Classes of the .NET Framework class library are available in multiple *namespaces*. Namespaces, In turn, are available In one or more *assemblies*. This section includes a description of assemblies and namespaces.

ASSEMBLIES

Assemblies are the basic units of the .NET Framework. They provide the necessary namespaces and types that can be used to create .NET applications. Assemblies are useful in defining the scope of namespaces.

Assemblies can be one of two types—static or dynamic. *Static assemblies* are stored on the hard disk. They typically include interfaces, classes, and the resources required to implement the interfaces and classes. On the other hand, *dynamic assemblies* contain classes that are run directly from memory and optionally stored on the hard disk after the classes have been accessed.

NAMESPACES

Classes are organized in namespaces based on their functionality. For example, classes pertaining to Web applications are available in the System.Web namespace.

Similarly, classes pertaining to debugging and tracing are available in the System.Diagnostics namespace. When you create an application, you can import the namespaces that correspond to the classes you want to use in your application. To differentiate between namespaces and classes, the .NET Framework uses a . (dot) to separate the two. Therefore, System.Console represents the Console class in the System namespace.

> **NOTE**
>
> A namespace can include a number of namespaces within it. For example, System.Diagnostics represents the Diagnostics namespace within the System namespace.

ASP.NET

ASP.NET is a Web development technology. It includes a number of new features that make it much different than ASP 3.0. Some of the new and important features of ASP.NET include

- **Support for multiple programming languages**. In ASP 3.0, all server-side programming is done using VBScript. In ASP.NET, you have the option to use Visual Basic .NET and Visual C# to develop your applications. You can use both languages in the same application as long as they are used in different Web pages.

- **Separation of HTML code from logic**. In ASP.NET, you can write the HTML code in the .aspx file and the code for programming logic in the code-behind file (.aspx.vb if you use Visual Basic .NET or .aspx.cs if you use Visual C#). The advantage of separating code from programming logic is that you don't need to worry about how the output will be rendered in the Web page; Web designers can handle that task.

- **Configuration of XML-based applications**. You can configure ASP.NET applications using the Web.config file, which is an XML-based file. The advantage of using the Web.config file for storing application configurations is that you can specify different configuration settings for different subdirectories of an application. Therefore, Web pages that should be viewed by authorized users only can be placed in a separate directory from Web pages that can be viewed by unauthenticated users. You can then apply different configuration settings to pages in these subdirectories.

NOTE

ASP 3.0 applications were configured using IIS (*Internet Information Server*). In addition to configuring ASP.NET applications using the Web.config file, you can also configure them using IIS, if you choose. ASP.NET provides you with the flexibility of using the Web.config file or IIS.

- **Enhanced debugging support**. ASP.NET applications can be debugged using the Visual Studio .NET debugger, which provides a set of useful debugging tools that can help you detect problems in your application code and rectify them with minimal effort. In addition to the debugging tools provided by Visual Studio .NET, you can use the Debug and Trace classes of the System.Diagnostics namespace to debug your application.

These features of ASP.NET are only the tip of the iceberg. This book will allow you to explore the other features of ASP.NET and gain hands-on expertise in the areas mentioned.

Visual Studio .NET

Visual Studio .NET is the development suite for creating .NET applications. Using Visual Studio .NET, you can create applications in Visual C++ .NET, Visual C#, and Visual Basic .NET. Visual C# and Visual Basic .NET enable you to use the ASP.NET technology for creating Web applications. However, if you need to create Web applications in Visual C++ .NET, you need to use ATL Server.

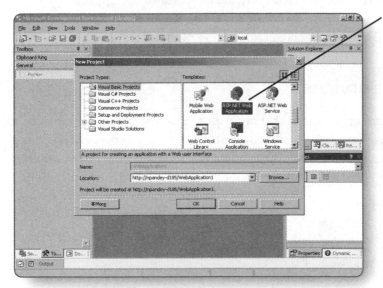

In this book, you will use Visual Studio .NET to create ASP.NET applications. As you will see, Visual Studio .NET greatly simplifies the development of ASP.NET applications. It enables you to create ASP.NET Web applications, ASP.NET Web services, and controls for Web applications. Of these applications, ASP.NET Web applications and ASP.NET Web services are the key components that are used for implementing the .NET initiative.

Applications Created in ASP.NET

In ASP.NET, you primarily create two types of applications—ASP.NET Web applications and ASP.NET Web services. The procedures for developing these applications aren't much different, especially when you use Visual Studio .NET. However, the implementation of these applications differs significantly. In this section, I'll discuss Web applications and Web services and explain how the two, along with the other components of the .NET initiative, meet the objectives of the .NET initiative.

ASP.NET Web Applications

Applications that you commonly browse on the Internet are ASP.NET Web applications. For example, if you create a Web site in ASP.NET and host it on the Internet to be accessed directly by users, your Web site is an ASP.NET Web application.

ASP.NET Web applications are made up of one or more Web forms. Web forms are ASP.NET components that allow you to display the interface of the application and interact with users to accept or display information. See Chapter 3, "Exploring the New Features of ASP.NET," for a detailed explanation of Web forms.

ASP.NET Web Services

ASP.NET Web services are applications that are exposed on the Internet. However, users do not access these applications directly. Instead, they are accessed by other applications through the Internet. The applications that access Web services use them to display the applications to users. Thus, Web services are services provided to applications for making data accessible.

Consider an online book retailer who stocks books published by 10 publishers. Suppose the retailer requires an updated list of books that are being published and also needs to send the details of all orders to publishers. Implementing this scenario using Web applications is not easy.

However, in this scenario, Web services find an ideal implementation.

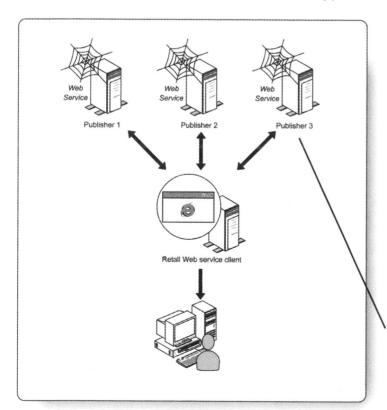

Each publisher can host a Web service, which allows Web service clients to retrieve catalogs of available books. The retailer can host a Web service client that implements each Web service and displays the catalogs of books on the Web site. For a detailed explanation of creating and implementing Web services, see Chapter 15, "Building ASP.NET Web Services."

Implementing the .NET Initiative

Up to this point, I have talked about the components of the .NET initiative separately. The components of .NET Framework blend together to achieve the common objectives for the .NET initiative, which were discussed in the "Products and Technologies in the .NET Initiative" section of this chapter. Now you need to understand how these components blend to offer a customized solution.

One of the foremost objectives of the .NET initiative is to provide a customized solution that results in an enriching user experience. For example, if a user visits a Web site, the Web site should be able to identify the user and load the user's preferences. To enable this functionality, Microsoft provides a set of services that are referred to as My Services. A part of these services is Microsoft's .NET Passport authentication service, which is the default authentication service used by Microsoft Hotmail and MSN.

You can integrate a Web application with the .NET Passport authentication service to enable passport authentication on your Web site.

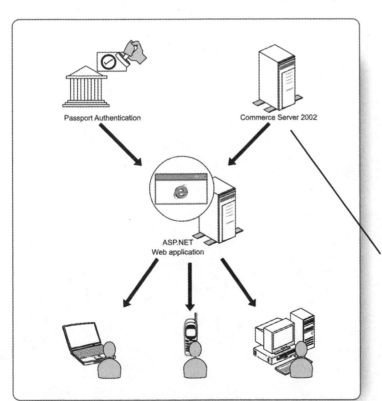

Passport Authentication

Commerce Server 2002

ASP.NET
Web application

Commerce Server 2002, a .NET enterprise server, offers integration with Microsoft's .NET Passport authentication service. Therefore, you can create an ASP.NET Commerce Server Web site using Visual Studio .NET and implement passport authentication on the site. If a user who has logged on to the Passport authentication service visits your Web site, he is automatically recognized on the Web site, and his preferences are automatically loaded. You can also offer other customized services, such as mobile access, to enable users to access your Web site through mobile applications.

As you go on reading this book, you will learn that a solution similar to this one is easy to create with ASP.NET.

2

Installing and Configuring Visual Studio .NET

To create ASP.NET applications, all you need is a text editor. However, that is not the recommended way to create applications, and it is certainly not an easy one. When you code ASP pages using a text editor such as Notepad, you need to code the HTML (*Hypertext Markup Language*) and ASP.NET code without the help of any utility.

Instead of using a text editor, the easiest way to code ASP.NET applications is to use Microsoft's Visual Studio .NET development tool. Visual Studio .NET offers many advantages over a text editor. For example, it uses color schemes for keywords and values, which makes the code easier to read. It also includes an auto-complete feature that completes common entries as you type the code. You will discover many other advantages of using Visual Studio .NET to create ASP.NET applications as you proceed with this book. In this chapter, you'll learn how to:

- Install Visual Studio .NET
- Configure Visual Studio .NET

Installing Visual Studio .NET

To install Visual Studio .NET, you first need to ensure that your computer meets the necessary hardware and software requirements. Next, you need to install prerequisite software, which is bundled in the Visual Studio .NET installation package. Finally, you can install Visual Studio .NET.

This section covers the hardware and software requirements for installing Visual Studio. NET, as well as the installation steps.

Hardware and Software Requirements

Visual Studio .NET includes the Professional, Enterprise Developer, Enterprise Architect, and Academic editions. The components that are shipped with Visual Studio .NET vary depending on the edition that you purchase. For example, the Enterprise Architect edition includes Visio-based modeling tools that are not included in the Enterprise Developer version of Visual Studio .NET. Regardless of the edition of Visual Studio .NET, the hardware and software requirements are more or less same.

Hardware Requirements for Visual Studio .NET

The hardware requirements for installing Visual Studio .NET are

- 600 MHz Pentium II microprocessor
- 3.5 GB of available hard disk space
- 256 MB of RAM
- 52X CD-ROM drive
- Internet connection (to check for product updates)

Software Requirements for Visual Studio .NET

The software requirements for installing Visual Studio .NET are

- Windows 2000 (Server or Professional) or Windows XP Professional
- Windows .NET Server
- IIS (*Internet Information Server*) 5.0 or later

> **NOTE**
>
> Although Visual Studio .NET also can run on Windows NT 4.0 Server or Windows NT Workstation, these platforms do not support ASP.NET. Therefore, you cannot use these platforms to run ASP.NET applications.

Aside from the software requirements, Visual Studio .NET also requires updated versions of several Windows components, which are listed in the following section, "Installing Windows Update Components." However, if the updated versions are not available on your computer, they will be installed when you install Visual Studio .NET.

Having examined the requirements for installing Visual Studio .NET, you can proceed to the installation of the Windows components, which will update your system as a preliminary step to installing Visual Studio .NET.

Installing Windows Update Components

If you have not applied patches for Windows components that are installed on your computer, the setup program will install the following updated versions of the components.

- Windows 2000 Server Service Pack 2
- Microsoft FrontPage 2000 Server Extensions Service Release 1.2
- Microsoft Windows Installer 2.0
- Microsoft Windows Management Infrastructure
- Microsoft FrontPage 2000 Web Extensions Client
- Setup Runtime Files
- Microsoft Internet Explorer 6.0 and Internet Tools
- Microsoft Data Access Components 2.7
- Microsoft Jet 4.0 Service Pack 3
- Microsoft .NET Framework

> **NOTE**
>
> You do not need to determine which of these components you must install. The setup program automatically determines the configuration of your computer and installs the necessary software updates.

If you have purchased the CD-ROM package of Visual Studio .NET, the Windows Update components will be available on the last CD-ROM that is included in the package. If you have purchased the DVD package of Visual Studio .NET, Windows update components are available on the DVD-ROM that comes in the package. In either case, you will need to run the Setup.exe file from the CD-ROM or DVD-ROM.

To install Windows component updates, follow these steps.

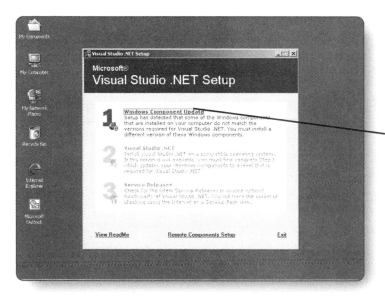

1. Double-click on the Setup.exe file in the installation package. The Microsoft Visual Studio .NET Setup dialog box will open.

2. Click on the Windows Component Update option. The End User License Agreement screen will appear.

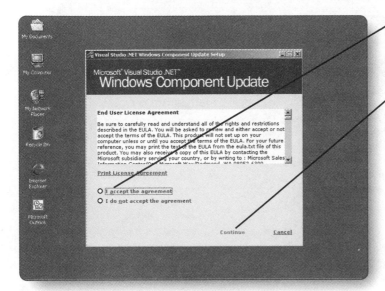

3. Click on the I Accept the Agreement radio button. The option will be selected.

4. Click on the Continue link. The Windows Component Update screen will appear, listing the Windows components that need to be updated.

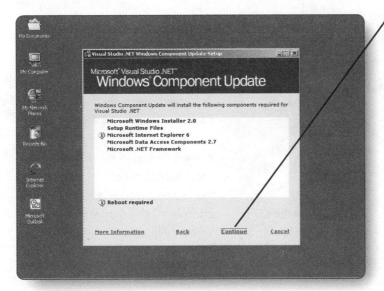

5. Click on the Continue link. The Optional Automatic Log On screen will appear.

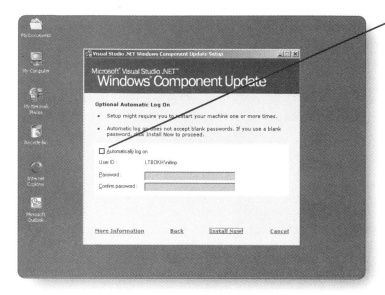

6. Specify log-on information to enable the computer to log you on every time your computer reboots during the installation process. To specify log-on information, click on the Automatically Log On check box. The option will be selected.

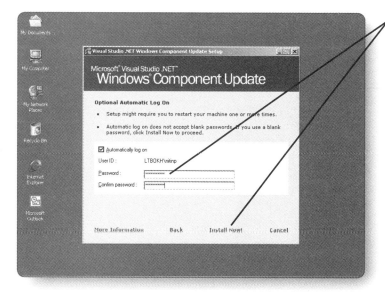

7. Type your Windows password in the Password and Confirm Password text boxes and click on Install Now! The setup program will install Visual Studio .NET on your computer and automatically restart your computer when required. When the installation of updated Windows components is complete, the Congratulations screen will appear.

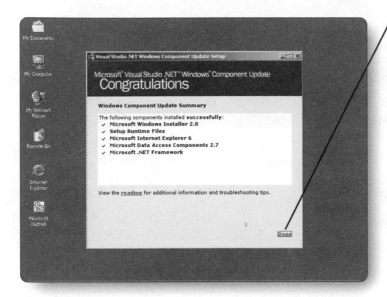

8. Click on Done. The Microsoft Visual Studio .NET Setup screen, which was the first screen to appear when you started the installation program, will reappear.

You have successfully completed the installation of Windows Update components. You can now proceed to installing Visual Studio .NET.

Visual Studio .NET Installation

To install Visual Studio .NET, simply start the setup program from where you left it after installing Windows Update components. Follow these steps to install Visual Studio .NET.

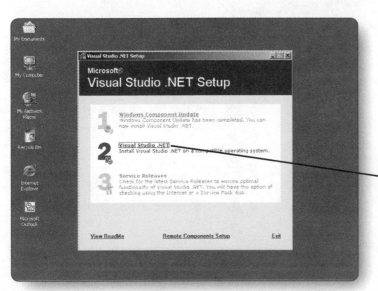

1. Double-click on the Setup.exe file on the DVD-ROM or the first CD-ROM that came with the installation package. The Microsoft Visual Studio .NET Setup dialog box will open.

2. Click on the Visual Studio .NET option. The Microsoft Visual Studio .NET Setup Start page will appear.

3. Click on the I Accept the Agreement option to accept the license agreement. The option will be selected.

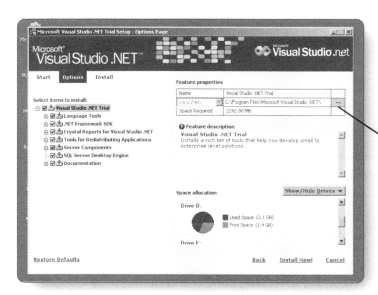

4. Specify the product key in the Product Key fields and click on Continue. The Microsoft Visual Studio .NET Setup Options page will appear.

5. The default location where Visual Studio .NET will be installed is given in the Local Path field. If you need to change this location, click on the Ellipsis button next to the Local Path field. The Select a Destination Folder dialog box will open.

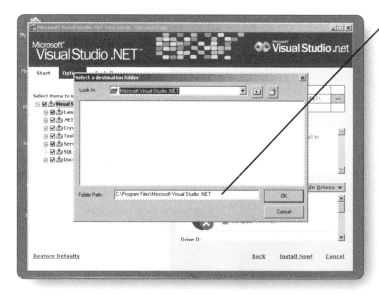

6. Type the location where you want to install Visual Studio .NET in the Folder Path text box and click on OK. The location that you selected will be displayed in the Local Path field of the Microsoft Visual Studio .NET Setup Options page.

7. Click on Install Now! When the installation is complete, the Setup is Complete screen will appear.

8. Click on Done to close the screen and complete the Visual Studio .NET setup. You will be returned to the Microsoft Visual Studio .NET Setup screen. The Service Releases link on this screen will be enabled, so you can check for software updates.

Checking for Product Upgrades

To check for updates to Visual Studio .NET, follow these steps.

1. Click on the Service Releases link on the Microsoft Visual Studio .NET Setup screen. The Service Releases dialog box will open.

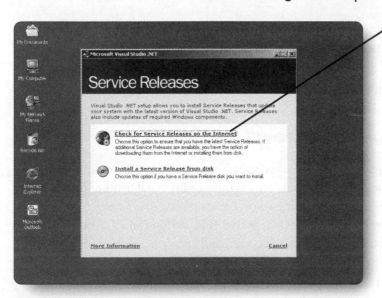

2. Click on the Check for Service Releases on the Internet link to check for Visual Studio .NET updates on the Internet. The setup program will check for software updates on the Internet and notify you about whether or not updates are available.

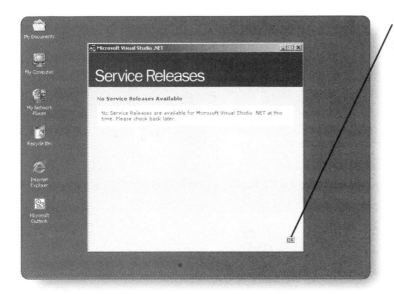

3. Click on OK to close the Service Releases dialog box.

Configuring Visual Studio .NET

Visual Studio .NET is highly customizable, which can simplify your work. The toolbars and windows in Visual Studio .NET can be conveniently positioned. You can also change the default code coloration scheme and the font size that is used for displaying code.

The objective of this section is to get you accustomed to the interface of Visual Studio .NET. In this section, you will read about the windows available in Visual Studio .NET and their purposes. You will also learn how to customize the Visual Studio .NET interface.

Visual Studio .NET Windows

Visual Studio .NET includes a number of windows that display information about your project and provide access to tools and resources in Visual Studio .NET and on the computer. For example, the Server Explorer provides access to the SQL Server databases, event logs, and performance counters that are on the local computer. The Toolbox enables you to access the clipboard and provides controls that you can add to an ASP.NET page. In this section, I will list the windows provided by Visual Studio .NET, their utilities, and how you can access them.

Server Explorer

The Server Explorer is used to access the resources on the local computer. To open the Server Explorer, click on the View menu and select Server Explorer.

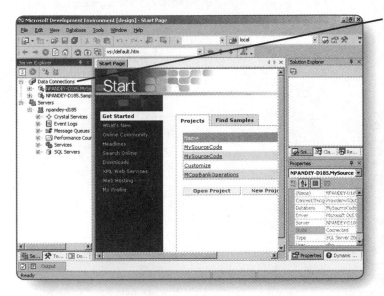

In the Server Explorer, the data connections that you establish to various databases while coding your application are listed in the Data Connections section. Next, the crystal services, event logs, message queues, performance counters, services, and SQL servers installed on the local computer are displayed.

One of the most common uses of the Server Explorer is for creating connections to SQL Server databases and tables. To create a connection to a SQL Server database, you simply drag the database from the Server Explorer to your Web form. To learn more about this technique, see Chapter 10, "Managing Data from ASP.NET Applications."

A common feature across all Visual Studio .NET windows is the Auto Hide feature. The Auto Hide feature enables you to collapse a window to increase the area available for working on your form. To enable the Auto Hide feature, click on the Auto Hide button on any window.

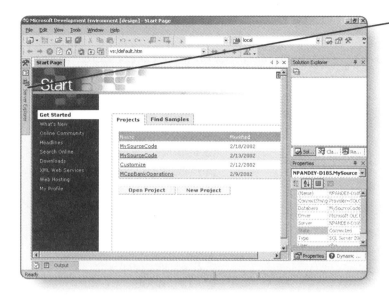

When you move the cursor away from a window, the window will automatically collapse to the side, thus increasing the area available on the screen for working. The full window will reappear every time you move the cursor over the collapsed window.

You can restore the original state of the window by clicking on the Auto Hide button again.

Toolbox

The Toolbox window, commonly referred to as the Toolbox, includes Web forms and HTML controls that you can add to your Web forms. It also includes controls that are used to interact with databases. To access the Toolbox, click on the View menu and select Toolbox.

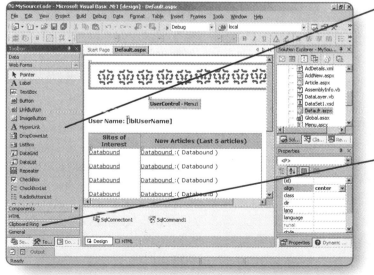

If you have not opened a .NET application, the Toolbox will not display any controls. However, when you open an application, the Toolbox will list the controls that you can add to your Web form.

The Toolbox also includes a Clipboard Ring section that is used for accessing the clipboard. All code snippets that you copy from your application are stored in the Clipboard Ring.

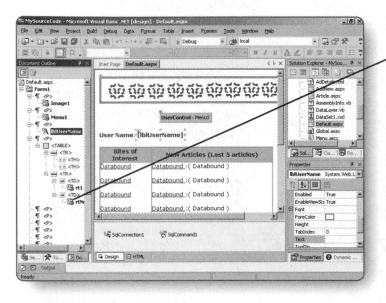

Document Outline

The Document Outline window can be accessed from the View menu. Just like the Toolbox, the Document Outline is only useful when you open an application. When you open a Web form in your application, the Document Outline displays the HTML tags and the controls that are used in the form. This window can be useful for identifying extra paragraph marks and unnecessary tags that you might have used while designing your form.

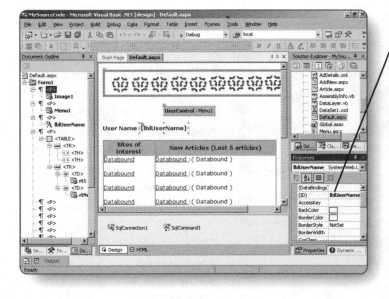

Properties

The Properties window is used to view and change the properties of currently selected elements on a form. For example, if you select a form, the Properties window will display the properties of the form. Similarly, if you select a database table from the Server Explorer, the Properties window will display the properties of the table. To access the Properties window, click on the View menu and select Properties Window.

As you will see, the Properties window is the most frequently used window in an application.

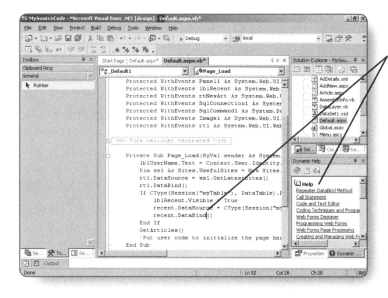

Dynamic Help

The Dynamic Help window is a handy tool to view help topics about the current task that you are performing in your application. For example, if you type the DataBind method of the Repeater class, the Dynamic Help window will display a link to the Repeater.DataBind method.

The Dynamic Help window is very useful when you are not sure of the definition of a function and you want to look it up in the documentation of Visual Studio .NET.

Solution Explorer

The Solution Explorer displays the details of references to other projects and Web forms that you have added to your application. You can also add references to

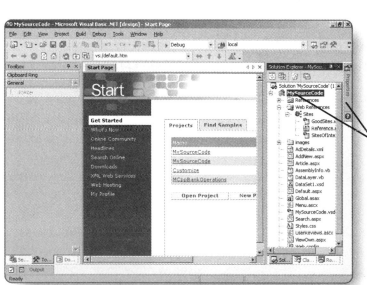

projects and add new forms and graphics to your application using the Solution Explorer. To open the Solution Explorer, click on the View menu and select Solution Explorer.

The files and references to other applications that have been added to an ASP.NET project are displayed in the Solution Explorer. Notice that I have hidden the Properties and Dynamic Help windows by using the Auto Hide feature.

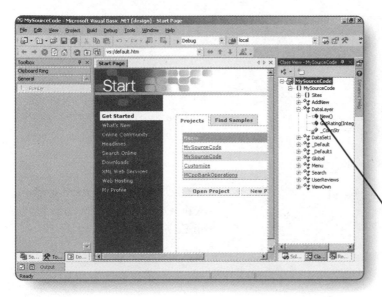

Class View

The Class View window shows the classes and namespaces that are defined in your application. You can use this window as a reference to the namespaces, classes, and functions that are available for your application.

To open the Class View window, click on the View menu and select Class View. The Class View window for an ASP.NET project is shown here. The DataLayer class has been expanded to show the methods and variables that are defined in the class.

Resource View

The Resource View window displays the resources that you have added to your application. This window is not really useful in ASP.NET applications. However, in Visual C++ .NET applications, you can use the Resource View window to view the bitmaps, dialog boxes, menus, and string tables that you have added to your application.

Customizing Visual Studio .NET

You use the Options dialog box to customize the Visual Studio .NET development environment. The Options dialog box includes several options that allow you to configure the font and color of the user interface elements and the startup settings of Visual Studio .NET. To access the Options dialog box, follow these steps.

1. Click on Tools. The Tools menu will appear.

2. Click on Options. The Options dialog box will open.

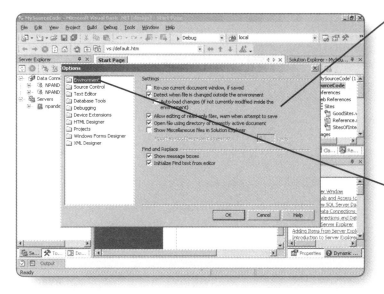

A number of sections are available in the left panel. When you click on a section, the property pages that correspond to the section will appear in the right panel. You can select one or more property pages to view properties and change them.

3. Click on the Environment section. The property pages in the Environment section will appear.

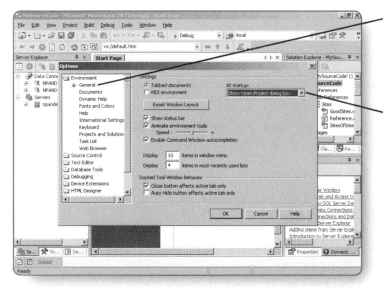

4. Click on the General property page. The properties in the General property page will appear.

5. You can change one or more properties in the General property page. For example, to show the Open Project dialog box every time you open Visual Studio .NET, click on the At Startup drop-down list. The contents of the At Startup list will appear.

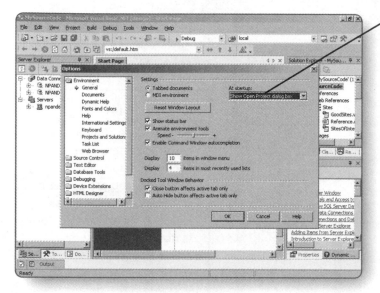

6. Click on Show Open Project Dialog Box option. The option will be selected.

7. You can configure many other properties of Visual Studio .NET using the Options dialog box. For example, click on the Auto-Load Changes check box in the Documents property page to load changes to the .aspx files when these files are changed outside of the Visual Studio .NET development environment.

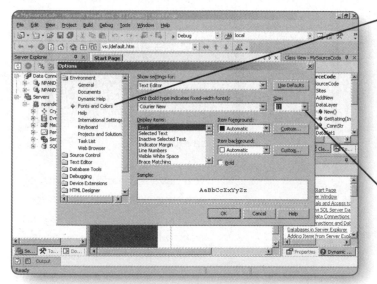

8. You can also change the default font size and the color that is used to display code if you have difficulty reading small fonts. To change the font size, click on the Fonts and Colors property page. The property page will be displayed.

9. Click on the Size drop-down list. The available font sizes will appear.

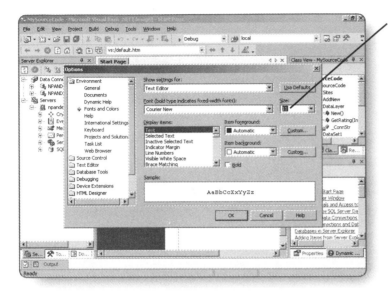

10. Click on 11. The font size for the Code Editor window will be set to 11.

TIP

You can also change the color scheme that is used for code coloration. For example, you can select a different color for break-points if the existing color is not legible. However, to ensure optimal clarity of code, I recommend that you retain the default color scheme.

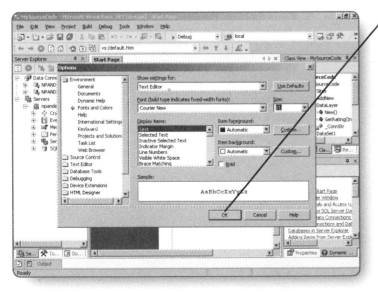

11. After making the required changes in the Options dialog box, click on OK. The Options dialog box will close and the changes that you made will be saved.

You have learned the basics of configuring the Visual Studio .NET environment. The easiest way to learn to use advanced features for configuring the environment is to practice using these features. You will have ample opportunity to gain hands-on expertise in Visual Studio .NET as you read this book.

3

Exploring the New Features of ASP.NET

You can use Visual Studio .NET to create different types of Web applications. The Web applications that you can create include simple Web sites containing simple HTML pages, Web services that provide access to data, and complex business-to-business applications that integrate one or more business processes across organizations. ASP.NET is the technology that makes creating all of these applications possible.

This chapter introduces you to the features and advantages of ASP.NET. In this chapter, you'll learn how to:

- Get started with the basics of ASP.NET
- Use Web forms

Getting Started with ASP.NET

ASP.NET is a compiled programming environment that uses the .NET Framework to create Web applications. Thus, all of the features of the .NET platform are available to an ASP.NET application.

ASP.NET is flexible in that it allows developers to write applications in any language offered by the .NET Framework, such as Visual Basic .NET and Visual C#. ASP.NET also has a powerful event-driven architecture that is based on the .NET CLR environment. See Chapter 1, "Introducing the .NET Initiative," for more information on the CLR. To get started with ASP.NET, you need to understand its architecture.

Understanding the ASP.NET Application Architecture

An ASP.NET page is composed of three elements—directives, layout, and code. Explanations of these elements follow.

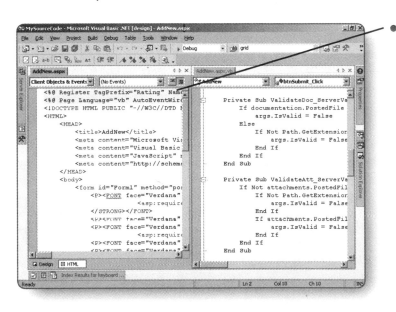

- **Directives**. You can use directives to insert messages for instructing the compiler and browser when they process a page. Directives specify the language used, indicate the transaction support required, and specify the page to which a user should be redirected in case of an error in the page that is being processed.

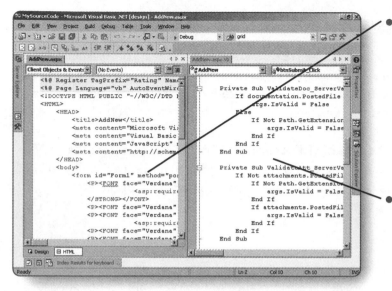

Layout. The layout of a page determines which HTML elements are present on a Web page and how they should be arranged. You can write the HTML code for defining the layout or drag controls from the Toolbox to the form.

Code. The code defines the classes, functions, and controls that are shared by multiple pages of an application or by different applications on the same server.

Web applications created in ASP.NET are composed of many files with different file names and extensions. This is because ASP.NET stores code for the user interface and the program logic in different files. Code separation ensures that the application is well structured and performs optimally.

ASP.NET files by default have an .aspx or .ascx extension. The .aspx files represent the Web forms, and the .ascx files represent the user controls created for a Web application. In addition to these files, there are other files that contain the code for an application. The extensions of the code files depend on the programming language used. For example, a C# file would have the extension .aspx.cs.

Examining the Features of ASP.NET

ASP.NET allows developers to create Web applications in the programming language of their choice. It also offers a number of other features that make creating Web applications easy. The following sections briefly discuss some of the important features of ASP.NET.

Common Language Runtime

ASP.NET runs in the context of the .NET CLR. A CLR provides a programming interface between the .NET Framework and the programming languages available for the .NET platform. The CLR simplifies application development and provides a robust and secure execution environment.

By being a component of the .NET Framework, ASP.NET benefits from the .NET Framework's features, such as cross-language integration and exception handling, automatic memory management, and enhanced deployment support.

Caching

Caching is a technique for storing frequently used data in an application. By caching data, you can improve the performance of your Web application, because retrieving data stored within an application is faster than retrieving data from any other location, such as a database. ASP.NET provides three types of caching support for Web applications.

- **Page-output caching**. Page-output caching is a powerful technique that increases request/response throughput by caching the content generated from dynamic pages. This technique is useful when the contents of an entire page can be cached.

- **Fragment caching**. Fragment caching is used to cache portions of a response generated by a request. This kind of caching is helpful when it is not practical to cache an entire page.

- **Data caching**. Data caching is used to cache arbitrary objects programmatically. To support this type of caching, ASP.NET provides a cache engine that allows programmers to easily retain data across requests.

For more information on implementing these types of caching, see Chapter 18, "Caching in ASP.NET Applications."

Debugging and Tracing

ASP.NET provides a rich debugging environment. It provides cross-language and cross-computer debugging support for your applications. ASP.NET is compiled, which enables you to debug ASP.NET applications as you would debug any other application created in Visual Studio .NET. To debug ASP.NET applications, you can use the Visual Studio .NET debugger. See Chapter 20, "Debugging ASP.NET Applications," for more information on using the Visual Studio .NET debugger.

ASP.NET also introduces a new feature, known as *tracing*, which allows you to write debug statements in the code. Even when you port the code to the production environment, you can retain the debug statements because these statements are not executed when tracing is turned off. Tracing allows you to write variables or structures in a page, assert whether a condition is met, or simply trace through the execution path of your page or application. See Chapter 19, "Tracing ASP.NET Applications," for more information on tracing applications.

Session and Application State Management

ASP.NET provides easy-to-use session and application state management. Session management enables you to track which user is requesting a resource on your Web application. It also enables you to load the profile of a user when the user logs on to your Web application. A session is restricted to a logical application and defines the context in which a user communicates with a server.

Application state management enables you to track the use of application variables in an ASP.NET application. For example, consider a situation in which you have stored the connection strings to data sources in text files. When the application is executed for the first time, you can retrieve the connection strings from text files and store them in application variables. These connection strings can then be requested by all pages of the Web application.

See Chapter 17, "Managing State in ASP.NET Applications," for more information on managing session and application states.

File-Based Application Configuration

ASP.NET uses XML-based files to store configuration data pertaining to an application. The configuration of an application determines the authentication mode and the list of users who are allowed to access the Web application.

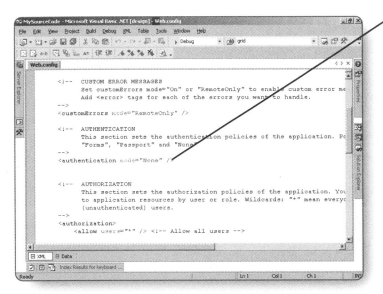

ASP.NET configuration files, being XML-based, are stored in text format and can be easily read and edited by site administrators. One important feature of a Web application that can be managed using the application configuration file is authentication. The configuration file includes an <authentication> element that specifies how users are authenticated on the Web application. See Chapter 22, "Securing ASP.NET Applications," for more information on authentication in ASP.NET.

User and Composite Controls

Developers can create their own custom and reusable controls called *user controls*. User controls are self-contained and can be placed on a Web page just like any other controls. These controls can also have a set of their own attributes.

Composite controls are created by combining existing controls and rendering them as a single control at run time. These controls reuse the functionality of the existing controls. See Chapter 12, "Creating a User Control in ASP.NET," and Chapter 13, "Creating a Composite Control in ASP.NET," for more information on user and composite controls.

Now that I've explained the features of ASP.NET, I'll discuss some of its advantages.

Advantages of ASP.NET

ASP.NET provides several advantages that enable you to develop and manage your Web applications efficiently. Of these advantages, the most important ones are support for multiple scripting languages, integration with Visual Studio .NET, and the ability to use server controls. These advantages, as well as a few others, are explained below.

- **Compiled execution**. The code of an ASP.NET page is compiled and cached on the server when the page is requested for the first time. This helps speed up execution of ASP.NET pages.

- **Multiple language support**. In ASP 3.0, server-side scripting was done using VBScript. However, in ASP.NET developers have the option to use either Visual Basic .NET or Visual C#. You can also use a combination of both languages to develop your application, as long as you use only one programming language on a page.

- **Extensive support by Visual Studio .NET**. ASP.NET applications can be developed in Visual Studio .NET, which allows WYSIWYG (*What You See Is What You Get*) editing for Web forms and provides drag-and-drop support to enable you to place controls on Web forms.

- **Server controls**. The .NET Framework provides server controls that simplify the task of creating Web pages. Server controls perform tasks that include validating form information, displaying data from a database, and displaying complex user interface elements such as interactive calendars.

- **Improved security**. ASP.NET provides different types of authentication mechanisms for Web applications. Developers can select a custom authentication mechanism and secure their Web applications.

Introducing Web Forms

Web forms are a part of the ASP.NET technology used to create programmable Web pages. Web forms can present information to users who access the Web application using a Web browser. The code in a Web form enables you to process information submitted by the users on the Web server.

A Web form is composed of two components—the visual elements and the code. Visual elements include controls and text, and the code refers to the program logic. Both of these components are stored in separate files. By default, the visual elements are stored in an .aspx file, and the code is stored in the code-behind file (.aspx.vb or .aspx.cs). However, when you create a Web form, you have the option to create the visual elements and code in the same file, as it was done in ASP 3.0.

A Web form utilizes the Page class to display data to users. The Page class includes several directives that are used to configure the Web form. The Page class and its directives are explained in the following sections.

Understanding the Page Class

A Web form contains different files for visual elements and code. However, when you compile a Web form, these files act as a single unit. While compiling, ASP.NET parses the Web form and its code, generates a new class dynamically, and then compiles the new class. The dynamically generated class is derived from the Page class of ASP.NET.

Put in simple terms, the Page class represents a single .aspx file that is requested from a server on which the ASP.NET Web application is hosted. The .aspx files are compiled at run time as Page objects and are cached in server memory.

Understanding Page Directives

Page directives specify the settings used by the page and the user control compiler when they process ASP.NET Web-form pages (.aspx) and user control (.ascx) files. Page directives can be located anywhere in an .aspx or .ascx file, and each directive can contain one or more attributes (paired with values) that are specific to that directive.

Two important directives that are used on a page are the @ Page and @ Control directives. These directives are used to define a Web form and a user control, respectively. The next two sections describe these directives in detail.

Working with the @ Page Directive

The @ Page directive defines page-specific attributes that are used by the ASP.NET page parser and compiler to determine certain attributes associated with a page, such as the scripting language used on the page. This directive can be used only in .aspx files. The .aspx file is compiled dynamically when a user browses the page. Therefore, the class associated with a Web form is also determined using the @ Page directive.

The syntax of the @ Page directive is

```
<%@ Page attribute="value" [attribute="value"] %>
```

Some attributes of the @ Page directive include

- **ClassName**. The ClassName attribute specifies the name of the class that will be compiled when the Web form is requested.

- **CodePage**. The CodePage attribute indicates the name of the code-behind file that is associated with the Web form.

- **Debug**. The Debug attribute indicates whether the page should be compiled with debug symbols.

- **Description**. The Description attribute provides a brief description of the Web form.

- **EnableSessionState**. The EnableSessionState attribute specifies whether session state is enabled for a Web form.

- **EnableViewState**. The EnableViewState attribute indicates whether view state is maintained across page requests.

Working with the @ Control Directive

The @ Control directive defines control-specific attributes used by the ASP.NET page parser and compiler. This directive can only be used in .ascx files, which signify user controls.

The syntax of the @ Control directive is

```
<%@Control attribute="value" [attribute="value"] %>
```

Some attributes of the directive include

- **ClassName**. The ClassName attribute specifies the name of the class that will be compiled when the user control is requested.

- **CompilerOptions**. The CompilerOptions attribute specifies compiler switches that are used to compile the user control.

- **Debug**. The Debug attribute indicates whether the page should be compiled with debug symbols.

- **Description**. The Description attribute provides a brief description of the user control.

- **EnableViewState**. The EnableViewState attribute indicates whether view state for the user control is maintained across requests.

Understanding Postbacks and Round Trips

Consider a scenario in which a Web form is requested by a browser. A form is displayed on the browser, and the user interacts with the controls on the form, which causes the form to post back to the server. (The form must be posted to the server because all processing must occur on the server.) The form is processed at the server and returned to the browser. This sequence of events is referred to as a *round trip*. Therefore, actions such as clicking a button result in a round trip.

Considering this scenario, Web-form pages are recreated with every round trip. As soon as the server finishes processing and sending the page to the browser, it discards the page information.

The freeing of server resources after each request can help Web applications scale and support hundreds or thousands of simultaneous users. The next time the page is posted, the server starts over in creating and processing it, which is primarily due to the transfer protocol (HTTP) being a stateless protocol. This results in the values of a page's variables and controls being lost between multiple requests.

However, in some cases you might need to store data between round trips. ASP.NET provides an EnableViewState property for controls. If you set this property to True, the information specified by a user on the Web form is stored between round trips. This process is referred to as saving the view state of the control; it is done using a hidden field on the form itself.

Understanding Cookies

A cookie represents data that is stored either in a text file on the client or in memory in the client's browser session. Cookies can be temporary (with specific expiration times and dates) or persistent.

You can use cookies to store information about a particular client, session, or application. The cookies are saved on the client device; when the browser requests a page, it sends information stored in the cookie along with the request. The server can read the cookie and extract a value to determine the user's credentials or user preferences.

Understanding Query Strings

A query string is the part of the information that is appended to the address of a Web form. A typical query string might be

```
http://www.querysample.com/querystring.aspx?username=john
```

In this Web-form address, the query string starts with the question mark and includes an attribute-value pair—username=john, in which *username* is the key and *john* is its value.

Query strings provide a simple but limited way of maintaining some state information. They also provide an easy way to submit information from one page to another. For example, you can pass a product ID from one page to another, where the product ID might be used to retrieve product details on the second page.

Query strings have a few drawbacks. Most browsers and client devices impose a 255-character limit on the length of the URL. Also, the query values are exposed to the Internet via the URL. Therefore, query strings are not a secure and convenient way to post data between Web forms in a Web application.

Another drawback of query strings is that to make query string values available during page processing, you must submit the page using an HTTP get method. You cannot take advantage of a query string if a page is processed in response to an HTTP post method.

The concepts discussed in this chapter provided an introduction to the major features of ASP.NET. In the remaining chapters of the book, you will learn about the implementation of each feature in detail.

4

Visual Basic .NET Basics

In Chapter 3, "Exploring the New Features of ASP.NET," you were introduced to some new features of ASP.NET. Before you begin creating your ASP.NET applications, you should get acquainted with the basics of Visual Basic .NET, because it is the language you will use to create your ASP.NET applications. This chapter will take you through some basic Visual Basic. NET concepts related to data types, variables, arrays, decision structures, and looping constructs. Specifically, in this chapter, you'll learn how to:

- Use variables and data types
- Work with arrays
- Use decision structures and loops

An Introduction to Visual Basic .NET

Visual Basic .NET is one of the programming languages of .NET Framework. Visual Basic .NET is the latest version of Visual Basic, and it introduces many new features. Some of the new features of Visual Basic .NET follow.

- **Object-oriented language**. Visual Basic .NET is an object-oriented language and thus supports abstraction, encapsulation, inheritance, and polymorphism.

- **Multi-threaded**. Visual Basic .NET supports multi-threading and thus allows you to create multi-threaded and scalable applications.

- **Structured exception handling**. Visual Basic .NET supports structured exception handling by providing Try and Catch statements.

- **CLS-compliant**. Visual Basic .NET is compliant with CLS (*Common Language Specification*), which means that Visual Basic .NET can use any class, object, or component created in any other CLS-compliant language, and vice versa.

Using Variables and Data Types

Consider a simple application that accepts data from a user, performs some operations on this data, and displays the result. This pattern is common with most applications that you create, regardless of the programming language. In other words, most applications deal with data in one way or another. This is where variables and data types come into the picture.

A variable is a temporary memory location that is assigned a name and can hold a specific type of data. Visual Basic .NET provides a number of data types that can be used to specify the type of data. Some of the data types include Integer, String, Long, and Double. Table 4.1 lists some of the commonly used data types in Visual Basic .NET.

Table 4.1   Commonly Used Data Types in Visual Basic .NET

Data Type	Type of Data Stored
Integer	Numeric data in the range of –2,147,483,648 to 2,147,483,647
Long	Numeric data that exceeds the range supported by the Integer data type
Short	A smaller range of numeric data (between –32,678 and 32,767)
Single	Single-precision floating-point numbers
Double	Large floating-point numbers
Decimal	Very large floating-point numbers
Boolean	Boolean values, which are either True or False
String	Alphanumeric data (text and numbers)
Object	Data of any data type
Char	A single character
DateTime	Date- and time-related data

Declaring Variables

To declare a variable in Visual Basic .NET, you use the Dim statement. The syntax for declaring a variable is

```
Dim VarName [As Type]
```

In this syntax, VarName is the name of the variable and As Type is an optional clause that specifies the data type of the variable being declared. Take a look at the following statements.

```
Dim MyNumber As Integer
Dim MyString As String
```

The first statement declares an Integer variable by the name MyNumber; the second statement declares a String variable by the name MyString.

You can also declare several variables at the same time, using a single Dim statement.

```
Dim MyNumber1, MyNumber2, MyNumber3 As Integer
```

This statement declares three Integer variables using a single Dim statement.

I will now discuss some ground rules for naming variables, because it is very important to give meaningful names to variables. There are various naming conventions used by programmers around the world. Although it is not necessary to follow a naming convention, following one does make coding easier and is considered good programming practice.

One of the most common naming conventions is to include the data type in the name of the variable. For example, an Integer variable can be declared as intResult. Another common practice is to capitalize the first character of each word in a variable name if it has multiple words. For example, intNumOfItems is an Integer variable whose name consists of three words—Num, Of, and Items. I have capitalized the three words in the name of the variable to make it easier to read. Yet another convention is to *not* use the data type in the name of the variable (for example, NumOfItems). Regardless of the convention used, here are some rules that you should follow.

- A variable name cannot contain spaces, periods, or identifier type characters.
- A variable name must begin with an alphanumeric character.
- A variable name cannot contain more than 255 characters.

Visual Basic .NET allows you to use identifier type characters while declaring variables. As the name suggests, identifier type characters specify the data type of the variable. To better understand this concept, consider the following statement.

```
Dim MyNumber%
```

This statement declares an Integer variable named MyNumber. Note the % character, which is the identifier type character for declaring Integer variables. Table 4.2 lists the various identifier type characters that you can use.

Table 4.2 Identifier Type Characters in Visual Basic .NET

Data Type	Identifier Type Character
Integer	%
Single	!
Long	&
Double	#
Decimal	@
String	$

Initializing Variables

When you declare a variable, it contains a value by default. For example, an Integer variable contains a value of 0. You can also initialize a variable, as shown here.

```
Dim MyNumber As Integer
MyNumber=100
```

Instead of using the preceding two statements, you can use a single statement, as shown here.

```
Dim MyNumber As Integer = 100
```

Using the Option Explicit Statement

In the previous sections, you looked at how to declare and initialize variables. Now, take a look at a situation in which you don't have to declare variables and you can start using them in your program. Visual Basic .NET supports this feature. In other words, you don't have to use the Dim statement at all.

In Visual Basic .NET, variable declarations can be categorized as explicit and implicit. *Explicit declaration* means that you declare a variable before using it; *implicit declaration* refers to using a variable without declaring it. However, implicit declarations can lead to unpredictable program results and can pose a problem while debugging. For example, you could misspell the name of an implicitly declared variable at some point in the code. To avoid the problems that can arise from implicit variable declaration, you should declare variables explicitly. To enforce explicit declaration, use the Option Explicit statement.

```
Option Explicit [On | Off ]
```

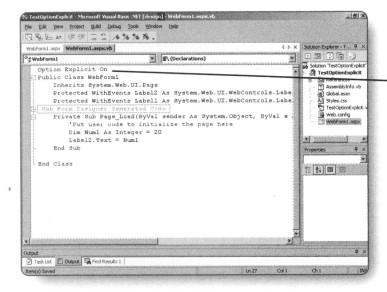

The On keyword ensures that variables are declared before being used, and the Off keyword ensures that variables can be used without being declared. By default, Option Explicit is On. To better understand this concept, consider an application that displays the value of a variable.

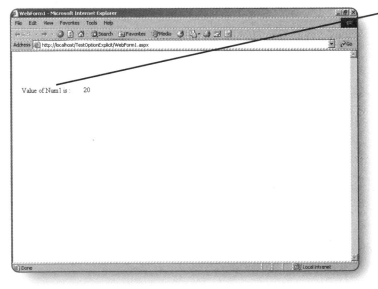

Option Explicit is On, and the variable Num1 is declared before being used, which results in the output shown here.

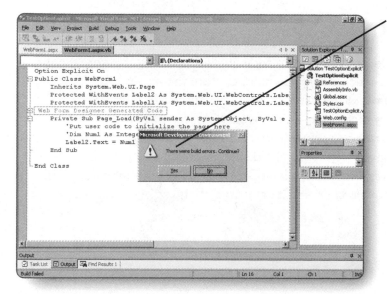

However, if you do not declare the variable Num1 and you compile the application, a build error will be returned.

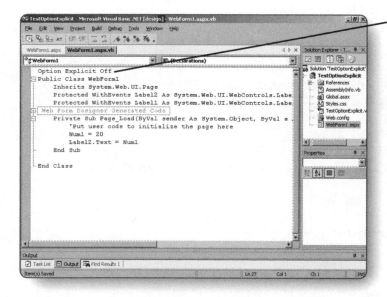

If the same application were compiled with the Option Explicit directive set to Off, there would not have been a build error. Notice that the variable Num1 is not declared using the Dim statement. The application runs fine, and the required output is displayed correctly.

Working with Arrays

In the last section, you learned to declare and initialize variables of different data types. Consider an application where you need to store the names of 100 employees. To store names of 100 employees, you would need to use 100 variables—one for every employee—which would be very tedious and time-consuming. However, arrays provide an easy solution. An *array* is a collection of variables of the same data type that can hold several values. Each variable in an array is called an *array element* and is identified by its position in the array. This position is called an *index number*, and it helps to distinguish one array element from another.

Declaring an Array

Just as you declare other variables, you also need to declare arrays. The declaration of arrays is not much different from the declaration of a variable. The syntax for declaring an array is

```
Dim ArrayName (NumOfElements) [As DataType]
```

In the preceding line of code, ArrayName is the name of the array. NumOfElements is the number of elements the array can hold, and DataType is the data type of the array elements. Consider the following statement.

```
Dim MyArray(5) As Integer
```

This statement declares an Integer array named MyArray, which can hold six elements.

NOTE

MyArray can hold six elements because arrays are zero-based. Therefore, the index number of the first element is 0 and the index number of the last element is 5, making a total of six elements.

Initializing an Array

To initialize an array, you need to assign values at each index of the array. After you declare an array, use the following syntax to initialize it.

```
Dim MyArray(2) As String
MyArray(0)="Mary Jones"
MyArray(1)="Paul Adams"
MyArray(2)="Henry John"
```

The first statement in the code declares an array named MyArray. The next three statements initialize each element of the array. These lines of code can also be written as:

```
Dim MyArray() As String = {"Mary Jones","Paul Adams","Henry John"}
```

You use the index number to retrieve the values from an array. In the case of MyArray, which holds three String values, you would use the following statement to retrieve the value stored at index position 1.

```
Dim MyString As String
MyString=MyArray(1)
```

After the execution of the code statements, MyString contains the value "Paul Adams," which is stored at index number 1 in MyArray.

Working with Multi-Dimensional Arrays

In Visual Basic .NET, you can also declare multi-dimensional arrays. As the name suggests, *multi-dimensional arrays* are arrays with more than one dimension. Visual Basic .NET supports up to 32 dimensions in an array. However, most often you will use two- or three-dimensional arrays. The syntax to declare a two-dimensional array is

```
Dim MyArray(3,4) As String
```

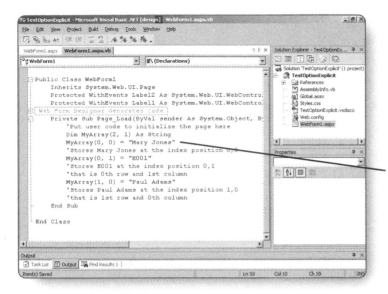

Here, MyArray is a two-dimensional array that can hold up to 20 elements. 20 is the product of four (the size of the first dimension plus one) multiplied by 5 (the size of the second dimension plus one).

The code to initialize a multi-dimensional array is simple. All you need to do is use the index numbers of the array to assign values to it.

Understanding Dynamic Arrays

There might be times when you do not know how large an array should be. For example, suppose you needed to store the training details of each employee in an organization. You couldn't specify a size for this array because the number of trainings attended by each employee will vary. For such an application, you could use dynamic arrays. As the name suggests, a *dynamic array* is an array whose size changes dynamically. You can change the size of a dynamic array during the execution of the program.

The following code sample shows the declaration of a dynamic array.

```
Dim MyArray() As String
```

Here, a String array named MyArray is declared. Note that the size of the array is not specified; it can change at run time. To resize an array, you use the ReDim statement. This syntax of this statement is

```
ReDim MyArray(5)
```

This example was for a one-dimensional array; you can also resize multi-dimensional arrays. However, you cannot change the number of dimensions for a dynamic multi-dimensional array. To better understand this concept, consider the following statements.

```
Dim MyArray(1,2) As String
ReDim MyArray(3,4)
```

The first statement declares a two-dimensional array with the dimensions 1, 2. The second statement changes the first dimension from 1 to 3 and the second dimension from 2 to 4.

When you use a ReDim statement, an array loses all of its existing data, and the elements of the resized array are initialized with the default value of their data type. To prevent data loss, you can use the Preserve keyword. The syntax for using this keyword is

```
ReDim Preserve ArrayName (NumOfElements)
```

Here, ArrayName is the name of the array that you want to resize. The Preserve keyword can also be used for multi-dimensional arrays. However, you can only resize the last dimension in a multi-dimensional array. To better understand this concept, consider the following statements.

```
Dim MyArray(2,3) As Integer
ReDim Preserve MyArray(3,4)
```

This statement will generate an error because you are trying to change the dimensions of the array and preserve the existing data. However, you can use the following statement to resize the last dimension in a multi-dimensional array.

```
ReDim Preserve MyArray(2,4)
```

Here only the last dimension is resized, and the existing data is preserved.

Now that you have learned about arrays, you'll want to learn about the next important element of programming—decision structures.

Working with Decision Structures

Decision structures enable you to make decisions based on a programming condition. In other words, they ensure execution of a set of statements based on the result of a condition. In this section, I'll discuss two decision structures—If...Then...Else and Select...Case.

Using If...Then...Else Statements

The If...Then...Else statement is the most commonly used decision structure. It is used to execute one or more statements based on a condition. The condition used in the If...Then...Else statement is a Boolean expression that returns either True or False. The syntax for the If...Then...Else statement is

```
If Condition(s) Then
        Statement(s)
[Else
        Statement(s)]
End If
```

Here, Condition(s) is the expression to be evaluated. If this expression returns True, the Statement(s) following Then are executed. If this expression returns False, the Statement(s) following Else are executed. End If marks the end of an If...Then...Else statement.

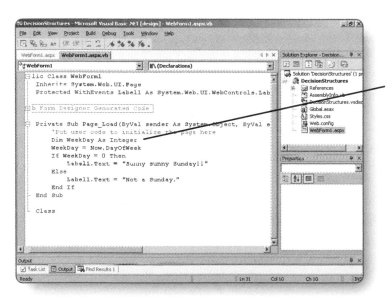

To better understand this concept, consider this code. I've declared an Integer variable named WeekDay to store the weekday. To determine the current weekday, I've used the Now.DayOfWeek property, in which Now returns the current date and time, and DayOfWeek returns the number of the weekday between 0 (for Sunday) and 6 (for Saturday).

Note the If…Then…Else statement in the code. This statement checks for the value of the WeekDay variable. If the value of this variable is 0, the expression in the If statement returns True, and the statements following the If statement are executed. In this case, the label displays the text "Sunny sunny Sunday!!" If the expression in the If statement returns False, the statements following the Else statement are executed. In this case, the label displays the text "Not a Sunday."

There is another form of the If…Then…Else statement in which you can check for multiple conditions. The syntax for this form of the statement follows.

```
If Condition1(s) Then
        Statement1(s)
[ElseIf Condition2(s) Then
        Statement2(s)
Else
        Statement3(s)]
End If
```

In the preceding syntax, Condition1(s) is evaluated. If it is True, Statement1(s) is executed. If it is False, the control moves to the ElseIf statement, and Condition2(s) is evaluated. If Condition2(s) is True, Statement2(s) is executed; otherwise, Statement3(s) (which follows the Else clause) is executed.

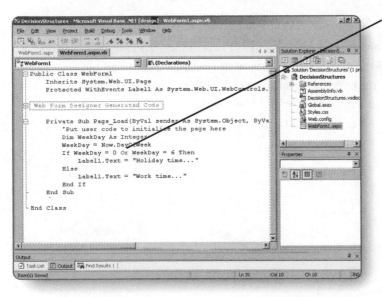

You can also use logical operators to combine multiple conditions in an If…Then…Else statement. An example of the Or operator is shown here.

In Visual Basic .NET, you can use the logical operators And, AndAlso, Or, OrElse, and Not. Out of these, And, Or, and Not are self-explanatory. The AndAlso operator checks for the first condition in the expression. If the condition evaluates as False, the AndAlso operator returns False; otherwise, a logical And operation is performed on the two conditions.

In the case of an OrElse operator, if the first condition evaluates to True, the OrElse operator returns True. Otherwise, a logical Or operation is performed on the two conditions.

Using Select…Case Statements

The Select…Case statement is another decision structure. The Select…Case statement checks for a condition and then executes a set of statements based on the result of that condition. A Select…Case statement is preferred when you need to check for multiple values of an expression. The syntax for the statement is

```
Select Case Expression
    Case ValueList
        Statement1(s)
    [Case Else
        Statement2(s)]
End Select
```

Here, the Expression is evaluated, and the result is compared against the values specified in ValueList of the Case statements. If the result matches any of the values specified in the Case statement, the statements following that Case statement are executed. If the result doesn't match any of the values in the Case statements, the statements following the Case Else statement are executed.

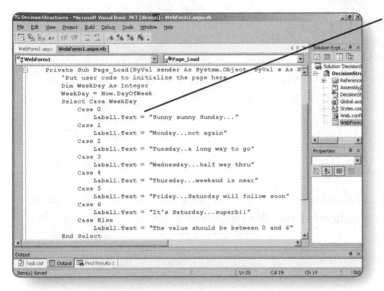

For a practical implementation of the Select...Case statement, consider the code shown here. In the code, the value of the WeekDay variable is checked for values between 0 and 6 in separate Case statements. The label is displayed based on the value of the WeekDay variable.

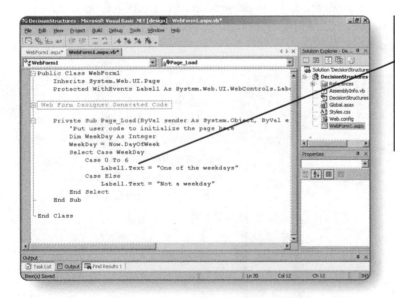

TIP

Instead of testing for each value separately in the Case statements, you can specify a range of values, as shown here.

Looping Constructs

Like other programming languages, Visual Basic .NET also supports various looping constructs, which include While...End While, Do...Loop, For...Next, and For Each...Next statements. Take a look at each one of these constructs in detail in the next few sections.

Understanding While...End While Statements

The While...End While statement specifies that a set of statements should repeat as long as the condition specified is true. The syntax for a While...End While statement is

```
While Condition(s)
        Statement(s)
End While
```

In this syntax, Condition(s) is evaluated at the beginning of the While loop and can be True or False. If it is True, Statement(s) is executed. The End While statement is used to exit a While loop.

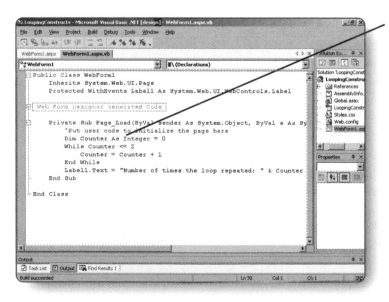

In this example, an Integer variable called Counter is declared and initialized with 0. The While loop executes as long as the value of Counter is less than or equal to 2. Therefore, the While loop repeats three times.

Understanding Do…Loop Statements

There are two forms of Do…Loop statements available in Visual Basic .NET. The first form checks for a condition before executing the loop. The syntax for this form is

```
Do While | Until Condition(s)
     Statement(s)
     [Exit Do]
Loop
```

Notice that you can either use the While or Until keyword. Use the While keyword to execute the Statement(s) as long as the Condition(s) are True. Use the Until keyword to execute the Statement(s) as long as the Condition(s) are False. The Exit Do statement is used to exit the Do loop.

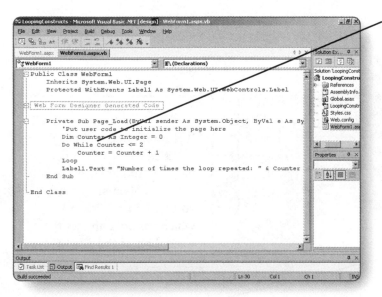

The same code that was written earlier for the While loop can be written for the Do loop. This loop also repeats three times, and the output of the code is the same as the output for the While loop.

The second form of the Do…Loop statement checks for the condition after executing the loop once. The syntax for this form of the Do…Loop statement is

```
Do
     Statement(s)
     [Exit Do]
Loop While | Until Condition(s)
```

Understanding For...Next Statements

For...Next statements are used to repeat a set of statements a specific number of times. The syntax for these statements is

```
For Counter = <StartValue> to <EndValue> [StepValue]
    Statement(s)
    [Exit For]
Next Counter
```

Here, Counter is a numeric variable, StartValue is the initial value of Counter, and EndValue is the final value of Counter. The For loop repeats as long as the value of Counter is between StartValue and EndValue. StepValue can be positive or negative; it is the value by which Counter, needs to be incremented. StepValue is optional and, if omitted, is assumed to be 1.

The Next statement marks the end of a For loop. When this statement executes, StepValue is added to Counter, and the For loop repeats if the value of Counter is between StartValue and EndValue.

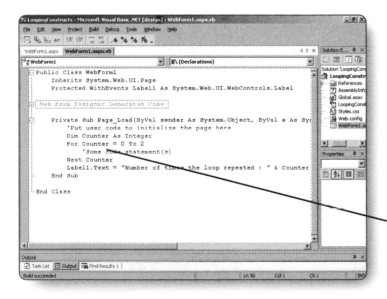

TIP

It is good programming practice to specify the name of the counter variable in a Next statement, so that you can identify which variable affects the execution of the For loop.

In the statements shown here, the For loop in the code repeats three times because Counter takes the values 0, 1, and 2.

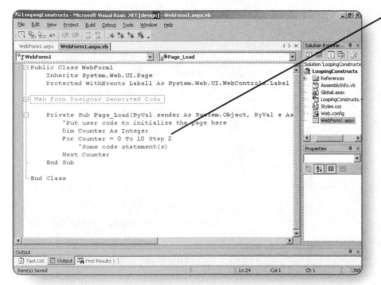

Consider a scenario in which the For loop is incremented with a value greater than 1. The increment value determines the number of times the For loop will execute. In this case, the For loop would execute six times, with Counter taking the values 0, 2, 4, 6, 8, and 10.

NOTE

For loops can be nested. This means that you can include one For loop inside another For loop. However, when nesting For loops, make sure that you use different counter variables, and that the sequence of the Next statements is correct.

Understanding For Each...Next Statements

A different implementation of the For loop is the For Each...Next statement. The For Each...Next statement is used to iterate through an array or a collection. The syntax for the For Each...Next statement is

```
For Each Element in List
    Statement(s)
    [Exit For]
Next [Element]
```

In this syntax, Element refers to individual elements in List. List can be an array or a collection.

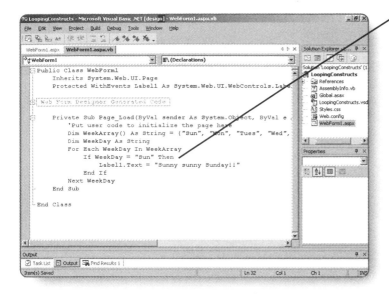

As an example of the For Each loop, consider this code, which uses a For Each loop to iterate through each element in WeekArray. When iterating through the array, the WeekDay variable is used to refer to individual elements of the array.

This completes the discussion of the basics of Visual Basic .NET. As you read through the other chapters of this book, you will use the concepts you learned in this chapter to write code for your applications.

5

Beginning with a Simple ASP.NET Application

In the last two chapters, you were introduced to the basics of Visual Basic .NET and ASP.NET. In this chapter, you will apply the skills that you learned in the previous two chapters to create an ASP.NET application.

Creating an ASP.NET application in Visual Studio .NET is fast and easy. The common tasks that you perform while creating your application, such as adding Web forms to an application, placing controls on a form, and responding to events generated when users interact with a form, are most easily performed in Visual Studio .NET. The objective of this chapter is to get you acquainted with how these tasks are performed in Visual Studio .NET. In this chapter, you'll learn how to:

- Create ASP.NET Web applications
- Design forms for Web applications
- Respond to user interaction

Creating ASP.NET Web Application Projects

An ASP.NET application is installed in a virtual directory in IIS. You can design stand-alone ASP.NET pages and copy these pages to a virtual directory in IIS to run them. However, when you use Visual Studio .NET, you can create a solution that includes a number of projects. Each project can include a number of ASP.NET applications.

The advantage of creating a solution is that you do not need to explicitly create a virtual directory for deploying the ASP.NET pages of your Web application. A solution enables you to create a deployment project and move your application from the development to the production environment.

In this section, I will explain the steps to create a new solution and add a project to it. The project will include one or more Web forms that can be displayed on a Web site.

Creating a New Project

To create a new project in Visual Studio .NET, follow these steps.

1. Click on Start. The Start menu will appear.

2. Move the mouse pointer to Programs, and then to Microsoft Visual Studio .NET. The Microsoft Visual Studio .NET submenu will appear.

3. Click on Microsoft Visual Studio .NET. The Microsoft Visual Studio .NET application will launch.

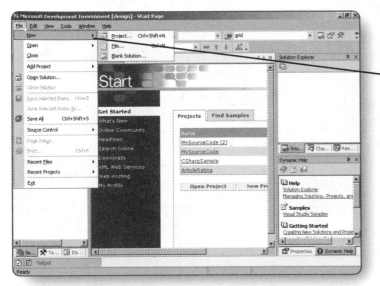

4. Click on File. The File menu will appear.

5. Move the mouse pointer to New. The New submenu will appear.

6. Click on Project. The New Project dialog box will open.

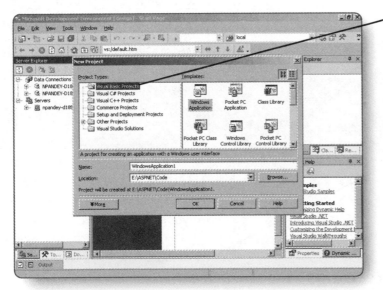

7. Click on the Visual Basic Projects folder. The templates available for creating Visual Basic .NET projects will appear in the Templates list.

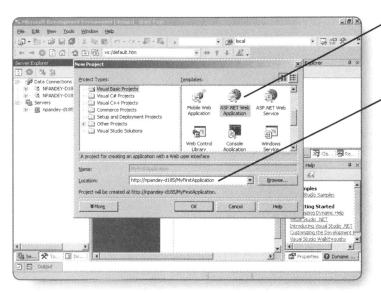

8. In the list of templates, click on ASP.NET Web Application. The option will be selected.

9. Type the name of the Web application in the Location text box.

> ### TIP
>
> When you type the name of the Web application, make sure that you retain the location of the Web application and change only the name. For example, if the original location and name of the Web application is http://npandey-d185/WebApplication1, change only the name by replacing only the WebApplication1 substring in the Location text box.

10. Click on OK. Visual Studio .NET will create a new project for you at the specified location.

By default, when you create a new ASP.NET Web application, Visual Studio .NET adds a Web form (WebForm1.aspx) to your application.

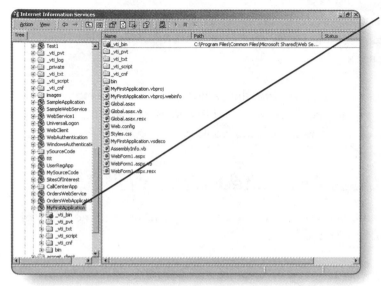

When you create a new project, a virtual directory for your project is created in the IIS root directory. By default, the root directory for IIS is located at C:\Inetpub\wwwroot. You can view the virtual directory for your application by using the Internet Services Manager. All Web forms that you add to your application will be listed in the virtual directory for your application. Notice that WebForm1.aspx, which was added to your project by default, appears in the virtual directory for your Web application.

Renaming a Web Form

By default, a blank Web form named WebForm1.aspx is added to your application when you create it. However, when you create applications, you will probably name the Web forms based on their utility. For example, the search form in a Web

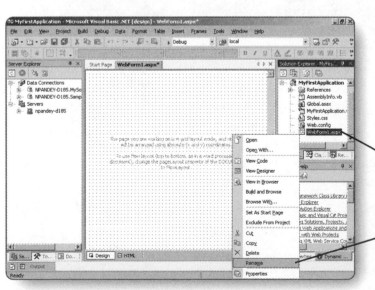

application might be named Search.aspx. Similarly, the default form in a Web application might be named Default.aspx. To change the name of a Web form, follow these steps.

1. Right-click on the name of the form in the Solution Explorer. A shortcut menu will appear.

2. Click on Rename. The name of the Web form will be selected.

3. Type a new name for the Web form and press Enter. When renaming a Web form, make sure that you type the file extension for the Web form as well. For example, type **Default.aspx**.

When you change the name of a Web form, the name of the code-behind file also changes accordingly. For example, if you specified the name of the Web form as Default.aspx, the name of the code-behind file would change to Default.aspx.vb.

Changing the Class Associated with a Web Form

After you change the name of a Web form, the next step is to change the name of the class that is associated with the form.

Namespaces and Classes in ASP.NET Applications

Visual Basic .NET is an object-oriented language. By default, all code in your application is organized into classes. Therefore, when you create a new application, a namespace with the name of your application is created. Each form that you add to the application is treated as a class in the namespace. For example, if you have a Web form named WebForm1.aspx for an application that is named MyFirstApplication, a MyFirstApplication namespace will be created for your application, and a class (WebForm1) that corresponds to the WebForm1.aspx page will be created in the MyFirstApplication namespace. The classes for Web forms are always created in the code-behind files.

When you change the name of a form, it is a good idea also to change the name of the class associated with the form so that the development team can easily identify which class is linked to which form.

To change the name of the class for a Web form, follow these steps.

1. Double-click on a form in the Design view. The code-behind file for the form will open.

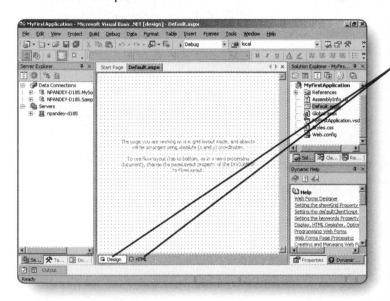

NOTE

In Visual Studio .NET, a Web form has two views—Design and HTML. The Design view shows the controls that you have added to the form. At run time, your form will appear as it is in the Design view. On the other hand, the HTML view shows the HTML code that is generated for your form. You can switch between the two views for a form by clicking on the Design and HTML buttons located in the lower-left corner of the Web form.

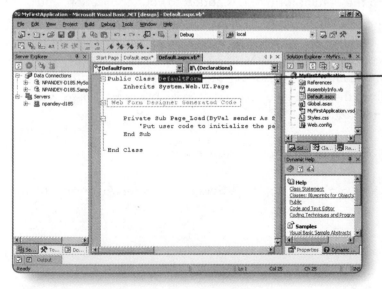

2. In the code-behind file for the form, change the name of the class (which appears after the Public Class declaration). For example, I have changed the name of the class for the form to DefaultForm.

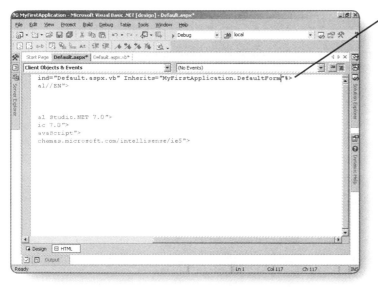

3. When you change the class name of a form in the code-behind file, you also need to change the class name in the @ Page directive of the Web form. To do so, locate the @ Page directive in the HTML view of the form and change the name of the class.

> **TIP**
>
> The name of the class is the last word in the @ Page directive.

Adding a New Form

So far, I have described the steps to change the name of a form and the default class associated with it. A Web application usually includes a number of Web forms. Therefore, in addition to the default form that is added to your application, you need to add forms to your application.

You probably don't need to change the name of any subsequent forms that you add to your application because you will specify the form name when you add it to the application. Therefore, the effort involved in customizing a new form for your application is significantly reduced.

To add a new form to your application, follow these steps.

1. Right-click on the name of the project in the Solution Explorer. A shortcut menu will appear.

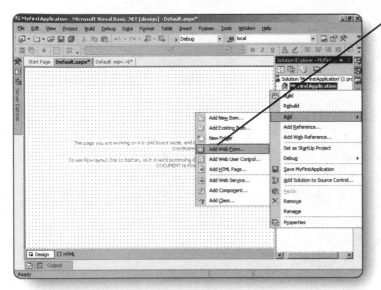

2. Move the mouse pointer to Add and then select Add Web Form from the Add submenu. The Add New Item dialog box will open.

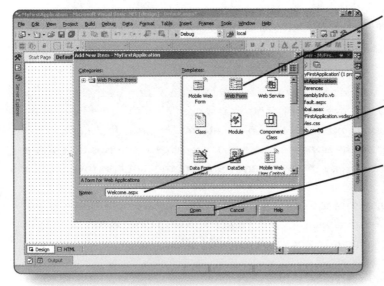

3. Make sure that the Web Form option is selected in the Templates section of the Add New Item dialog box.

4. Type the name of the Web form in the Name text box.

5. Click on Open. A new form will be created for you.

In the code-behind file and @ Page directive for the new form, notice that the class name is the same as the name of the Web form. Therefore, you don't need to change this name explicitly.

Designing Forms

The Toolbox in Visual Studio .NET is handy for designing Web forms. When using the Toolbox, all you need to do is drag controls and arrange them on a Web form.

You design a form in the Design view. Visual Studio .NET provides two layouts for a form in the Design view—GridLayout and FlowLayout. The interface of your application can depend upon the layout that was used to design the application's forms. In this section, you will examine the difference between the GridLayout and the FlowLayout of a form, and how you can design a form by dragging controls to it from the Toolbox.

Selecting a Layout for a Form

You can use GridLayout or FlowLayout to design a form. Following are brief descriptions of these layouts.

- **GridLayout**. GridLayout uses absolute coordinates to position controls on a Web form. For example, if you place a control at the coordinates (10,20), the position of the control will not change with respect to other controls or the size of the form.

- **FlowLayout**. FlowLayout does not position controls on a form by their coordinates. Instead, the position of controls is automatically determined with respect to the position of other controls on the form. Thus, the first control is automatically placed on the upper-left corner of the screen. The position of the next control is determined by the width and height of the first control.

Each layout has its own advantages and disadvantages. For example, if you know the exact size of the form that will be used, you can go with GridLayout because you don't need to worry about the how the controls will appear when your form is resized.

However, GridLayout poses a problem when you need to display or hide controls on the form dynamically. For example, you might have a search page that displays a calendar if the user needs to search by date. The results of the search might be displayed in a table. Using GridLayout, each control would retain its respective position even when other controls are removed from the form.

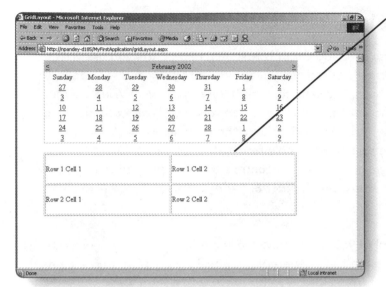

As long as both elements (the calendar and the table) are displayed on the form, the form appears normal in GridLayout and FlowLayout.

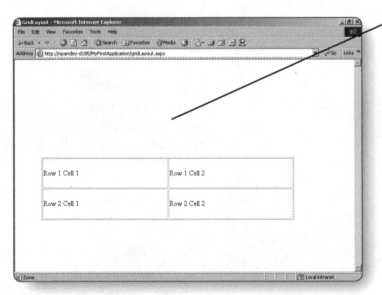

However, when the calendar control is removed from the form dynamically, GridLayout poses a problem. The position of the table remains the same, and the space that should have been occupied by the form is left empty. This problem does not arise in FlowLayout because the table occupies the position of the calendar when the calendar control is removed.

Adding Controls to a Form

When you design a form, you add controls to it. In a text editor, you use HTML tags to add controls to a form. For example, you use the <TABLE> and </TABLE> tags to add a table to your form. You can accomplish the same task in Visual Studio .NET by using the Toolbox. You can add Web form controls and HTML controls to your form by dragging them from the Toolbox onto the form. In this section, I will describe the procedure to create a simple form to accept information from users. For more detailed information about the controls that you can add to a form and their configurable properties, see Chapter 6, "Adding Server Controls to a Web Form."

When you add a control to your form using the Toolbox, the corresponding HTML code for the form is automatically generated. Try designing a form that accepts the user name and password from a user. To add controls to a form, open the form and follow these steps.

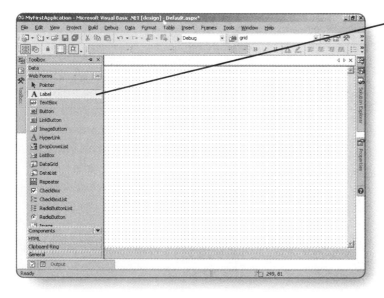

1. Click on the Label control in the Toolbox. The Label control will be selected.

2. Press and hold the mouse button and drag the Label control to the form. Release the mouse button to place the Label control on the form.

3. Right-click on the Label control. A shortcut menu will appear.

4. Click on Properties. The Properties window for the control will appear.

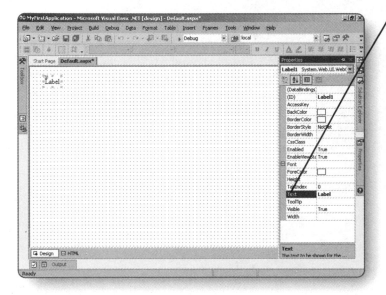

5. Double-click on the Text property. The Text property will be highlighted.

6. Type **User Name** in the Text field and press Enter. The text displayed on the Label control will change to User Name.

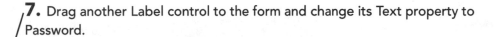

7. Drag another Label control to the form and change its Text property to Password.

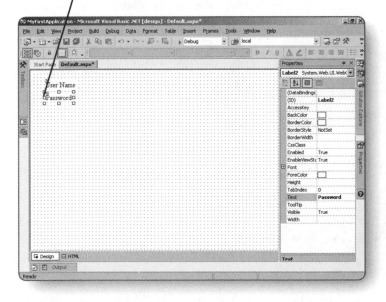

8. Drag a TextBox control from the Toolbox to the form and open the control's Properties window.

9. In the Properties window, type txtUserName as the ID of the control.

10. Drag another TextBox control from the Toolbox to the form.

11. Change the ID property of the control to txtPassword.

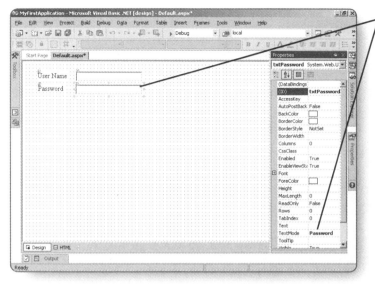

12. Change the TextMode property of the control to Password. This change will ensure that when the form is run, the control will mask the characters that are typed into it.

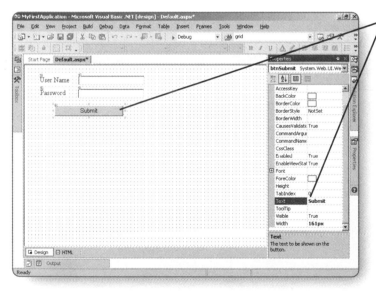

13. Drag a Button control from the Toolbox to the form and change its ID and Text properties to btnSubmit and Submit, respectively.

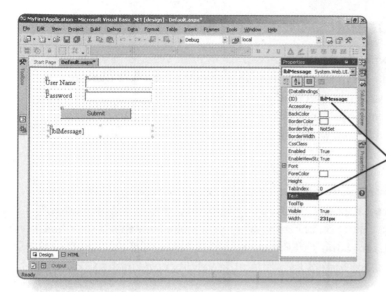

14. To display a message to users when they enter an incorrect user name or pass-word, drag another Label control onto the form from the Toolbox.

15. Clear the Text property of the label and change the value of the ID property to lblMessage.

NOTE

When you add a Label control to the form and clear the text that is displayed in the label, the form displays the name of the label in parentheses, so that you can place the label accurately at design time.

The form that you have just designed accepts the user name and password from a user. Next you'll learn about the steps to respond to user interactions with the form.

Responding to User Interaction

The primary function of a Web form is to accept information from users and display information based on the users' selections. Some of the ways in which users might provide information include clicking on a hyperlink, specifying information in a text box, or clicking on a button.

In this section, I will describe the steps to validate the user name and password specified by a user. If the user name and password are correct, the user will be redirected to another form. Otherwise, an error message will be displayed.

Redirecting a User to Another Web Form

Consider a scenario in which users are directed to another Web form when they specify a valid user name and password. In such a scenario, you first need to determine whether the user has specified any values in the User Name and Password fields. When a user has specified valid values, you need to determine whether the user name and password are correct and then redirect the user to the new form.

You can use validation controls to determine whether users have specified a user name and password. See Chapter 7, "Accepting Information Using Web Forms," for more information on validation controls. After you make sure that a user has specified values in the User Name and Password fields, you can check whether the user name and password are correct by writing the validity code in the Click event of the Submit button.

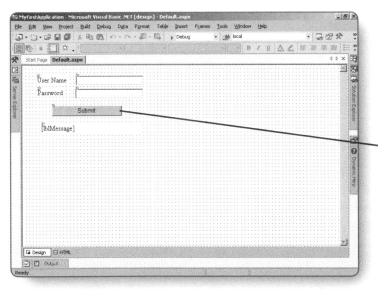

The following steps demonstrate how to validate a user name and password. For this example, I have used the same form that you designed in the previous section.

1. Double-click on the Submit button in the form. The Code Editor window will open, and the declaration for the Click event of the Submit button will be added to the code-behind file for the form.

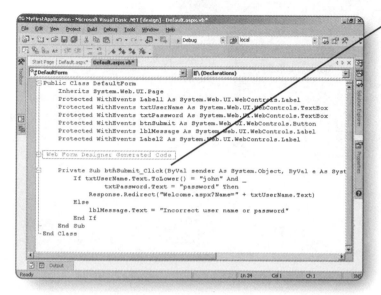

2. Write the code for the Click event of the Submit button. Notice that I have checked whether the user name and password are john and password, respectively. If they are, the user is redirected to the Welcome.aspx page, and the name of the user is passed to the Welcome.aspx page as a query string. If the user name or password is not valid, the lblMessage label displays an error message to the user.

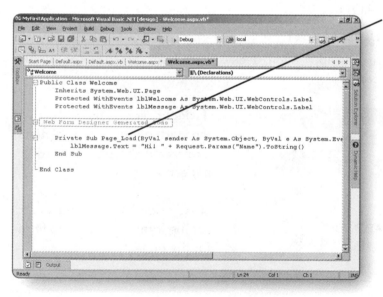

On the Welcome.aspx page, the user name is retrieved from the query string in the Load event of the form.

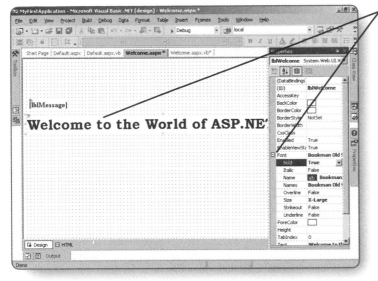

When the user runs the form, the user name and a welcome message will be displayed with the help of two Label controls. Notice that I have changed the Font property of the welcome message.

Executing the Application

You need to specify a startup form to be displayed when the application is run. To set a startup form and run the application, decide which form should be the startup form and follow these steps.

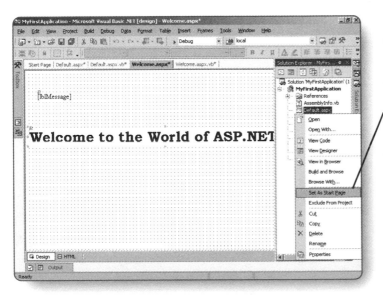

1. Right-click on the name of the startup form in the Solution Explorer. A shortcut menu will appear.

2. Click on Set As Start Page to set the form as the startup form for the project.

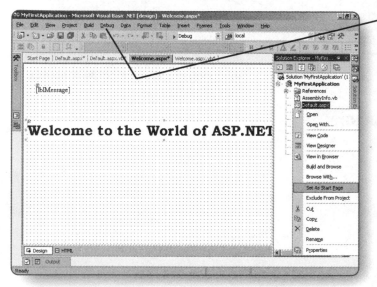

3. Click on Debug. The Debug menu will appear.

4. Click on Start. Your project will be compiled and the startup form of the project will open.

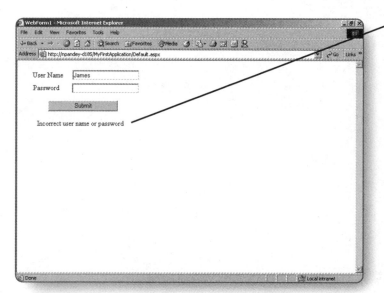

When the form is run, the user is prompted to enter a user name and password. If the user name or password is incorrect, an error message is displayed.

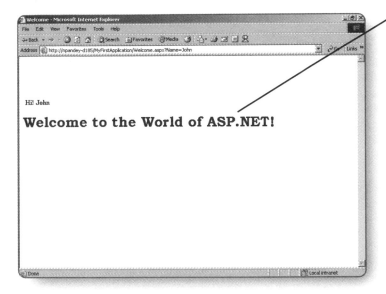

If the user name and password are correct, the user is redirected to the Welcome.aspx page, and a welcome message is displayed.

6

Adding Server Controls to a Web Form

Server controls (or Web form controls, as they are commonly known) are used to design the interface and code the functionality of an application. As the name suggests, these controls use a server-side programming model in which events are generated and processed at the server end.

Server controls provide many advantages over the traditional HTML controls that you might have used in your ASP 3.0 Web applications. One important advantage is that the server-side script has complete control over the state of server controls even after a page has been rendered. Thus, even after a page is displayed to a user, the text that appears on a label or the contents of a list box can be altered by round trips, which occur when Web forms are returned to clients after data processing occurs at the server. This provides flexibility and improved performance to your application. In this chapter, you'll learn how to:

- Use ASP.NET server controls
- Code the functionality of a Web form

Using ASP.NET Server Controls

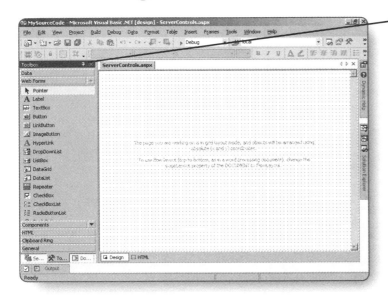

ASP.NET provides about 30 server controls to help you design your form. To view the list of controls, you can open a Web form in any ASP.NET application and access the Toolbox.

Some of the controls that you see in the Toolbox are similar in their functionality. For example, the Button, LinkButton, and ImageButton controls display buttons on the Web form. Similarly, the CheckBoxList and RadioButtonList controls display a number of options on the screen. The difference between these two controls is that the CheckBoxList control allows you to select multiple options from a list, while the RadioButtonList control only allows you to select one option. In this section, I will discuss one control for each type of functionality and describe the steps to configure the control by changing its properties.

As I explain the concepts in this chapter, you can create a sample application. Then you can build on the application as you study the later chapters of this book. When you finish reading this book, you will have created a completely functional application.

NOTE

Even though the same application is built upon as you read this book, the chapters are independent of each other. Each chapter includes concepts pertaining only to specific features of the application.

I have created an ASP.NET application, MySourceCode, and changed the name of the application's default form to Search.aspx. I have also changed the pageLayout property of the Web form to FlowLayout. Read on to learn how to design the Search form by adding controls to the form.

Working with the Label Control

The Label control is used to display information on a Web form. It is often used to label other controls on a Web form. For example, you might use the Label control to label a text box. However, you can also use the Label control to alter text that is displayed on a Web form, as you might do when you want to display an error message on a form. To add the Label control to a form, follow these steps.

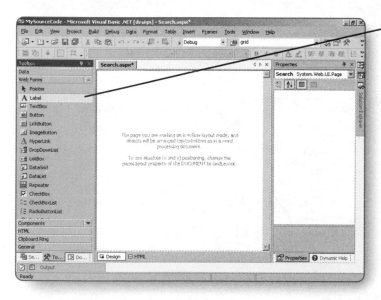

1. Click on the Label control in the Toolbox. The Label control will be selected.

TIP

If the Toolbox is not visible, click on the View menu and select Toolbox.

---

2. Press and hold the mouse button and drag the Label control to the form. The Label control will be placed on the form.

3. Right-click on the Label control. A shortcut menu will appear.

4. Click on Properties. The Properties window will appear.

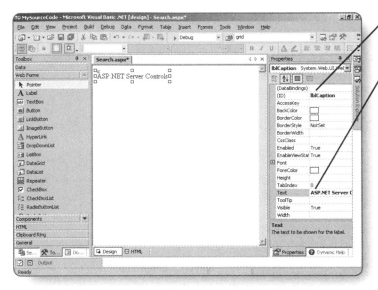

5. Type **lblCaption** in the ID property field for the label.

6. Type **ASP.NET Server Controls** in the Text property field for the label.

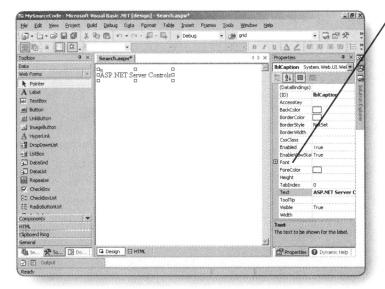

7. Double-click on the Font property. The properties for the font will appear.

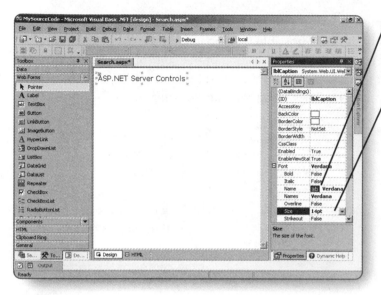

8. Click on the Name field and select Verdana from the list of fonts.

9. Type **14** in the Size property field.

NOTE

When specifying the size of the font, you can either type a numeric value or select a size from the drop-down menu. If you specify a numeric value, such as 14, it is converted to the size in points. However, if you select a size from the size list (for example, XX-Large), the size of the text will depend upon the settings of the browser.

For example, a font set to 36 points or XX-Large appears the same at design time. However, if a user has set the text size to smallest on his or her machine, at run time the font size will remain the same for text that is set to 36 points, but will change for text that is set to XX-Large.

When you use FlowLayout to design your form, you can use the Formatting toolbar to format it. In GridLayout, it is not possible to align your controls centrally on a form because you must specify the exact position of the control on the form. However, in FlowLayout you can align controls using the Formatting toolbar. The steps to align controls using the Formatting toolbar are given here.

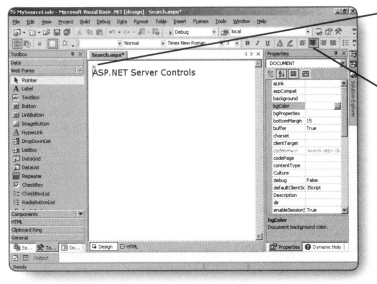

1. Click to the left of the lblCaption label. A caret will be placed at the point of click.

2. Click on the Center button on the Formatting toolbar. The lblCaption label will be aligned at the center of the form.

In the FlowLayout view, you can also type directly onto a form. Therefore, instead of adding the Label control to the form, you could've typed the text that you wanted on the form. However, I added the Label control to the form so you could see how to use the Label control and the steps to change the common properties of controls on the form. You can remove this control before you proceed.

Working with the DropDownList Control

The Search form that you design in this chapter uses the DropDownList control to display the parameters by which a user can search for an article. The parameters by which articles can be searched are Author, Topic, Level of Difficulty, and Date of Upload. The user can select one option from the drop-down list and search using that option. To add a DropDownList control to your application, follow these steps.

1. Click on the DropDownList control in the Toolbox. The control will be selected.

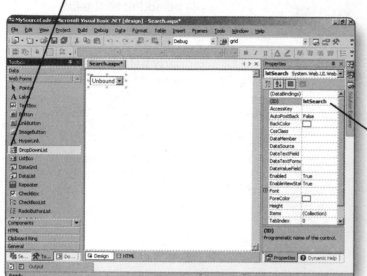

2. Press and hold the mouse button and drag the control to the form. The DropDownList control will be added to the form.

3. In the Properties window for the DropDownList control, change the ID property of the control to lstSearch.

4. To specify a label for the lstSearch control, click to the left of the control. A caret will appear.

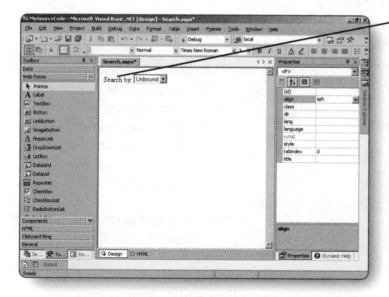

5. Type **Search by:**.

After you add the DropDownList control to the form, you need to add items to the list. To do so, use the Items Collection of the DropDownList control.

1. Click on the lstSearch control. The control will be selected.

2. Click on the Items Collection in the Properties window. An Ellipsis button will appear in the Items Collection.

3. Click on the Ellipsis button. The ListItem Collection Editor dialog box will open.

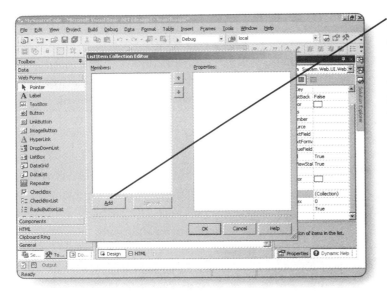

4. Click on Add. A new item will be added to the list.

5. Type Author in the Text property field for the first item in the list.

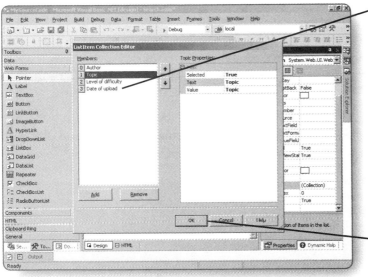

6. Repeat steps 4 and 5 to add three more items to the list. Specify Topic, Level of Difficulty, and Date of Upload in the Text properties for these controls. When you add the Topic item to the list, change the value of the Selected property from False to True. This will ensure that when the Web form is run, the Topic option is selected by default.

7. Click on OK. The ListItem Collection Editor dialog box will close.

After you add the DropDownList control to the form, you can change its properties, such as Font and ForeColor. For consistency, I always specify Verdana, X-Small as the font for controls.

Working with the Button Control

The Button control is used to submit a form to the server for processing. For example, users can fill in a registration form and submit it using a Submit button. In the Search.aspx form, the Button control is used to display a set of controls depending upon the option that the user has selected in the lstSearch control. For example, if the user has selected the Author option, the form will display a text box in which the user can type the name of the author.

To add the Button control to a form, follow these steps.

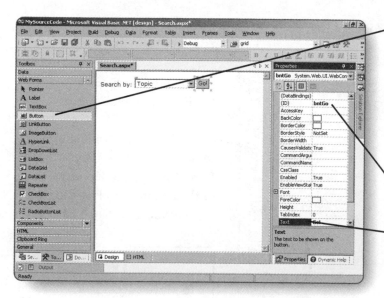

1. Drag the Button control from the Toolbox to the form. The control will be added to the form.

2. Invoke the Properties window for the control.

3. Change the ID of the control to btnGo.

4. Change the Text property of the control to Go!

After adding the Go! button to the form, you can check the option selected by the user in the Click event of the form and display other controls on the form accordingly.

Working with the Panel Control

When you want to group a number of controls, you can use a Panel control. For example, in the case of the Search form, you need to display different controls depending on the search option that the user has selected. You can group controls that pertain to each search option in a Panel control and display or hide the Panel control depending on the option selected by the user.

You have four search options. Therefore, you need to add four Panel controls to the form.

1. Drag the Panel control from the Toolbox to the form. The Panel control will appear on the form.

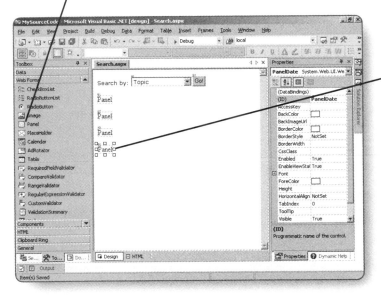

2. Change the ID property of the Panel to PanelAuthor.

3. Follow steps 1 and 2 above to add three more panels to the form. Change the ID properties of these panels to PanelTopic, PanelLevel, and PanelDate.

> **TIP**
>
> To move successive controls to new lines on the form, click to the right of a control and press the Enter key.

Each Panel control is labeled Panel by default. When you add controls to a panel, you can select the text and delete it. Keep reading to learn how to design each panel of the form.

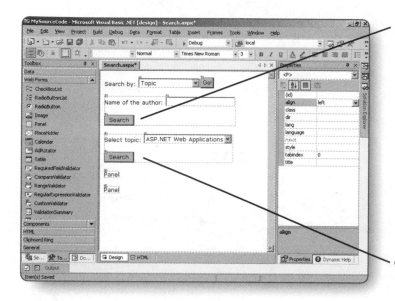

- **PanelAuthor**. The PanelAuthor panel allows the user to specify the name of the author and search for articles written by the author. Therefore, this panel includes a TextBox control and a Button control. You can drag these controls from the Toolbox. I have named the TextBox control txtAuthor and the Search button btnAuthor.

- **PanelTopic**. The PanelTopic panel includes a DropDownList control that lists the topics that can be used to search for articles. The steps to add a DropDownList control were discussed earlier, in the "Working with the DropDownList Control" section of this chapter. After you add the DropDownList control to the form, change its ID to lstTopic and add five items to it: ASP.NET Web Applications, ASP.NET Web Services, Visual Basic and Visual C#, Visual C++ .NET, and .NET Framework SDK.

The PanelLevel and PanelDate panels include the RadioButtonList and Calendar controls. I will discuss these controls in the following sections.

Working with the RadioButtonList Control

The RadioButtonList control is used to add a group of radio buttons to the form. For example, if you need to accept the age group of users, you can use the RadioButtonList control and add different radio buttons that signify different age groups.

In the MySourceCode application, the articles that are added to the form are rated on the basis of their difficulty. Articles can be for beginning, intermediate, or advanced users. When searching for articles, users can set the difficulty level as a parameter. When they do so, the PanelLevel control is displayed to the user. This panel contains a RadioButtonList control that allows the user to select the difficulty of the article. To add the RadioButtonList control to a form, follow these steps.

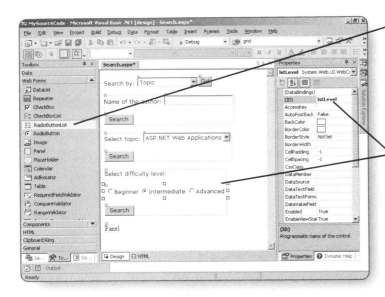

1. Drag a RadioButtonList control from the Toolbox to the PanelLevel control on the form. The RadioButtonList control will be placed in the PanelLevel control.

2. Change the ID of the control to lstLevel and add three items to the control—Beginner, Intermediate, and Advanced.

TIP

The procedure to add items to a RadioButtonList control is the same as the procedure to add items to a DropDownList control.

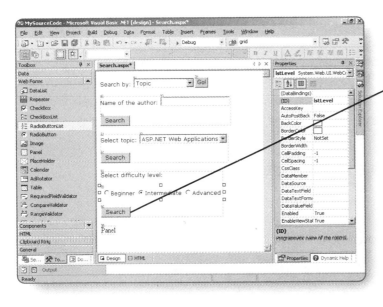

3. Add a Search button and type the label for the RadioButtonList control to complete the PanelLevel control.

Working with the Calendar Control

The Calendar control is used to select a date. In the MySourceCode application, users can select a date to retrieve the articles that have been updated later than the date specified.

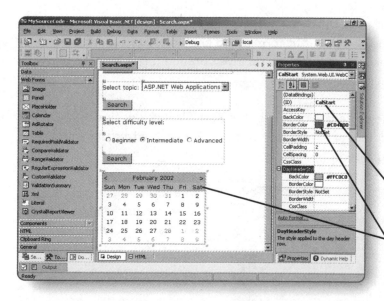

You need to add the Calendar control to the PanelDate panel. To do so, follow these steps.

1. Drag the Calendar control from the Toolbox to the PanelDate panel. The control will be added to the form.

2. Change the ID of the Calendar control to CalStart.

3. You can change the appearance of a Calendar control to make it blend with your Web form. For example, you can change the color of the title bar and the border of the calendar to match your preferences. For this calendar, I have changed the BorderColor property to #C04000, the BackColor property in the TitleStyle to #DFA894, and the BackColor property in the DayHeaderStyle to #FFC0C0.

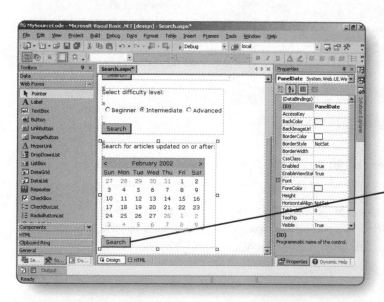

4. Complete the PanelDate panel by adding a title for the calendar and a Search button.

Working with the AdRotator Control

Aside from the controls discussed previously, another useful control that you can use on your form is the AdRotator control. This control enables you to randomly select and display advertisements on a Web form.

The advertisements that need to appear in the AdRotator control are specified in an XML file. The XML file is in a specific format and enables you to specify the location of advertisement banners and the relative duration for which each banner should appear.

A sample XML file is shown here. Notice that the XML file includes three Ad elements that specify details of each advertisement. For each advertisement, the following elements are present.

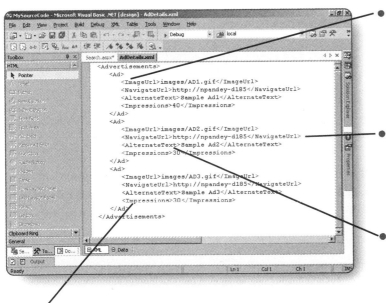

- **ImageUrl**. The ImageUrl element specifies the URL of an image file. The URL that you specify is relative to the root directory of the Web site.

- **NavigateUrl**. The NavigateUrl element specifies the URL to which users should be redirected when they click on an advertisement banner.

- **AlternateText**. The AlternateText element specifies the text that should be displayed if the advertisement banner cannot be found. This text is also displayed as a tool tip when the user hovers the mouse pointer over an advertisement.

- **Impressions**. The Impressions element specifies the relative time for which each advertisement should be displayed. For example, the values for the Impressions element for the three advertisements are 40, 30, and 30. Therefore, these advertisements would be displayed in the ratio 4:3:3.

In order to use the AdRotator control, you need to add the XML file to your application. Save the XML file to the same directory as your application and follow these steps.

1. Click on View. The View menu will appear.

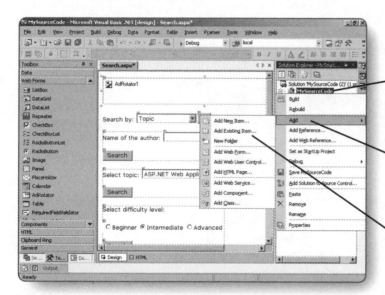

2. Click on Solution Explorer. The Solution Explorer will open.

3. Right-click on the name of the project. A shortcut menu will appear.

4. Move the mouse pointer to Add. The Add submenu will appear.

5. Click on Add Existing Item. The Add Existing Item - MySourceCode dialog box will open.

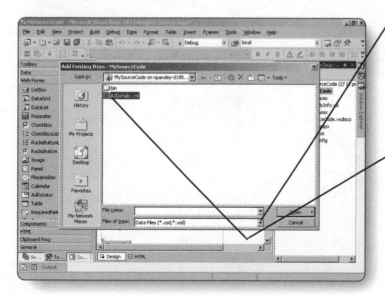

6. Click on the Files of Type down arrow and select Data Files (*.xsd;*.xml) from the list. The XML file that you added to the application's root directory will appear.

7. Click on the XML file and click on Open to add it to your project.

After you add the XML file to your project, you can add an AdRotator control to the Search.aspx form.

1. Place a caret before the first element on the Search.aspx form and press Enter to move the element to the next line.

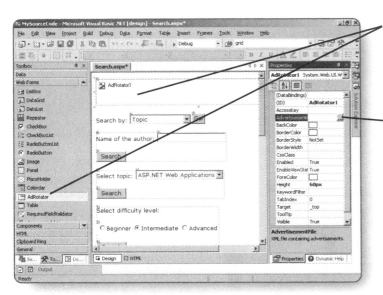

2. Drag the AdRotator control from the Toolbox to the form. The control will be placed on the form.

3. Click on the Ellipsis button for the AdvertisementFile property. The Select XML File dialog box will appear.

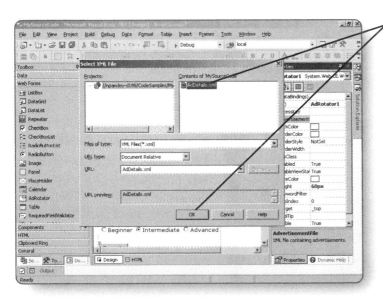

4. Click on the XML file and click on OK to define the XML file associated with the AdRotator control.

After you add the AdRotator control to the form, the design of the form is complete. Next, you need to write the code for displaying selective controls on the form depending upon the search parameter that a user selects. You'll learn how to do that in the next section.

Coding the Functionality of a Web Form

You typically write the code to implement the functionality of an ASP.NET Web application either in the Load event of a form or in the Click event of one or more buttons on the form. In this section, I will explain the steps to code the functionality of the Search.aspx form, which enables a user to specify a parameter and a value by which articles should be searched in the application.

Coding the Load Event of a Form

The Load event of a form is often used to configure the initial state of a Web form before the form is displayed to the user. For example, you might want to retrieve data from a database and display it on the home page of a Web application.

In the Search.aspx form, the Load event of the form is used to hide all the panels from the form except the PanelTopic panel, which is associated with the Topic item of the Search By list.

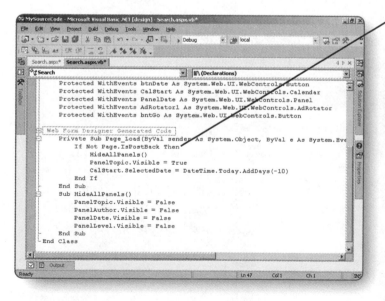

In the code for the Load event of the form, you'll notice that I first use the IsPostBack property of the Page class to check whether the form is being posted back, which occurs when the user clicks on a button to submit a form for processing by the server. When the form is posted back, you need to ensure that the code of the Load event is not run. Otherwise, the same panel will be displayed every time the user selects a search parameter and clicks on the Search button.

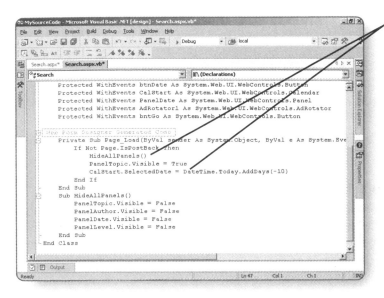

Next, the HideAllPanels() function hides all of the panels. Since the Topic option is selected in the Search By list, the PanelTopic panel is made visible. Finally, a date that is 10 days before the current date is selected in the CalStart calendar.

Hiding and Displaying Panels on a Form

You need to display or hide panels depending on the search parameter selected by a user. For example, if a user wants to search for articles by the name of the author, you need to hide all other panels except PanelAuthor.

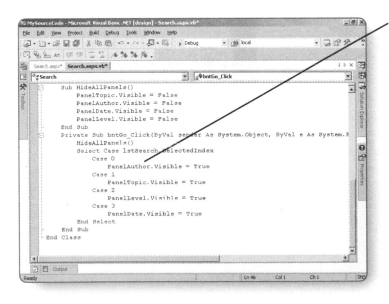

To determine which panel should be displayed, I've added the Go! button to the form. In the Click event of the Go! button, you can determine the option that the user has selected in the Search By list and load the appropriate panel.

After you write the code to determine which panel to display, set the Search.aspx form as the startup form and run the application. See Chapter 5, "Beginning with a Simple ASP.NET Application," for more information about specifying a startup form and running the application.

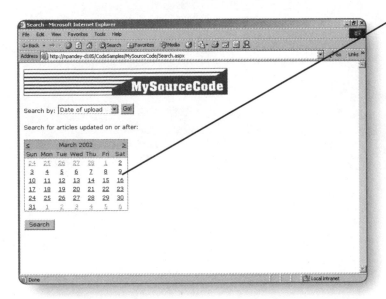

When you run the form, the Topic option is selected in the Search By list by default. Select a different option and click on Go! The panel corresponding to the option you selected will be automatically displayed and the panel that was previously displayed will be hidden.

You will notice that the Search form is not complete yet. You still need to write the code for the Search button in each panel. However, this involves connectivity to a database and the use of data binding server controls. See Chapter 11, "Displaying Data Using Data Binding Server Controls," to complete the Search.aspx form by adding the code to retrieve data from the database and display it on the form.

7

Accepting Information Using Web Forms

In ASP.NET applications, you often accept information from users. To accept information from users, you can use the ASP.NET server controls, as well as HTML controls. Often, it becomes necessary to use server controls and HTML controls in conjunction to accept information. For example, if a user wants to upload a file to the Web server, it is best done using HTML controls.

An ASP.NET form that accepts information from a user needs to be validated. You need to ensure that the user has provided values for mandatory fields of a form, and that the provided values are valid. ASP.NET includes a number of validation controls that enable you to validate information specified by users. For example, you can ensure that a field has not been left blank, and that the values specified by the user are in the correct format. In this chapter, you'll learn how to:

- Design forms to accept information
- Validate information on a form

Designing Forms to Accept Information

You can design customized forms to accept information from users. The design of the form and the validation rules will depend on the purpose of the information you are accepting from users. You might also make it optional for users to specify certain information.

Regardless of the design of your form, the concepts for accepting information from users are the same. In this section, I will design a Web form for accepting the details of a new article that a user wants to add to a Web application. When the user specifies the details of the new article, he will also have the option to upload source files for the article using HTML controls.

Understanding Form Structure

The form that you will design in this section is used to accept details of a new article that is added to an application. The form, AddNew.aspx, is a component of the MySourceCode application. The application is a corporate portal that is used to share programming code with developers. You created the Search.aspx form for this application in Chapter 6, "Adding Server Controls to a Web Form;" see Chapter 6 for more information.

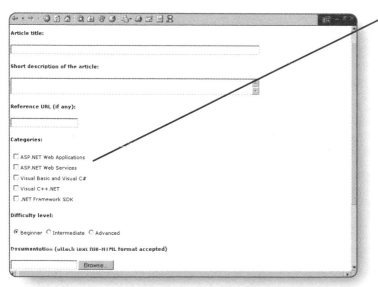

The details of the article accepted on the AddNew.aspx form are the title and description of the article, the category and difficulty level of the article, the documentation, and the source code for the article. I will now walk you through the steps to create a form.

Adding Server Controls to a Form

Server controls are server-side components that are used to display information on Web forms. They are also used for processing information that is provided by users. Most of the server controls were discussed in Chapter 6, "Adding Server Controls to a Web Form." The AddNew.aspx form uses four types of server controls: TextBox, CheckBoxList, RadioButtonList, and Button.

Before you add server controls to a form, open the MySourceCode application. If you have not created the MySourceCode application, create a new ASP.NET Web application, and then add a Web form to the application and name it AddNew.aspx. See Chapter 5, "Beginning with a Simple ASP.NET Application" for more information about adding Web forms to a project.

After you add the Web form to your project, follow these steps to add server controls to the Web form.

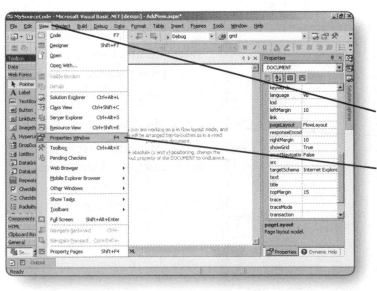

1. Double-click on the AddNew.aspx form in the Solution Explorer. The form will open in Design view.

2. Click on View. The View menu will appear.

3. Click on Properties Window. The Properties window will appear.

4. Change the pageLayout property from GridLayout to FlowLayout. The layout of the page will change.

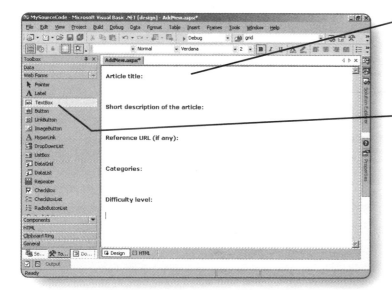

5. Type the label for each server control that you want to add to the Web form. Leave a blank line after each label.

6. Add TextBox controls to accept the title, description, and reference URL of an article.

7. Change the ID properties of the TextBox controls to txtTitle, txtDescription, and txtURL, respectively.

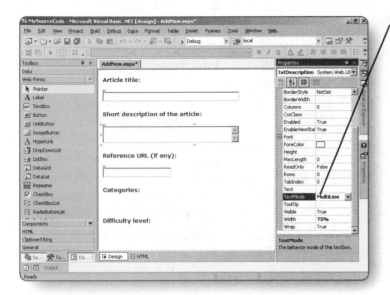

8. Change the TextMode property of the txtDescription control to MultiLine.

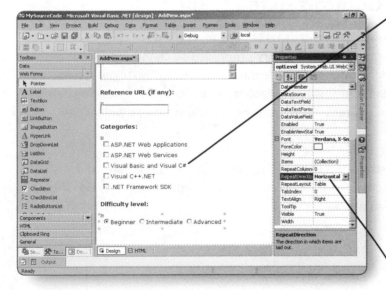

9. Add a CheckBoxList control to the form. Change the ID property of the control to optCategory and add five items to the list: ASP.NET Web Applications, ASP.NET Web Services, Visual Basic and Visual C#, Visual C++ .NET, and .NET Framework SDK. See Chapter 6, "Adding Server Controls to a Web Form," for more information about adding items to a list.

10. Add a RadioButtonList control to the form. Change the ID property of the control to optLevel and the RepeatDirection property to Horizontal.

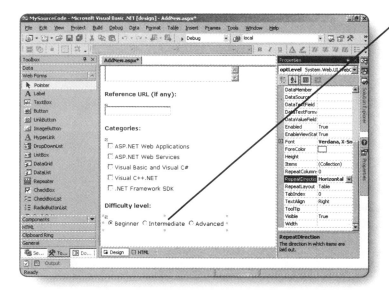

11. Add three items to the optLevel control: Beginner, Intermediate, and Advanced.

A Submit button must be added to the form to enable the user to submit the form for processing when it is completed. However, I will add this button after I complete the design of the form by adding HTML controls to incorporate the functionality of uploading files to the Web server.

Adding HTML Controls to the Form

HTML controls are controls that map to HTML elements used for designing Web forms. HTML controls provide the necessary properties to change the state of the control on the client side. However, these controls can be easily run as server controls by specifying the runat=server directive. Therefore, these controls are useful when you want to process information on the client side as well as the server side.

In this section, I will illustrate the use of HTML controls to upload files to a Web server. I will use these controls to accept the documentation, source code, and graphic files, if any, for an article.

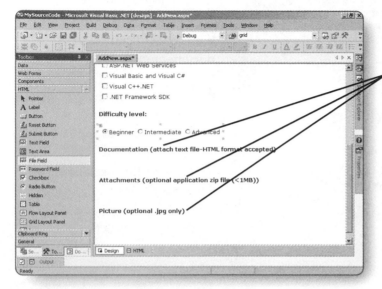

To add HTML controls to a form, follow these steps.

1. Type the labels for the documentation, attachments, and picture file controls that you want to add to the form.

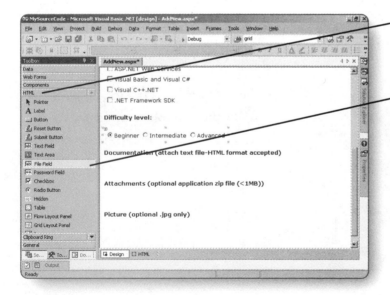

2. Click on the HTML tab in the Toolbox. The available HTML controls will appear.

3. Click on the File Field control. The control will be selected.

4. Press and hold the mouse button and drag the control to the form. The File Field control will be added to the form.

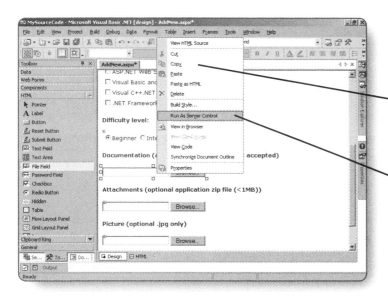

5. Change the ID property of the File Field control to documentation.

6. Right-click on the documentation control. A shortcut menu will appear.

7. Click on Run as Server Control.

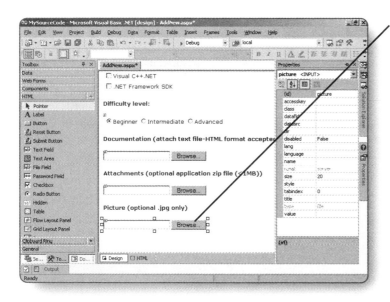

8. Repeat steps 5–7 to add two additional File Field controls to the form.

9. Change the ID properties of the controls to attachments and picture, respectively.

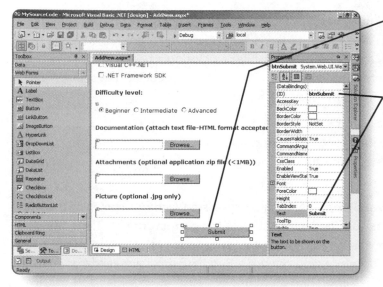

10. Select a Button control from the Web Forms tab of the Toolbox and add it to the form.

11. Change the ID property of the Button control to btnSubmit and the Text property to Submit.

Validating Information on a Form

By now, you are familiar with the need to validate a form. ASP.NET provides a number of validation controls that enable you to validate information provided by users in server and HTML controls.

In this section, I will introduce you to the validation controls that are provided by ASP.NET. I will then use these controls on a form and perform validation.

Understanding Validation Controls in ASP.NET

ASP.NET provides six validation controls. These controls include

● **RequiredFieldValidator**. The RequiredFieldValidator control is used to ensure that a user has not left a field blank. For example, you can associate a RequiredFieldValidator control with the user name field to ensure that the user does not leave the field blank.

- **CompareValidator**. The CompareValidator control is used to compare the value specified by a user in one control with values in another control, or with a predefined set of values. For example, while registering a user, you can use the CompareValidator control to ensure that the user has specified the same values in the Password and Confirm Password fields.

- **RangeValidator**. The RangeValidator control is used to compare the values specified by a user with a range of values. For example, you can use the RangeValidator control to ensure that the age specified by a user is between 1 and 100.

- **RegularExpressionValidator**. The RegularExpressionValidator control is used to ensure that a user has specified information in the correct format. There are a number of expressions, such as URLs and e-mail addresses, which follow a predefined format. Therefore, you can use a RegularExpressionValidator control to ensure that a user has entered a piece of data, such as an e-mail address, in the predefined format.

- **CustomValidator**. The CustomValidator control is used to specify a script for validation. Sometimes you will realize that none of the validation controls that are provided by ASP.NET meet your requirements. For example, how would you ensure that a user has specified a valid file for uploading? You can specify a script for the CustomValidator control. The script is then executed each time the Web form is submitted to the server for processing. If the values specified by the user do not meet the required criteria, an error message is displayed on the Web form.

- **ValidationSummary**. The ValidationSummary control is used to summarize all incorrect values on a Web form. For example, you might use a number of validation controls on the same form. When a user submits the form, you can use the ValidationSummary control to summarize all of the error messages or display all of the error messages in a message box.

Now that you have examined all of the validation controls, you need to add these controls to a Web form.

Adding Validation Controls to a Form

In this section, I will add different types of validation controls to validate data specified by a user in the AddNew.aspx form. To add validation controls to the form, follow these steps.

1. Click on the RequiredFieldValidator control in the Toolbox.

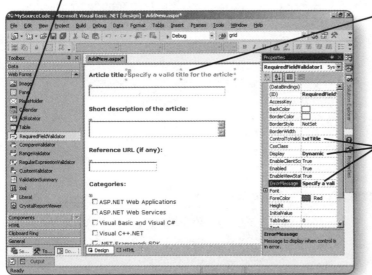

2. Press and hold the mouse button and drag the control beyond the label of the first text box on the form. A RequiredFieldValidator control will be added to the form.

3. Change the ControlToValidate property of the RequiredFieldValidator control to txtTitle. Change the Display property to Dynamic, and change the ErrorMessage property to Specify a Valid Title for the Article.

NOTE

Take a moment to consider the properties of the RequiredFieldValidator control that you have changed. The ControlToValidate property specifies the control to be validated. Setting the Display property to Dynamic adjusts the position of the error message that is displayed depending upon the width of the form. Finally, the ErrorMessage property specifies the error message that is displayed if a control is not validated successfully.

---

4. Repeat steps 1–3 to add another RequiredFieldValidator control for validating the txtDescription control.

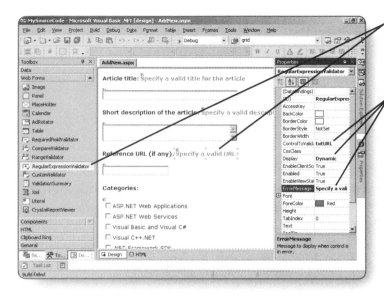

5. Add a RegularExpression Validator control to validate the txtURL control.

6. Change the ControlTo Validate, Display, and ErrorMessage properties to txtURL, Dynamic, and Specify a Valid URL, respectively.

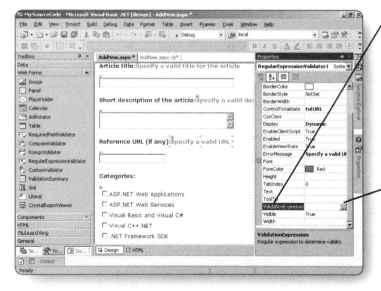

7. For the RegularExpression Validator control, you also need to specify the validation expression. Click on the ValidationExpression property. An Ellipsis button will appear next to the ValidationExpression property.

8. Click on the Ellipsis button. The Regular Expression Editor dialog box will open.

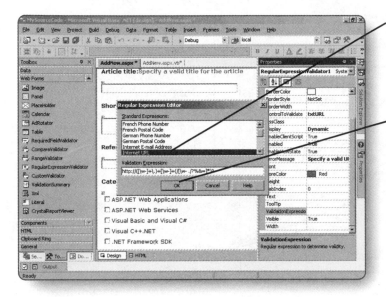

9. Click on the Internet URL option in the Standard Expressions list. The option will be selected.

10. Click on OK. An expression that corresponds to an Internet URL will be added to the ValidationExpression property.

TIP

Often users do not include the http:// prefix when specifying a URL. To accept a URL from the user without the http:// prefix, you can change the ValidationExpression property from http://([\w-]+\.)+[\w-]+(/[\w- ./?%&=]*)? to ([\w-]+\.)+[\w-]+(/[\w- ./?%&=]*)?

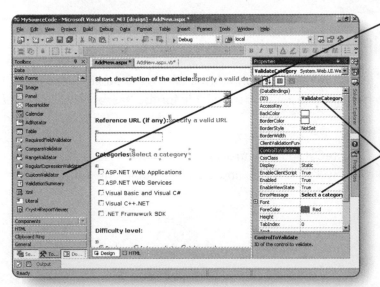

11. You also need to validate the optCategory, documentation, attachments, and picture controls. Drag the CustomValidator control from the Toolbox to the form.

12. Change the ID property of the control to ValidateCategory. Change the Display property to Dynamic, and change the ErrorMessage property to Select a Category.

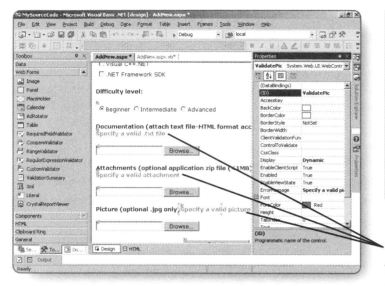

13. Repeat steps 11 and 12 to add CustomValidator controls for the documentation, attachments, and picture controls. The IDs for the validation controls should be ValidateDoc, ValidateAtt, and ValidatePic, respectively.

For CustomValidator controls, you need to specify a validation script. The script is executed every time the page is submitted. If the control with which the CustomValidator control is associated is not validated successfully, an error message will be displayed. I will now write the script for the CustomValidator controls that you added in steps 11–13.

Coding the Validation Logic

The validation logic for a CustomValidator control is coded in the Server_Validate event of the control. To begin, write the validation logic for the ValidateCategory control.

1. Double-click on the ValidateCategory control in Design view. The declaration for the Server_Validate event will be created, and the code-behind file for the form will open.

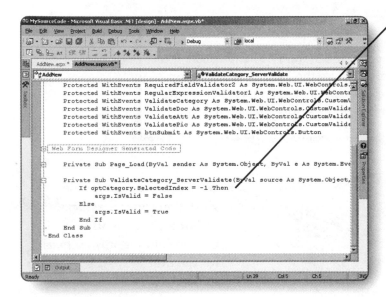

2. Write the code for the Server_Validate event. The code written here determines whether any option is selected in the optCategory list. When no option is selected in the list, the value of the SelectedIndex property is −1. When the value is −1, the IsValid property for the control that is being validated is set to False.

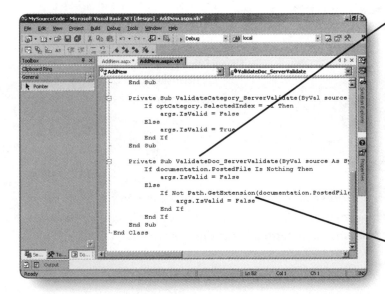

3. Write the code for the ValidateDoc CustomValidator control. The code written here determines whether the user has a file name. If the user has not specified a file name (which is determined by examining the PostedFile property of the documentation control), the IsValid property of the control is set to False.

4. Use the GetExtension function of the Path class to check the file extension, which will determine the validity of the file entered by the user. If the extension of the file is not .txt, the IsValid property of the documentation control is set to False.

> **NOTE**
>
> Make sure that you import the System.IO namespace into your application before you use the Path class. To import the System.IO namespace, specify the Imports System.IO statement as the first line of the AddNew.aspx.vb file.

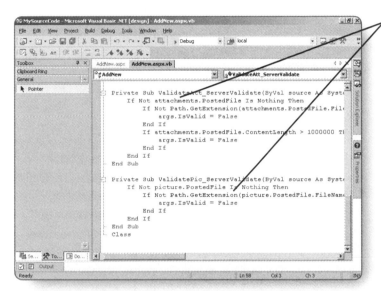

5. Write the code for the validation controls associated with the attachments and picture controls. It is optional for the user to specify a value in these controls. Therefore, validate the controls only when the user has specified values in the control. You should also check whether the size of the uploaded file is less than 1 MB. This is determined by the ContentLength property of the attachments control.

Running the Form

Now you can run the form to determine whether the validation controls work as desired. Click on the Debug menu and select Start. When the application executes, type the address of the AddNew.aspx form in your Web browser.

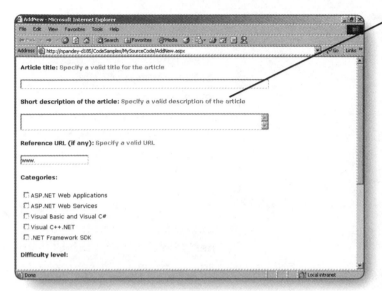

Click on the Submit button without specifying any values in the controls on the form. The error messages that you specified for the RequiredFieldValidator controls will be displayed. If you supply values for the first two controls and then click on Submit, the other validations will be performed and error messages, if any, will be displayed.

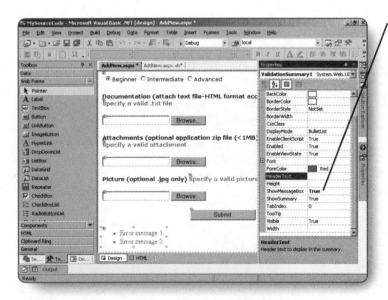

To display the error messages in a message box, add the ValidationSummary control to the form and change its ShowMessageBox property to True.

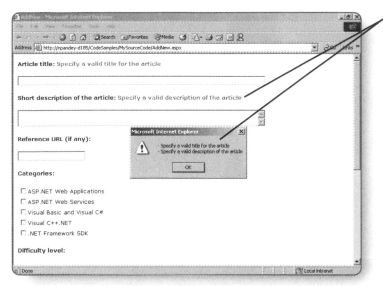

After you add the ValidationSummary control to the form and click on the Submit button without specifying valid values for any of the controls, a message box will appear. Notice that the error message that appears in the message box also appears on the form.

This completes our discussion of the validation controls. In the next two chapters, you will learn about the basics of database access. You will use those concepts to code the complete functionality of the forms in your application.

8

SQL Server Basics

In addition to the source code of an application in ASP.NET, you also need databases and tables in which to store data for the application. These databases need to be compatible with the application to ensure that data can be easily added, modified, and retrieved.

ASP.NET is compatible with SQL Server and can store and retrieve data from SQL Server using SQL commands. Before you begin using SQL Server in ASP.NET applications, you should know the basics of creating and managing SQL Server databases. In this chapter, you'll learn how to:

- Create databases and tables using the SQL Server Enterprise Manager
- Insert, update, and delete data from databases using the Query Analyzer
- Retrieve data from databases using the Query Analyzer
- Create stored procedures using the Query Analyzer

Creating Databases and Tables

Before you can store data for an ASP.NET application in SQL Server, you need to create a database and add tables to it.

In this section, you will learn how to create a database in SQL Server using the SQL Server Enterprise Manager. Then you will learn to create a table in the database.

Creating a Database

When you install SQL Server 2000, you can register more than one instance of SQL Server on the same computer. After registering the SQL servers, you can use the SQL Server Enterprise Manager to manage them. SQL Server Enterprise Manager is an MMC (*Microsoft Management Console*)-based tool that provides a GUI (*Graphical User Interface*) for managing SQL servers and databases. Two important tasks performed by SQL Server Enterprise Manager are database and table creation.

You can open the SQL Server Enterprise Manager from the Microsoft SQL Server submenu in the Programs menu. To create a database in SQL Server using the SQL Enterprise Manager, follow these steps.

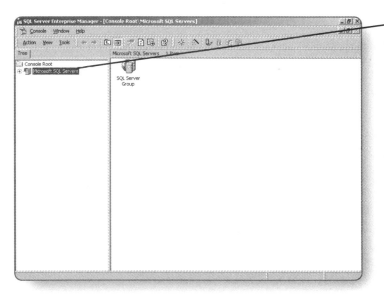

1. Click on the plus sign next to the Microsoft SQL Servers option. The list of SQL server groups created on the computer will be displayed.

2. Click on the plus sign next to the SQL Server Group option. The list of SQL servers installed on the computer will be displayed.

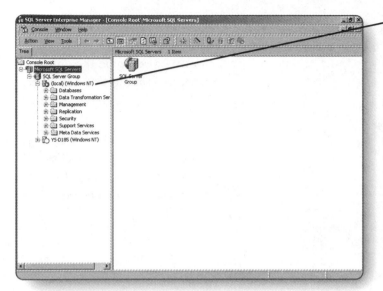

3. Click on the plus sign next to the server on which you want to create the database. The components of the database will be displayed, and more buttons will appear on the toolbar in the Console window.

4. Click on Action. The Action menu will appear.

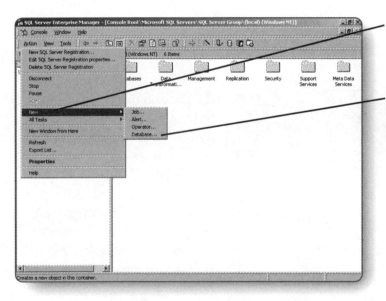

5. Move the mouse pointer to New. The New submenu will appear.

6. Click on Database. The Database Properties dialog box will open.

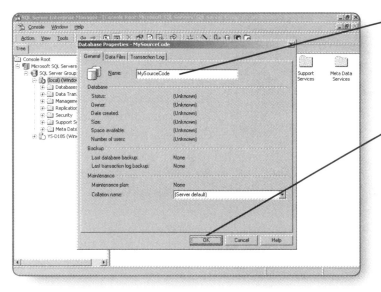

7. Type the name of the database that you want to create. As you type the name, it will appear in the title bar of the Database Properties dialog box.

8. Click on OK. The Database Properties dialog box will close, and a new database will be created with the name you specified.

Creating a Table

To create a table in SQL Server using SQL Enterprise Manager, simply follow these steps.

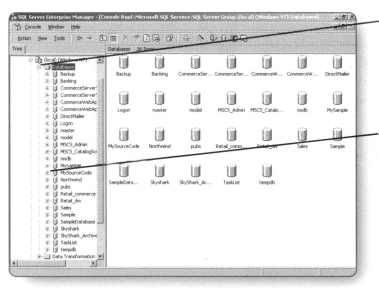

1. Click on the plus sign next to the Databases option. The databases on the server to which you are connected will be displayed.

2. Click on the plus sign next to the database in which you want to create a table. The contents of the database will be displayed.

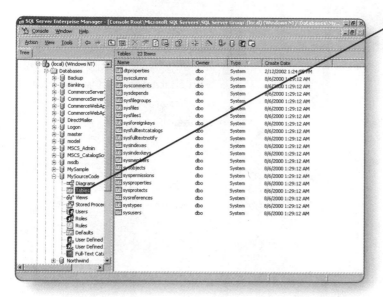

3. Click on the Tables option. A list of all the tables in the selected database will be displayed in the right pane of the console window.

4. Click on Action. The Action menu will appear.

5. Click on New Table. A new console window will appear.

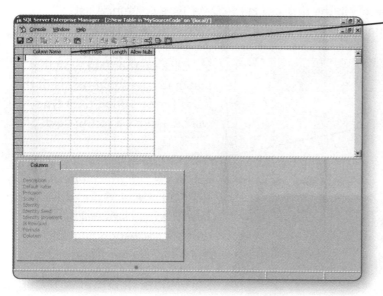

6. In the rows contained in the window, specify the details of the fields that are to be included in the table. For each field you need to specify the field name, the data type of the field, the length of the field, and whether or not the field will contain null values.

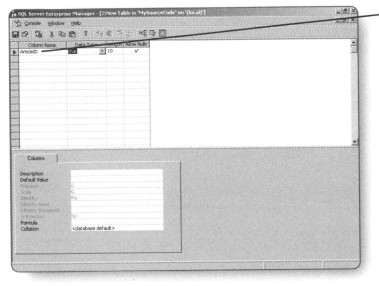

7. Type the name of the first field in the table and press the Tab key. By default, the field will be a character field with a size of 10 characters that allows null values.

8. Click on the down arrow in the first cell in the Data Type column. A list containing all possible field types will be displayed.

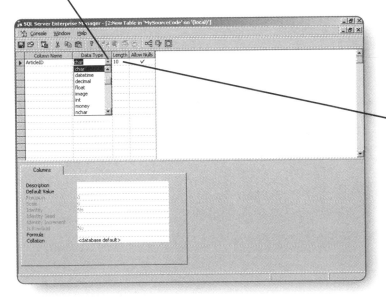

9. Click on the data type that matches the requirements of the field. The specified data type will be assigned to the field.

10. Double-click on the first cell in the Length column, type the field size, and press the Tab key. The field size will be set, and the corresponding cell in the Allow Nulls column will be selected.

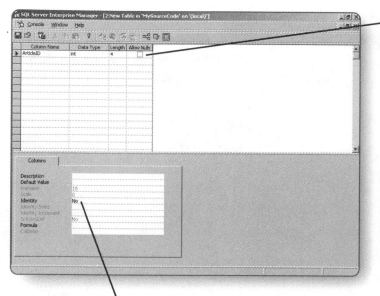

11. Click on the check box in the first cell of the Allow Nulls column. The check mark in the Allow Nulls column will be cleared. This ensures that you will not be able to specify null values for the field.

> **TIP**
>
> If you want to allow null values in a field, you should not clear the check box in the Allow Nulls field.

12. Click on the Identity field in the Columns section. A down arrow will appear. This box is active only if the int data type is specified for a field. Selecting this box ensures that you cannot insert or edit values in the selected field, and that a value is automatically specified for each new row.

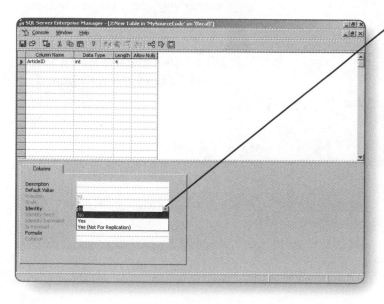

13. Click on the down arrow in the Identity field. A drop-down list of options will appear.

14. Click on Yes. This will ensure that the selected field will contain integer values that will be automatically incremented by 1 for each row of values.

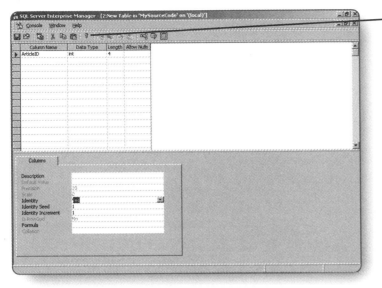

15. Click on the Set Primary Key button. The selected field will be set as the primary field of the table.

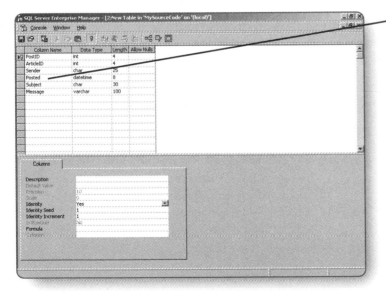

16. Create the rest of the fields of the database table the same way you created the first field.

17. Click on Save. The Choose Name dialog box will open.

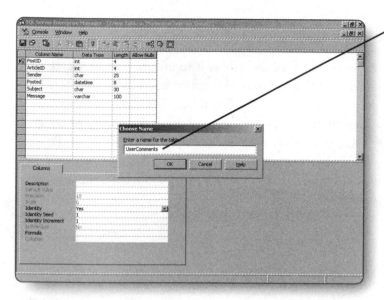

18. Type the name of the new table and click on OK. The table will be saved.

19. Click on Close. The window will close, and the updated table list for the selected database will appear.

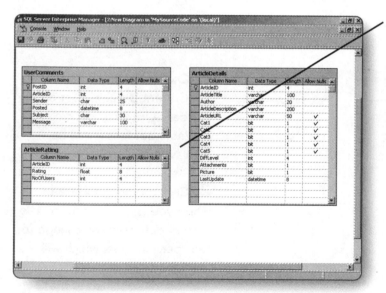

In the preceding steps, I created the UserComments table of the MySourceCode database. You can repeat these steps to create other tables for the database. As shown here, I have created three tables for the database.

Managing Data

The main purpose for creating databases and tables is to ensure that application data can be stored, updated, and deleted from the appropriate tables easily. You can insert, update, and delete data from the tables in SQL Server by running SQL commands in the Query Analyzer that can be displayed using the Query Analyzer option on the Microsoft SQL Server submenu.

In this section, you will learn to insert, update, and delete data from a table in SQL Server using the Query Analyzer.

Inserting Data

Before you insert data in a table using the Query Analyzer, you need to select the database that contains the table into which you want to insert data. You can open the Query Analyzer from the Microsoft SQL Server submenu in the Programs menu.

After you've opened the Query Analyzer, select the database that contains the appropriate table.

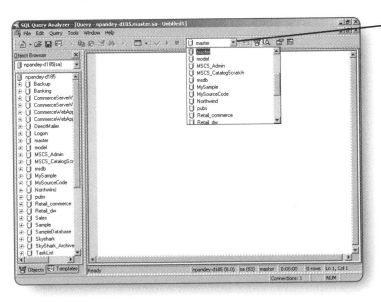

1. Click on the down arrow for the Current Database list on the toolbar. A list of all of the available databases will be displayed.

2. Click on the database to which you want to connect. The current database will change to the specified one, which will ensure that all of the SQL commands specified in the Query Analyzer will be run on that database.

After you connect to the database, you can type SQL commands in the Query window to manage data in the current database. Use the INSERT INTO command to insert data into a table using the Query Analyzer. The syntax of the command for inserting data into a table that contains three fields is

```
INSERT INTO TableName (FieldOneName, FieldTwoName, FieldThreeName) VALUES
                      (ValueOne,ValueTwo,ValueThree)
```

The TableName value represents the name of the table into which data will be added. Replace TableName with the appropriate table name.

The FieldOneName, FieldTwoName, and FieldThreeName values represent the fields in the table. Notice that these field names are enclosed in parentheses and separated by commas. Replace these values with the names of fields to which data will be added.

NOTE

You do not need to include all of the fields in the table in the INSERT statement. You can omit the fields that contain null values.

TIP

If you want to insert values that require characters or dates, you need to enclose them in quotes.

After you specify the name of the table and the names of the fields into which data will be added, you need to specify the values that will be added to each of the fields that follow the VALUES keyword. In this example, the values to be added to the table are represented by ValueOne, ValueTwo, and ValueThree. Notice that they are enclosed in parentheses and separated by commas. These values should be in the same order as the field names specified after the table name. In addition, they should be specified in accordance with the data types for their respective fields.

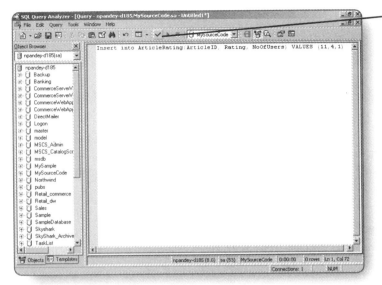

You can now insert a record into a table using the INSERT statement. A SQL query to insert a record into the ArticleRating table is shown here. After you type the SQL command to insert data into the specified table, you need to execute the command. Click on the Parse Query button. The Query Analyzer will check whether the syntax of the command you typed is correct.

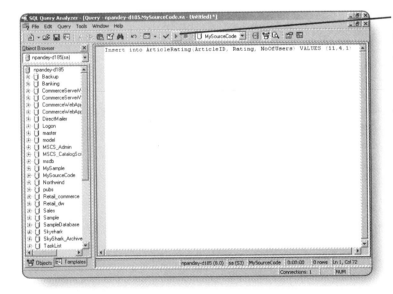

Click on the Execute Query button. The Query Analyzer will execute the specified command and add the values you specified to the table named in the command.

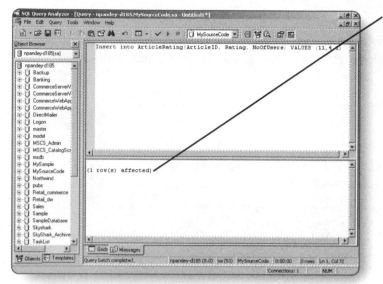

After the query executes, the result will be visible in the Messages tab of the Query Analyzer window.

Updating Data

You often need to change data in tables. For example, when a user rates your article, the rating should be reflected in the database. If the rating for an article already exists, then it needs to be updated. In this section, I will examine the steps to update data in a database.

Before you update data in a table using the Query Analyzer, you need to select the database that contains the table you want to update. After you connect to the database, you can type the SQL commands in the Query window to update table data.

1. Use the UPDATE command to update data in a table using the Query Analyzer. The syntax of the command for updating data in a table containing three fields is

```
UPDATE TableName SET FieldOneName = ValueOne, FieldTwoName = ValueTwo,
                FieldThreeName = ValueThree Where (FieldOne = Value1)
```

2. The TableName value represents the name of the table in which data will be updated. Replace this value with the appropriate table name.

3. After you specify the name of the table, you need to specify the keyword SET. FieldOneName, FieldTwoName, and FieldThreeName represent the fields in the table. Replace these values with the names of the fields in which data will be updated.

NOTE

You do not need to include all of the fields in the table in the UPDATE statement. The fields that are not specified in the UPDATE statement will retain their current values.

---

4. In this example, ValueOne, ValueTwo, and ValueThree represent values that need to be updated in the database. Replace these values with the values that will be updated in the database.

5. The WHERE clause determines the rows in which the updated values will be specified. It contains field names and values. However, these values represent the value that the specified field of an existing row should contain. The rows that match the criteria specified in the WHERE clause are updated according to the SET clause. If you omit the WHERE clause, the values of the specified fields are updated for all of the rows in the table.

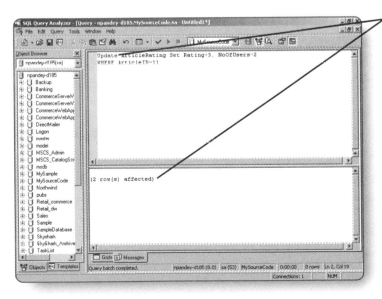

In this example, I have used the UPDATE statement to update data in the ArticleRating table. After you have typed the SQL command to update data in the specified table, you can execute the command. The result of the query will appear in the Messages tab of the Query Analyzer window.

Deleting Data

When there is a redundancy in the data in a table, you might need to delete information.

1. Use the DELETE command in the Query Analyzer to delete data from a table. The syntax of the command for deleting data from a table is

```
DELETE TableName Where (FieldOne = ValueOne) AND/OR/NOT (FieldTwo = ValueTwo)
```

2. TableName represents the name of the table from which data will be deleted. Replace TableName with the appropriate table name.

3. After you specify the table, you need to specify the WHERE clause. This clause is used to determine the rows that need to be deleted from the specified table. If you have multiple criteria, you can use the AND, OR, and NOT logical operators to select the rows to be deleted.

- **AND**. Use the AND clause to specify deletion for rows in the table that meet all of the criteria in the WHERE clause.

- **OR**. Use the OR clause to specify deletion for rows that meet any of the criteria in the WHERE clause.

- **NOT**. Use the NOT clause to specify deletion for rows that do not meet the criteria in the WHERE clause.

TIP	**NOTE**
You can use parentheses to specify two or more criteria and prioritize the logical operators.	If you omit the WHERE clause, all the rows of the specified table will be deleted.

4. After you have typed the SQL command to delete rows from a specified table, execute the command. The rows will be deleted from the table.

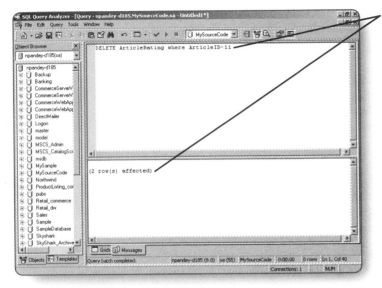

I have used the DELETE statement to delete records that have the ArticleID of 11 from the ArticleRating table. When you run this query, the records will be deleted from the ArticleDetails table, and the result will be displayed in the Messages tab of the Query Analyzer window.

Retrieving Data

In an ASP.NET application, you often retrieve data from a database and display it on a form using the SELECT statement. The SELECT statement can accept a parameter, or it can be run without any specified parameters.

In this section, you will learn to retrieve data from a table in SQL Server using the SELECT statement.

Retrieving Data Using the SELECT Query

The syntax for a simple SELECT query is

```
SELECT * FROM TableName
```

In this syntax, the * keyword signifies that all of the values from all rows of the table are to be retrieved from the table specified by TableName. However, if you need to retrieve only specific rows from the table, you can use the following syntax.

```
SELECT FieldOne, FieldTwo, FieldThree FROM TableName
```

Notice that a comma separates each field name. This syntax will retrieve the values from only the specified fields of all rows in the table.

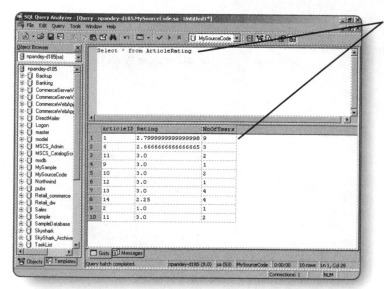

In this query, I have used the SELECT statement to retrieve all of the records from the ArticleRating table. Notice that the result is visible in the Grids window of Query Analyzer.

Retrieving Data Using a Conditional Query

To retrieve data from a table conditionally, use the SELECT command with the WHERE clause. The syntax for a conditional query is

```
SELECT FieldOne FROM TableName WHERE (FieldTwo > 10)
```

This syntax specifies that the value in the FieldOne field is to be retrieved from the table rows in which the FieldTwo value is greater than 10.

TIP

You can use logical operators and parentheses with the WHERE clause to specify multiple conditions.

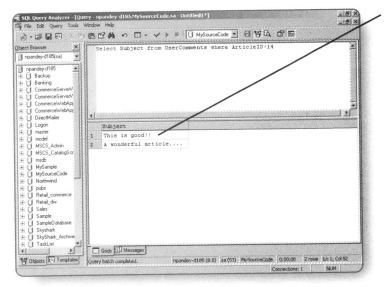

In this query, I have retrieved the Subject of user comments for an article with the ArticleID of 14.

Understanding Stored Procedures

In an application, many tasks are repetitive. For example, a task might involve canceling an airline ticket. This task is not only repetitive, but it also involves updating a number of tables in a database.

If you pass multiple SQL statements from an ASP.NET application to update a database, you risk increasing the load on the network and introducing errors while updating data. To prevent these problems, you can call a stored procedure, which includes one or more SQL statements that can update a database. In this section, you will learn how to create and execute a stored procedure.

Creating a Stored Procedure

A stored procedure contains the commands that are used to perform a specific task in an application. These commands can be executed by executing the stored procedure. You can create a stored procedure in a specific database by selecting the database in which the procedure is to be created and using the CREATE PROCEDURE command.

The syntax for creating a stored procedure is

```
CREATE PROCEDURE ProcedureName
//declarations
AS
//variable definitions
BEGIN
//commands
END
```

In this syntax, ProcedureName specifies the name of the procedure that will be created. After you specify the name of the procedure, you need to specify the variables that are required to execute the procedure.

After you have declared the variables that are to be accepted from the user, use the AS keyword to define variable declaration for the variables accepted from the user and other variables required by the stored procedure.

After you complete the variable declarations, specify the SQL commands that constitute the stored procedure. The commands start with the BEGIN keyword. After you have specified the SQL commands, you need to specify all of the commands required by the stored procedure. Use the END keyword to indicate that the stored procedure is complete.

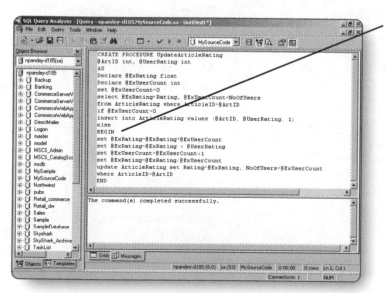

The stored procedure displayed here updates the rating of an article in the ArticleRating table. This procedure accepts the article ID and the rating given by a user as parameters. Run this query to create the stored procedure.

Executing a Stored Procedure

After you create a stored procedure, you can execute it to run all of the statements that you specified in it. To execute the procedure, select the database in which the procedure should be run, and then follow these steps.

1. Use the syntax for executing a stored procedure to run the procedure. The syntax for executing a stored procedure is

```
EXEC ProcedureName Parameter1, Parameter2
```

2. Use the EXEC command to execute the procedure. Follow the command with the name of the procedure that is to be executed. This example specifies that the values represented by Parameter1 and Parameter2 are to be passed to the procedure. These values need to be enclosed in quotation marks if they are not numeric values.

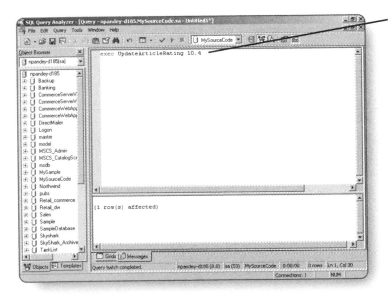

3. Execute the stored procedure that was created in the preceding section. Specify the command in the Query Analyzer window and click on the Execute Query button to run the stored procedure. The procedure will execute and the result will be displayed in the Messages tab of the Query Analyzer window.

This completes the discussion on SQL Server basics. In the next chapter, you will be introduced to the concepts of ADO.NET, one of the core components of data access in ASP.NET.

9

Getting Started with ADO.NET

You can store data in databases or other data sources, such as spreadsheets and text files. This data can then be accessed by the various data-centric applications. To access the data, these applications need to use a data access model. ADO.NET is one such data access model, designed for Web-based applications. By catering to Web applications specifically, ADO.NET allows you to implement data access in ASP.NET applications.

ADO.NET enables you to access data from various data sources. By using ADO.NET as a data access model, you can easily manipulate and update data. In this chapter, you'll learn how to:

- Utilize the features and architecture of ADO.NET
- Configure a data adapter

Understanding the Features of ADO.NET

ADO.NET is a highly efficient data access model based on the .NET Framework. It provides a uniform data access technology for local, client-server, and Web applications.

In this section, I'll discuss the main features that make ADO.NET an efficient data access model.

Non-Dependency on a Persistent Connection

An important feature of ADO.NET is that it is not dependent on a persistent connection with the database. This means that the applications connect to the database only when they need to access or update data. To understand the importance of this feature, you should be aware of how most traditional applications access data in a database.

In most of the traditional applications, a connection to the database is established and then kept open while the application processes data. However, such open connections might lead to:

- **Intensive use of system resources**. The number of open connections with the database might result in low performance of the application.

- **Limited scalability**. A significant requirement of an ASP.NET Web application is scalability, because the number of users accessing a Web site might increase tremendously within a short period of time. However, if connections are perpetually open, the site might no longer remain scalable.

- **Non-viability**. Exchange of data across applications is difficult and not viable if connected architecture is used. In such a case, the two components need to be perpetually connected to share data between them.

Open connections are not feasible, particularly for ASP.NET Web applications where the components are disconnected. In such applications, when a Web browser requests a Web page, the Web server sends the page after processing the request. Then, the server disconnects from the browser until it receives the next request. Therefore, open connections to databases are not required because it cannot be determined whether the client (the Web browser, in this case) needs any further access to data.

The architecture of ADO.NET promotes disconnected data architecture, thereby making it an efficient data access model.

Data Commands

Working with a database can involve various operations. These operations include reading or writing data and creating or modifying columns or tables in the database. Another operation that you commonly perform in a database is the calculation of a total or average by using aggregate functions. You perform these operations by executing SQL statements or stored procedures.

When you use ADO.NET, you can perform database operations using data commands. The data commands comprise a SQL statement or a stored procedure. This means that you create a data command and then configure it either with the SQL statement text or the stored procedure name that is used to perform the desired operation.

If you want to perform multiple database operations, you need to use multiple data commands—a separate data command for each operation. In addition, you can include parameters in data commands. Such parameters enable you to create parameterized queries.

Datasets

There are situations when an application needs to display data on a Web form or further process the data. Regardless of the way in which the application needs to use the data, it has to first retrieve the data from a database. This data can be a record or a group of records. Moreover, records might be stored in multiple tables in the database.

In such situations, the application needs to access the database multiple times to process each record. As you have learned, this is not feasible in the case of disconnected architecture. However, when you use ADO.NET, you have an alternative in the form of a dataset.

An ADO.NET dataset temporarily stores records that are retrieved from the database. It is a virtual miniature database that enables you to work with the data stored in it just as you would work with data in the database.

A dataset can be made up of a single table or multiple tables. If the dataset contains multiple tables, it also stores information about the relationships that exist between them. Moreover, a dataset can also include information about the constraints set for the tables.

To put it simply, a dataset, like a database, consists of tables that contain data, constraints, and relationships. Therefore, when an application works with data in a dataset, it has access to all of the elements of the data source and it doesn't need to maintain a connection with the database. If you want to make any modification to the data, you can do so in the dataset itself. These changes can later be written into the database easily.

Although data retrieved from a database is stored in a dataset, the task of moving the data between the database and the dataset is done using data adapters. A data adapter usually contains four commands that are related to Select, Insert, Update, and Delete statements. You will learn about these four commands later in this chapter. One or more of these data commands contained in a data adapter is used to load data in a table in a dataset and update the corresponding database table with the changes.

Another significant point that you should note is that a dataset is independent of the database or data source from which it retrieves the data. Since the dataset does not maintain any direct relationship with the original source, it is possible to store data from various data sources in a single dataset.

Support for XML

As you know, the data from a database needs to be transferred to a dataset, and then from the dataset to various other components. ADO.NET uses XML as the data format for such a transfer.

XML is an industry-accepted standard, approved by W3C (*World Wide Web Consortium*). It is used to store data in a text format. XML is commonly used to exchange data between applications based on different platforms.

Because XML is an industry-accepted data format and is text-based, ADO.NET support for XML makes ADO.NET the preferred data access model. Because conversion of data into and out of XML is automated, you do not need to have any knowledge of XML to work with data in ADO.NET.

ADO.NET uses XML as its internal data format. As a result, when you use ADO.NET, XML is used as the format for any transfer of data. If you want to store data in a file, it is stored as XML. You can also use an XML file as the data source for creating a dataset.

Now that you know about the main features of ADO.NET, I'll discuss the ADO.NET architecture.

Understanding the ADO.NET Architecture

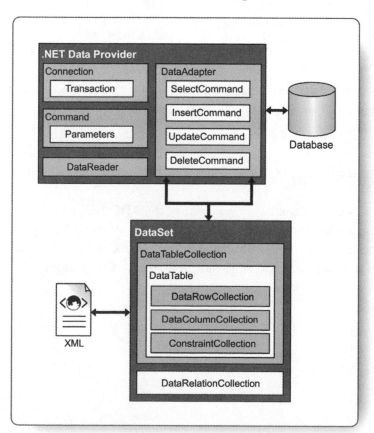

The ADO.NET architecture consists of two main components that are designed to enable data access and data manipulation. These two components are the dataset and the .NET data provider.

In the following sections, I will discuss each component of the ADO.NET architecture separately.

Datasets

A dataset acts as a primary component of the ADO.NET disconnected architecture. A dataset in ADO.NET is represented by the DataSet class, which is available in the System.Data namespace.

NOTE

A namespace refers to a naming scheme. It is used for logical grouping of related types, such as classes and structures. In the .NET Framework, namespaces follow a hierarchical, dot-syntax naming scheme. Since ADO.NET is a data access model, it uses data-related namespaces for accessing the data-related classes. The main namespace used by ADO.NET is System.Data. When you work with ADO.NET, you need to refer to this namespace in your applications.

The tables contained by a dataset are represented by DataTable objects. The DataTable objects contain DataRow and DataColumn objects that represent the rows and columns of a table, respectively.

The .NET Data Provider

The .NET data provider is another essential component of the ADO.NET architecture. It serves as a bridge between an application and the data source because it enables an application to connect to the data source, execute commands, retrieve results, and later update the data source with the changes. The .NET Framework currently provides two .NET data providers.

• **SQL Server .NET data provider**. This data provider is designed specifically for Microsoft SQL Server 7.0 or later databases. The System.Data.SqlClient namespace stores the classes of this data provider. You need to include this namespace in your applications when you use the SQL Server .NET data provider. The names of the classes of the SQL Server .NET data provider begin with the prefix "Sql."

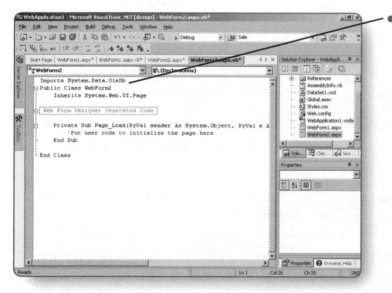

• **OLE DB .NET data provider**. This data provider enables interaction with any OLE DB data source. It provides support for various OLE DB providers, such as SQLOLEDB (SQL OLE DB provider), Microsoft.Jet.OLEDB.4.0 (Jet OLE DB provider), and MSDAORA (Oracle OLE DB provider). The System.Data.OleDb namespace stores the classes of the OLE DB .NET data provider. You must include this namespace in your applications when you use the OLE DB .NET data provider. The names of the classes of this provider begin with the prefix "OleDb."

The .NET data providers consist of four core components that enable you to manipulate data and provide quick, read-only, and forward-only data access. The following sections discuss these four components.

Connection Object

To enable an application to interact with a data source, you need to first establish a connection with the data source. To accomplish this, you use the Connection object.

ADO.NET provides you with the following two Connection objects.

- **SqlConnection.** The SqlConnection object enables you to directly create and manage a connection to a Microsoft SQL Server 7.0 or later database. The SqlConnection class, which indicates an open connection with a Microsoft SQL Server database, is stored in the System.Data.SqlClient namespace. Note that it is not possible to inherit the SqlConnection class.

- **OleDbConnection.** The OleDbConnection object enables you to create and manage a connection to a data source that is accessible through OLE DB. These data sources can be of various types, such as databases, spreadsheets, or text files. The OleDbConnection class, which indicates an open connection with the data source, is stored in the System.Data.OleDb namespace.

Both the SqlConnection and OleDbConnection classes include several properties, methods, and events. The members of both of the classes are almost identical. The most commonly used members of these classes are

- **ConnectionString property.** This property provides information necessary to create and manage a connection with the data source. Such information is in the form of a string that consists of several clauses and their values. The most important parameters of a connection string are Provider (which denotes the name of the data provider), Data Source (which denotes the server name), Initial Catalog or Database (which denote the database name), User ID or UID (which denote the user name to log on), and Password or Pwd (which denote the password).

> **NOTE**
>
> When you use the SqlConnection object, the only data provider that you use is SQL Server, so the SqlConnection object does not support the Provider clause.

- **Open method**. This method opens a connection to the data source by making use of the information in the ConnectionString property.

- **Close method**. This method closes a connection. Closing a connection after you perform the desired operations is important to minimize the use of valuable system resources.

Command Object

After you connect to the database, you need to process requests that are in the form of database commands and then return results for these requests. The requests might relate to retrieving data, modifying data, or executing stored procedures.

You can use the following two command objects to retrieve data.

- **SqlCommand**. The SqlCommand class enables you to create a data command object. This class, stored in the System.Data.SqlClient namespace, denotes a Transact-SQL statement or a stored procedure to be executed against a Microsoft SQL Server database.

- **OleDbCommand**. The OleDbCommand class enables you to create a data command object. This class, stored in the System.Data.OleDb namespace, denotes a SQL statement or a stored procedure to be executed against a data source.

DataReader Object

When you want to read data sequentially, you can use the DataReader object. This object enables you to retrieve a read-only, forward-only data stream from the data source. When you use the DataReader object, the performance of the application improves, and the system overhead is considerably reduced. This is because at any given time, there is only one row of data in the memory.

There are two data reader objects, including:

- **SqlDataReader**. The SqlDataReader class provides you with a data reader object for reading forward-only data from a Microsoft SQL Server database.

- **OleDbDataReader**. The OleDbDataReader class provides you with a data reader object for reading forward-only data from any data source.

DataAdapter Object

To work with a dataset, you need to transfer data from the data source to the dataset and later transfer it back to the data source to reflect the changes. To enable this communication between the dataset and the data source, ADO.NET provides the DataAdapter object.

If you want to use a data adapter, you need to first create and configure it. You have an option to configure the data adapter when you create it or at any later stage. When you configure a data adapter, you actually specify the SQL statements or stored procedures to be used to read and write data to the data source.

The two DataAdapter objects that ADO.NET provides are

- **SqlDataAdapter**. This object is used for communication between a dataset and a Microsoft SQL Server 7.0 or later database.

- **OleDbDataAdapter**. This object is used for communication between a dataset and any data source accessible through OLE DB.

Both the SqlDataAdapter and OleDbDataAdapter classes include several properties, methods, and events. The members of both classes are almost identical. The most commonly used members are

- **SelectCommand property**. This property enables you to select and retrieve data from the data source.

- **InsertCommand property**. This property allows you to insert data in the data source.

- **UpdateCommand property**. This property enables you to update data in the data source.

- **DeleteCommand property**. This property allows you to delete data from the dataset.

NOTE

The SelectCommand, InsertCommand, UpdateCommand, and DeleteCommand properties are instances of the Command class. Another point to remember is that in the case of OleDbDataAdapter, these properties refer to either a SQL statement or a stored procedure, whereas in the case of SqlDataAdapter, they refer to a Transact-SQL statement or a stored procedure.

- **TableMappings property**. This property retrieves a collection that represents mapping between a table in the data source and the corresponding data table in the dataset.

- **Fill method**. This method fills the dataset with data retrieved from the data source. When the DataAdapter object calls this method, it uses the SelectCommand property to select and retrieve the data with which the dataset will be filled.

- **Update method**. This method updates the data source with the modifications made to the data in the dataset. When the DataAdapter object calls this method, it uses the InsertCommand, UpdateCommand, and DeleteCommand properties for inserting, updating, and deleting data, respectively.

Now that I've explained the core components of the .NET data providers, I will discuss the steps to use these components on a Web form.

Configuring a Data Adapter

Visual Studio .NET provides the Data Adapter Configuration wizard, which helps you configure a connection and a data adapter to a data source. In this section, I will describe the utility of the wizard and the steps to run the wizard to connect to a data source.

Introducing the Data Adapter Configuration Wizard

The Data Adapter Configuration wizard provides you with simple steps to quickly create and configure a data adapter. The wizard performs several tasks for you. It will

- **Create a new connection to a database**. You can create a new connection to a database using the Data Adapter Configuration wizard.

- **Use an existing connection**. If you have already configured a connection to a data source, you can use the connection while configuring a data adapter.

- **Create SQL queries**. You can use the Query Builder to create queries that can be used for the Select, Insert, Update, and Delete commands of a data adapter.

Running the Wizard

To use the Data Adapter Configuration wizard, first create a form on which you want to run the wizard. Alternatively, open an existing form. Follow these steps to run the wizard.

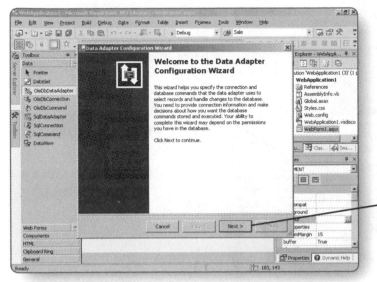

1. Click on a DataAdapter object (either OleDbDataAdapter or SqlDataAdapter) on the Data tab of the Toolbox and drag it to the form. An instance of the object will be created, and the first dialog box of Data Adapter Configuration wizard will open.

2. Click on Next. The Choose Your Data Connection dialog box will open.

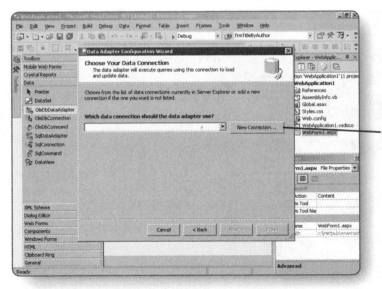

3a. Choose a connection from the list if you want to use an existing connection.

OR

3b. Click on New Connection if you want to create a new connection. The Data Link Properties dialog box will open.

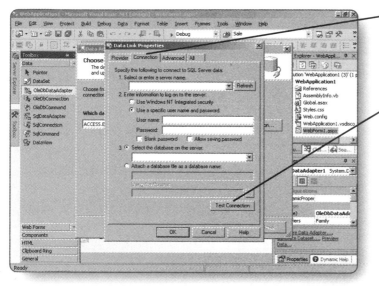

4. On the Connection tab, specify the server name, user name, password, and database name.

5. Click on Test Connection. A message will appear if the connection is successfully established.

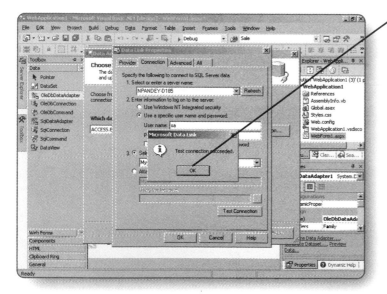

6. Click on OK. You will be returned to the Data Link Properties dialog box.

7. Click on OK. You will be returned to the Choose Your Data Connection dialog box.

8. Click on Next. The Choose a Query Type dialog box will open. This dialog box provides you with three options to specify the type of the query. You can specify whether you want to use SQL statements, create a new stored procedure, or use an existing stored procedure to access the database. By default, the Use SQL Statements option will be selected.

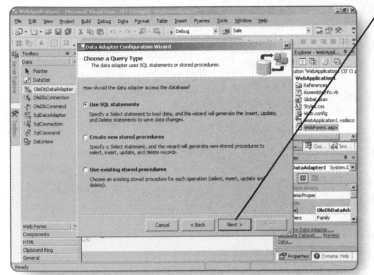

9. Click on Next. The Generate the SQL Statements dialog box will open. This dialog box enables you to specify the Select statement that will be used to automatically create the Insert, Update, and Delete statements.

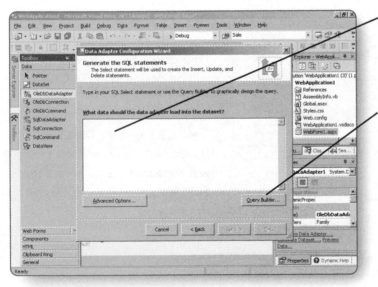

10a. Type the Select statement in the box.

OR

10b. Click on Query Builder if you want to design the query. The Add Table dialog box will open.

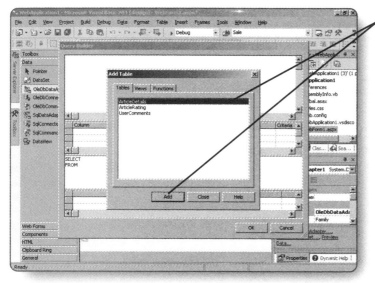

11. Click on the name of the table you want to use in your query, and then click on Add. The columns of the selected table will appear in the Query Builder.

12. After you add all of the tables that you want to use in your query, click on Close. The Add Table dialog box will close.

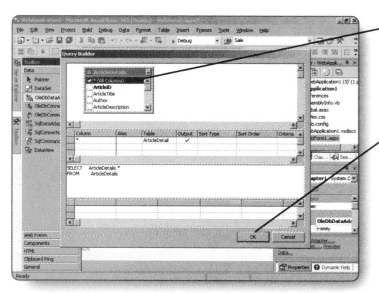

13. Click on the check box for each column that you want in your query. The selected queries will be designed in the Query Builder.

14. Click on OK. The Query Builder will close, and the query will appear in the Generate the SQL Statements dialog box of the wizard.

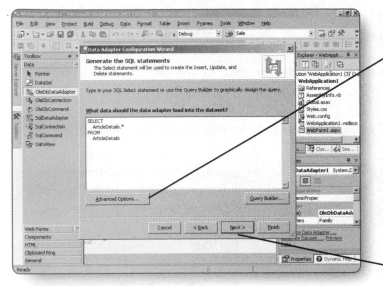

TIP

If you want to set advanced options for how the wizard should create the Insert, Update, and Delete statements, you can do so by clicking on the Advanced Options button to open the Advanced SQL Generation Options dialog box.

15. Click on Next. The View Wizard Results dialog box will open. This dialog box lists the tasks performed by the wizard.

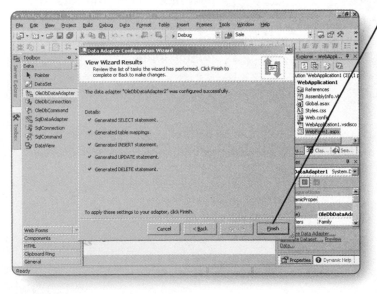

16. Click on Finish. The wizard will be completed and the configuration settings will be applied to the data adapter. An instance of the connection and data adapter objects will appear on the form.

The preceding steps used the Data Adapter Configuration wizard to configure a data adapter for the application. You can also configure a data adapter for your application by dragging a table from the Server Explorer to the form. See Chapter 10, "Managing Data from ASP.NET Applications," for more information on this technique.

After you complete the configuration of the data adapter using the Data Adapter Configuration wizard, you can generate a dataset by following these steps.

1. Right-click on the instance of the data adapter on the form. A shortcut menu will appear.

2. Click on Generate Dataset. The Generate Dataset dialog box will open.

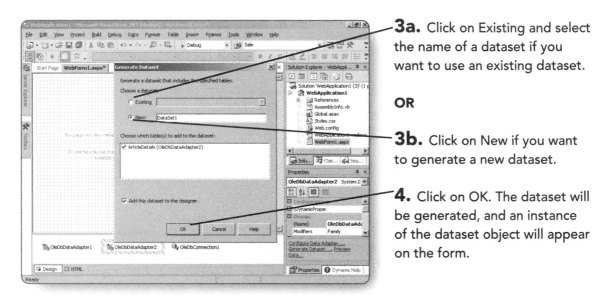

3a. Click on Existing and select the name of a dataset if you want to use an existing dataset.

OR

3b. Click on New if you want to generate a new dataset.

4. Click on OK. The dataset will be generated, and an instance of the dataset object will appear on the form.

This completes the discussion on ADO.NET. In the next chapter, you will learn how to use the components of the ADO.NET architecture to enable data access in an ASP.NET application.

10

Managing Data from ASP.NET Applications

In Chapter 9, "Getting Started with ADO.NET," you were introduced to the features and advantages of the ADO.NET architecture. ADO.NET provides data access components that are used for managing data in databases.

In ASP.NET, you can use the data access components that are provided by ADO.NET to data-enable your Web applications. By data-enabling your Web applications, you can add, update, retrieve, and delete data in data sources. This chapter describes the steps to data-enable your application by interacting with a SQL Server database. In this chapter, you'll learn how to:

- Add data to SQL Server databases
- Retrieve data from SQL Server databases

Adding Data to SQL Server Databases

Adding data to a database is a three-step process. First, you need to identify the table in the database to which you want to add data. Next, you need to design the form that will accept information from users. Finally, you need to use the ADO.NET data components to add data to the database.

In this section, you will learn to perform these three steps to add data to a database.

Designing a Database Table

You can create a database and add a table to it using SQL Server Enterprise Manager, which is the administration tool for SQL Server. (See Chapter 8, "SQL Server Basics," for more information on creating a database and adding a table to it.)

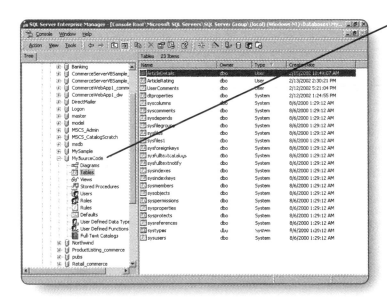

For this chapter, I have created a database called MySourceCode in SQL Server 2000. The database includes an ArticleDetails table, which is used to store the details of a new article that is added to the Web application.

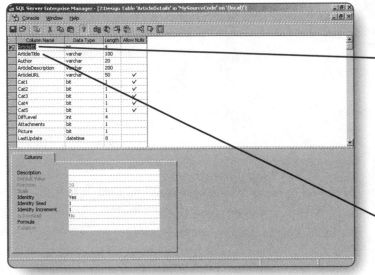

The ArticleDetails table includes the following fields:

- **ArticleID**. The ArticleID field is used to uniquely identify an article in the ArticleDetails table. This field is a primary key for the table and is automatically generated when a new article is added to the table.

- **ArticleTitle**. The ArticleTitle field stores the title of the article, as specified by the user.

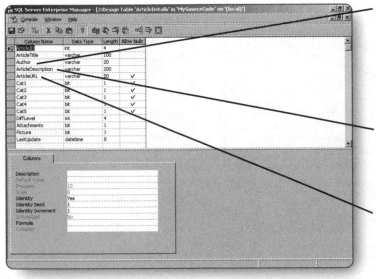

- **Author**. The Author field stores the name of the author of the article. As you will see later, this value is automatically retrieved from the user's Windows 2000 user ID.

- **ArticleDescription**. The ArticleDescription field stores a brief description of the article.

- **ArticleURL**. The ArticleURL field stores the address of a Web site to which the author of the article would like to refer the readers.

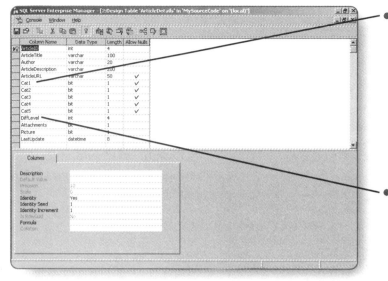

- **Cat1–Cat5**. The Cat1 to Cat5 fields store Boolean values that represent the categories to which the article belongs. For example, if the value of Cat1 is True, the article belongs to the first category. An article can belong to one or more categories.

- **DiffLevel**. Each article is rated in terms of difficulty level. An article can be for beginning, intermediate, or advanced users. The DiffLevel field stores an integer value that represents the difficulty level of the article.

- **Attachments and Picture**. The Attachments and Picture fields store Boolean values to specify whether the author has included an attachment and image file with the article.

- **LastUpdate**. The LastUpdate field stores the date and time when the article was last updated.

Designing a Form to Accept Information

To add data to the ArticleDetails table, I have added the AddNew.aspx form to an ASP.NET Web application. The form includes fields that correspond to each field in the ArticleDetails table. I have also added validation controls to the form to ensure that the user has specified valid information in all fields of the form.

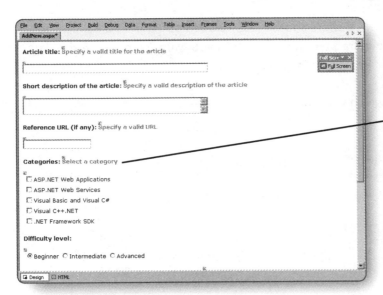

The detailed steps to create the form and add validation controls were discussed in Chapter 7, "Accepting Information Using Web Forms." After you design the form for your application, proceed to the next section.

Inserting Records into the Database Table

After you validate the data specified by a user, you can add the data to a database. Adding data to the database is a three-step process. First, you need to configure a data adapter for the form. Next, you need to configure the InsertCommand of the data adapter. Finally, you need to write the code to add the record to the database. The following sections will examine these steps one by one.

Adding a Data Adapter to the Form

You can use the SqlCommand object or the SqlDataAdapter object to add data to a database. When you use the SqlDataAdapter object, you can use the InsertCommand property of the object to specify the query for inserting records into the database.

I will use the SqlDataAdapter object to add data to the database. You can add the SqlDataAdapter object to your form using the Data Adapter Configuration wizard. (See Chapter 8, "SQL Server Basics," for more information on using the Data Adapter Configuration wizard.)

However, Visual Studio .NET offers another easy way to add the data adapter to your form. You can simply drag the table for which you want to configure the data adapter from the Server Explorer to the form.

1. Open the form for which you want to configure the data adapter. The form will open in Design view.

2. Click on View. The View menu will appear.

3. Click on Server Explorer. The Server Explorer will appear.

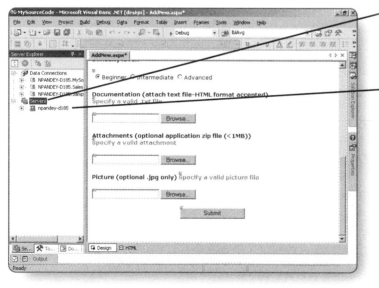

4. Double-click on Servers. The name of the local computer will appear in the Servers list.

5. Double-click on the name of the local computer. The components of the computer that are accessible from Visual Studio .NET will appear.

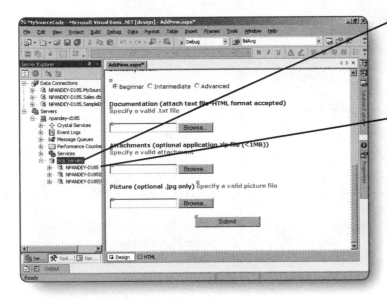

6. Double-click on SQL Servers. The SQL servers that are registered on the computer will appear.

7. Double-click on the server on which the database for the application is installed. A list of databases available on the server will be displayed.

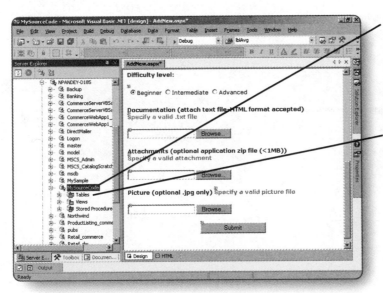

8. Double-click on the name of the database to be used in the application. The tables, views, and stored procedures in the database will appear.

9. Double-click on the Tables option. The tables available in the database will appear.

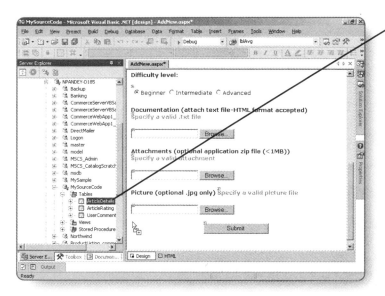

10. Press and hold the mouse button on the ArticleDetails table and drag it to the form. The SqlConnection1 and SqlDataAdapter1 controls will be added to the form.

Configuring the Data Adapter

After the SqlConnection1 and SqlDataAdapter1 controls have been added to the component tray of the form, you need to configure the InsertCommand property of the SqlDataAdapter1 control. To configure the property using the Properties window, perform the following steps.

1. Right-click on SqlData Adapter1. A shortcut menu will appear.

2. Click on Properties. The Properties window for the control will appear.

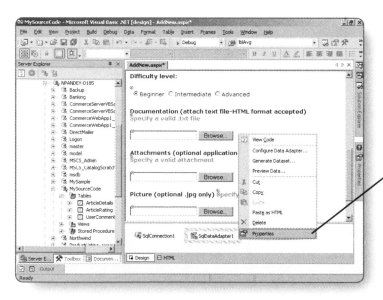

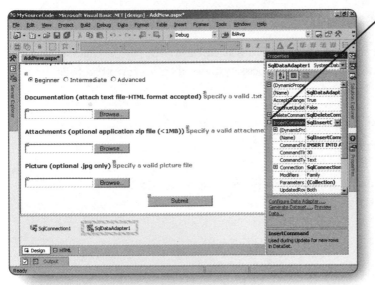

3. Click on the plus (+) sign next to the InsertCommand property. The details of the InsertCommand property will appear.

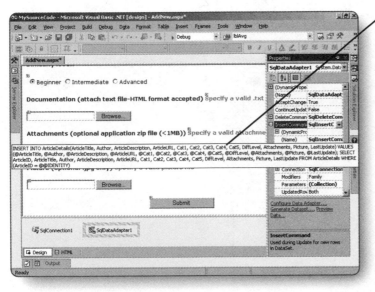

4. Move the mouse pointer to the CommandText property of InsertComamnd. The SQL query that is associated with InsertCommand will appear as a tool tip. Notice that you don't need to change the command text here, because the query suits your requirements.

Now that you have ensured that the data adapter control is configured, you can use the data adapter to add data to the database.

Coding the Form to Add Data

The code to add a record to the database needs to be written in the Click event of the Submit button. In the AddNew.aspx form, you need to perform the following tasks while adding data to the database.

1. Retrieve data from the controls on the form and assign these values to the parameters of InsertCommand.

2. Execute the query on the database to retrieve updated data in the database and the ID of the article that is added.

3. Use the ID of the article to save the attachments of the article.

To assign values to the parameters of the InsertCommand property, you need to know what the parameters are. To view the parameters of the InsertCommand property, follow these steps.

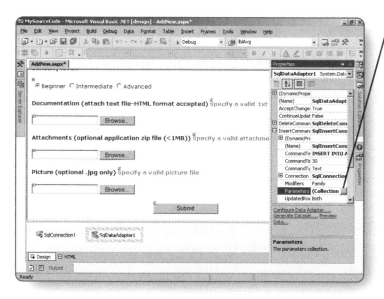

1. Click on the Ellipsis button in the Parameters property of InsertCommand. The SqlParameter Collection Editor dialog box will open.

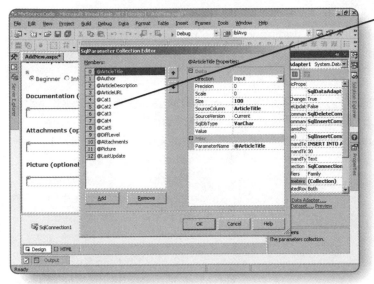

2. View the parameters expected by InsertCommand. Make a note of these parameters, because you need to refer to them while coding your application.

3. Click on OK to close the SqlParameter Collection Editor dialog box.

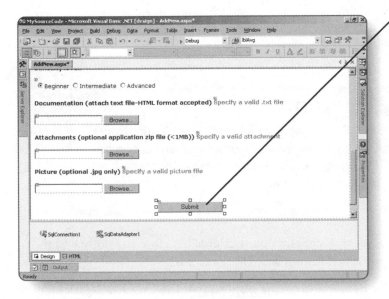

To code the functionality for adding records to the database, double-click on the Submit button in the Design view of the form. The code-behind file for the form will open.

The definition of the Click event of the Submit button is automatically created. In the definition, write the code for assigning values to the parameters of InsertCommand. In this example code, the following logic has been used to add values to parameters.

- The values for the first and second parameters (with index numbers 0 and 1), which represent the title and description of the article, are retrieved from the txtTitle and txtDescription text boxes.

- The third parameter, which represents the author of the article, is retrieved from the user's Windows 2000 domain account by using the Context.User.Identity.Name property.

NOTE

You can retrieve the user ID by using the Context.User.Identity.Name property only when you have disabled anonymous authentication on IIS. See Chapter 22, "Securing ASP.NET Applications," for more information on anonymous authentication.

- The fourth parameter, which represents the optional URL that the author of the article can specify, is retrieved from the txtURL text box.

- Parameters 5–9 are set depending on the options that the user has selected in the optCategory CheckBoxList. If an option is checked in the CheckBoxList control, the value of the corresponding parameter is set to 1. Otherwise, the value Is 0.

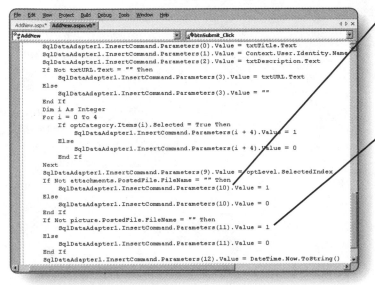

- The tenth parameter, which represents the level of difficulty of the article, is retrieved from the index of the selected item in the optLevel RadioButtonList.

- For the eleventh and twelfth parameters, the PostedFile property of the HTMLInputFile class determines whether the user has posted a file in the attachments and picture controls. If the user has posted a file, the parameters are assigned a value of 1; otherwise, the parameters are assigned a value of 0.

- The current date and time are assigned to the thirteenth parameter, which is the last parameter of the InsertCommand query.

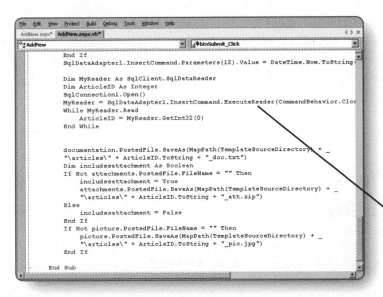

After assigning values to parameters, you run the query. You will notice that the query statement returns the article ID of the article that is added to the database. You need to retrieve this value so you can save the attachments of the article using the ID.

To add a record to the database and retrieve the article ID, you need to open the connection to the data source and use the ExecuteReader method to retrieve the article ID in an SqlDataReader object.

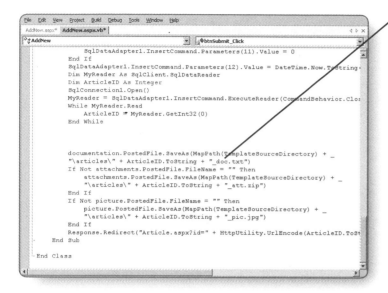

After the article ID has been retrieved, you can use it to store the files posted by the user on the Web server. In the code shown here, I have appended _doc.txt, _att.zip, and _pic.jpg to the article ID to generate the file names of the documentation, the attachment, and the image files. These files are then stored in the Articles subfolder in the root directory of the Web site.

> **TIP**
>
> Make sure that you have created an Articles folder in the root directory of your Web application.

After you store details of the article in the database, you can direct the user to another Web form that displays the details of the article that has been added to the application. In the MySourceCode application, I redirect the user to the Article.aspx form, which displays the details of the article that the user has added to the Web site. While redirecting the user to the Article.aspx form, I have added the article ID as a query string parameter using the UrlEncode method of the HttpUtility class.

Retrieving Data from SQL Server Databases

To retrieve data from the data source, identify the table from which you want to retrieve data and use the ADO.NET data objects to retrieve data from the database.

In this section, I will explain the steps to retrieve the details of an article that you added to a database in the previous section. You will first learn to design the Article.aspx form, which displays details of the article after retrieving them from the data source. Next, you will implement the data access logic.

Designing the Form to Display Data

The Article.aspx form is essentially composed of Label and Literal controls that will be used to display information retrieved from the database. Literal controls are similar to Label controls, but they allow you to format data using HTML tags. For example, if you specify <B>ASP.NET</B> for the Text property of the Literal control, the control will display ASP.NET in bold font.

The following list explains a few important controls that I have added to the form.

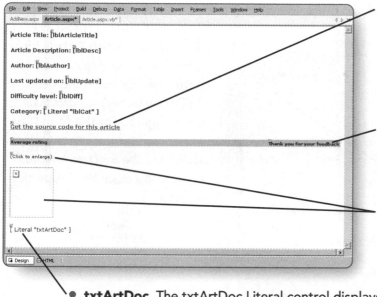

- **lnkCode**. The lnkCode Hyperlink control displays a hyperlink on the form if the author of the article has included the article's source code.

- **lblThankyou**. The lblThankyou label displays a message to the user after the user has rated an article.

- **imgLabel and ArtImg**. The imgLabel and ArtImg controls display an image file associated with a control.

- **txtArtDoc**. The txtArtDoc Literal control displays the documentation that accompanies new articles added to the Web site.

> ### TIP
>
> The lblThankyou label is displayed after the user has rated an article. To enable users to rate an article, you should create a composite control. Refer to Chapter 13, "Creating a Composite Control in ASP.NET," for more information on creating composite controls.

After you design the form to display data, proceed to the next section, which describes the steps to retrieve data from the database and display it on the form.

Displaying Data on a Form

To retrieve and display data on a form, you need to use the same logic that you used for adding data to the database. The only difference is that you need to use the SelectCommand instead of the InsertCommand.

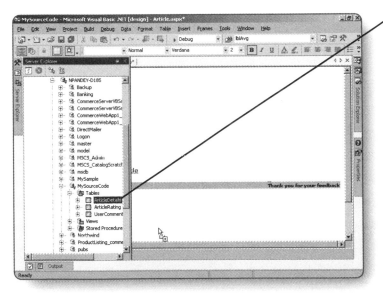

1. Drag the ArticleDetails table from the Server Explorer to the form. The SqlCommand1 and SqlDataAdapter1 controls will be configured for the form.

2. Select the SqlDataAdapter1 control and open the Properties window.

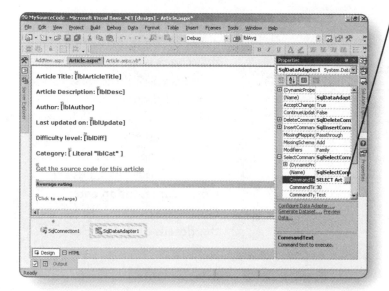

3. Click the Ellipsis button for the CommandText Property of the SelectCommand. The Query Builder dialog box will open.

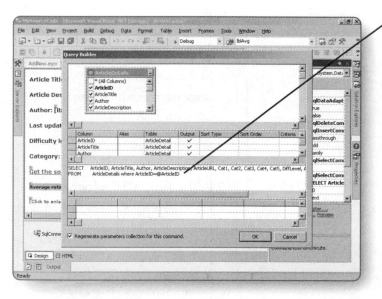

4. You need to retrieve the details of only one article for which the article ID has been passed in the query string. Therefore, append the phrase "where ArticleID=@ArticleID" in the SQL query.

5. Click on OK. The Query Builder dialog box will close.

6. Double-click on the form. The form will open in the Code Editor.

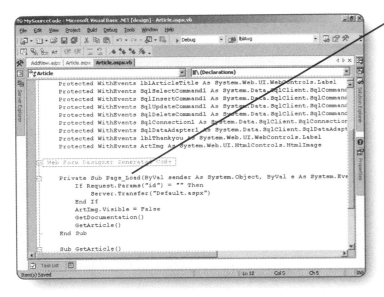

7. Write the code for the Load event of the form. Notice that I first check whether the query string is valid. If the query string is not valid, the user is redirected to the Default.aspx page, which is another page of the Web application. If the query string is valid, I use the GetDocumentation and GetArticle methods to retrieve the details of the article.

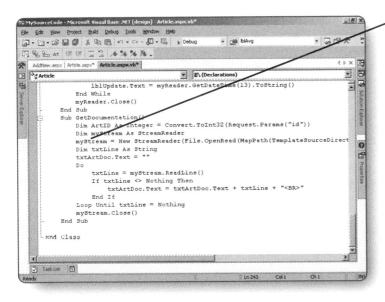

8. Write the code for the GetDocumentation method. This method reads the contents of the article from a file and displays them in a Literal control.

TIP

The Article.aspx form uses the StreamReader, File, and sqlDataReader classes. These classes are available in the System.IO and System.Data.SqlClient namespaces. Therefore, you should import the System.IO and System.Data.SqlClient namespaces into your application.

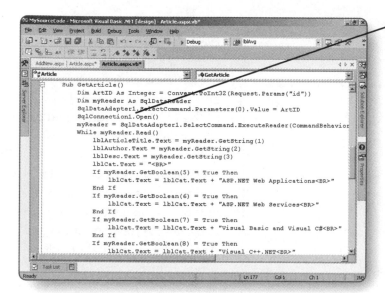

9. Write the code for the GetArticle method. The logic implemented by this code is not much different than the logic to add records to the database. The only difference is that the SelectCommand method is used to retrieve records, and the details of the article (which are retrieved in the object of the SqlDataReader class) are displayed on the form.

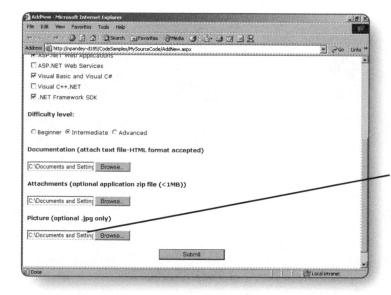

Running the Application

After you write the code to add and retrieve records from the data source, run the application to check its output.

Navigate to the AddNew.aspx form and specify the details of an article. Make sure that you specify a valid text file for the documentation of your article.

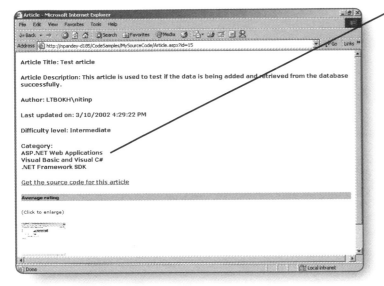

After you complete the form, click on Submit. If you have coded the application correctly, the Article.aspx form should appear and display the details of the article that you added on the AddNew.aspx form.

You now have learned how to add and retrieve data from a database. The next chapter explores the ways to format and display data using data binding server controls.

11

Displaying Data Using Data Binding Server Controls

Most often it is insufficient to retrieve data from a database and display it directly on a form. You generally need to format the data before displaying it on the form. Formatting data not only ensures that your form is visually appealing; it also ensures that the data is well organized. On a well-organized form, only the information that is relevant to the user is displayed at any given time. For example, you don't need to display all of the details of books available on your Web site. Instead, you can provide links to each book so the user can click on a link to explore more about a specific book.

ASP.NET provides a number of data binding server controls that are highly customizable. After you retrieve data from a data source, you can bind data to these server controls and display it on a form in a variety of formats. This chapter includes a detailed explanation about how to use each server control. In this chapter, you'll learn how to:

- Use the DataGrid control
- Use the Repeater control
- Use the DataList control

Using the DataGrid Control

The DataGrid control is the simplest of all the data binding controls. You can use the DataGrid control to display data in a tabular format. In this section, I will explain the steps to add and customize a DataGrid control for a form.

Displaying Data in a DataGrid Control

The DataGrid control is available in the Web Forms tab of the Toolbox. To demonstrate the use of the DataGrid control, I have added a Web form, ViewOwn.aspx, to the MySourceCode application. The form is used to display the details of articles that have been uploaded by a user who is logged on to the Web application.

Adding a DataGrid Control to a Form

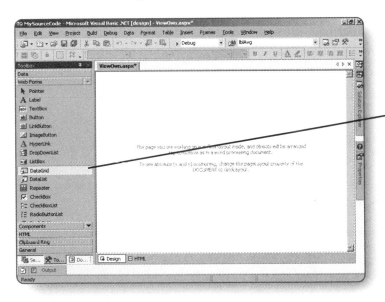

To add a DataGrid control to a form, add a Web form to an application and then follow these steps.

1. Click on the DataGrid control in the Toolbox. The control will be selected.

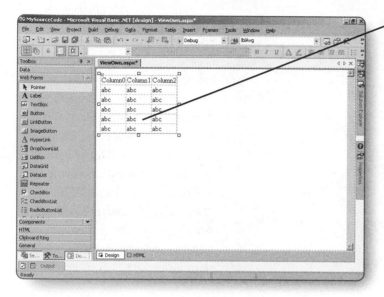

2. Press and hold the mouse button and drag the control to the form.

3. Right-click on the control. A shortcut menu will appear.

4. Click on Properties. The Properties window will appear.

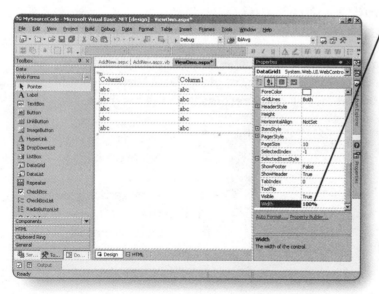

5. Change the Width property to 100%. The DataGrid control will occupy the entire width of the screen.

6. Optionally, change the ID property of the control so you can recognize it easily.

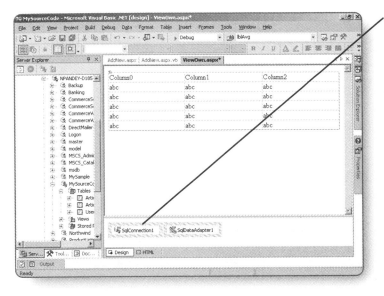

After you add the DataGrid control to the form, you need to create a data source that can be associated with the control. In this form, I have dragged the ArticleDetails table from the Server Explorer to the form to configure the SqlDataAdapter and SqlConnection controls for the form. See Chapter 10, "Managing Data from ASP.NET Applications," for more information about configuring a data adapter.

Changing the SelectCommand Property of a Data Adapter

After you add the SqlDataAdapter and SqlConnection controls to the form, you need to change the SelectCommand property of the SqlDataAdapter control, because you don't need to retrieve all of the records from the database.

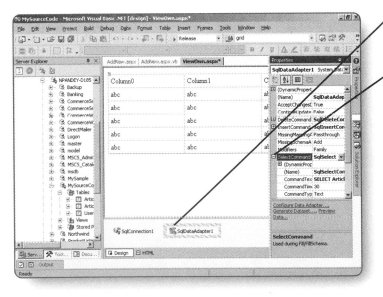

1. Click on the SqlDataAdapter1 control.

2. In the Properties window, click on the plus (+) sign next to the SelectCommand property. The contents of the SelectCommand property will be displayed.

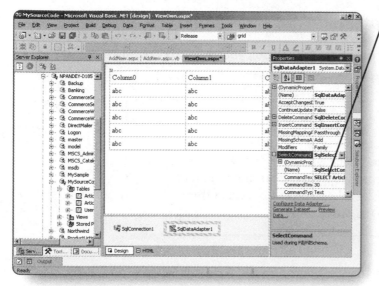

3. Type **SELECT ArticleID, ArticleTitle, Author, ArticleDescription, LastUpdate FROM ArticleDetails WHERE (Author = @Aid)** as the query for the CommandText property and press Enter. The Regenerate Parameters message box will appear.

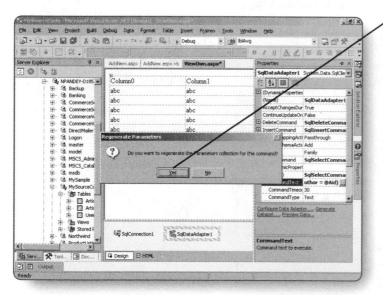

4. When you change the query associated with a command, the parameters expected by the query might change. To synchronize the parameters expected by the query with the command text, click on Yes. The Microsoft Development Environment dialog box will appear.

5. Click on Yes. The new query that you specified will be applied to the SelectCommand.

Generating a Dataset

After you configure the data adapter control, you need to generate a dataset to store data that is retrieved from the database.

> ### NOTE
> I did not use a dataset in Chapter 10, "Managing Data from ASP.NET Applications," because I did not need to store data in the application. I simply retrieved the data and presented it to the user. When you store data in the application, you need to use a dataset.

1. Click on the SqlDataAdapter control that was added to the form. The control will be selected.

2. Click on Data. The Data menu will appear.

3. Click on Generate Dataset. The Generate Dataset dialog box will open.

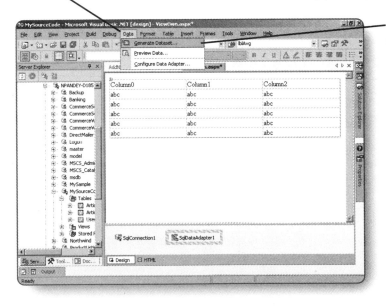

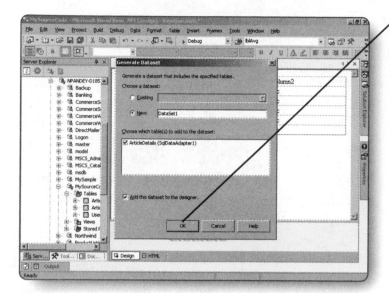

4. Retain the default options, which allow you to create a new dataset, add a table to the dataset, and add the dataset to the component designer. Click on OK. A new DataSet control will be added to your application.

Binding Data to the DataGrid Control

Now you are ready to use the DataGrid control. A DataGrid control includes a DataSource property that expects a DataView object as the data source.

When you configured the DataSet control in the preceding steps, you added the ArticleDetails table to the dataset. This table has a default view associated with it

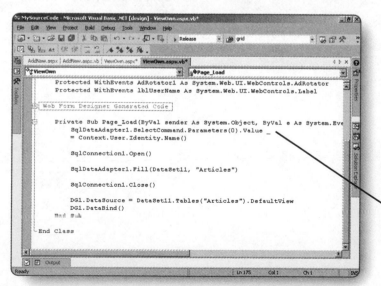

that can be assigned to the DataSource property of the DataGrid control. The steps to assign the default view of the table to the DataGrid control follow.

1. Double-click on the ViewOwn.aspx form to open the Code Editor.

2. Now you need to write the code in the Load event of the form. Retrieve the user name of the user who is currently logged on.

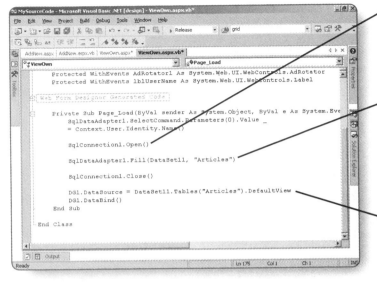

3. Assign the user name as a parameter to the SelectCommand and open the connection to the data source.

4. Execute the Fill method of the SqlDataAdapter class to retrieve details of articles uploaded by the user and add these details to the dataset.

5. Assign the default view of the dataset to the DataGrid control and call the DataBind method to display data on the form.

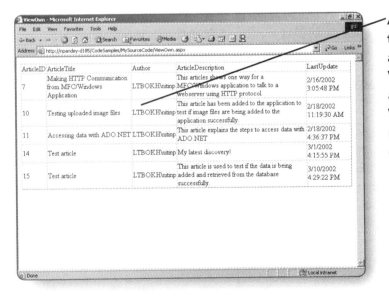

After you have added the code to the form, execute the application and navigate to the ViewOwn.aspx page. The articles that were added to the Web application by the current user will appear in the DataGrid control, as shown here.

Customizing a DataGrid Control

The DataGrid control presents many customization options. For example, you can change the appearance of the DataGrid control to make it blend with the color scheme of your Web application. In this section, I will show you how to customize the DataGrid control by changing its properties.

Changing the Appearance of the DataGrid Control

You can change the appearance of a DataGrid control using the Properties window.

1. Click on the DataGrid control on the form and open the Properties window.

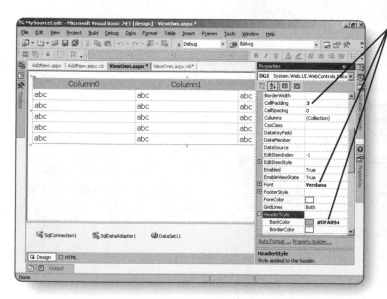

2. Change the style of the control. In this control, I have changed the CellPadding value to 3, the Font to Verdana, and the BackColor of the HeaderStyle property to #DFA894.

NOTE

The HeaderStyle property specifies the style of the header row in the DataGrid control.

I have configured only a few properties of the DataGrid control. You can configure other properties in the same manner. Take a moment to experiment with the properties, if you'd like.

Sorting Data in a DataGrid Control

When you enable sorting in a DataGrid control, each column in the header row of the DataGrid control appears as a hyperlink. When users click on a hyperlink, the data in the DataGrid control is sorted by the selected column.

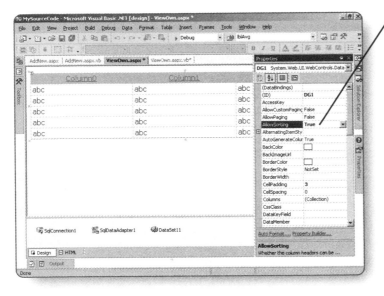

1. Double-click on the AllowSorting property in the Properties window. The value of the property will change from False to True.

2. Switch to the Code Editor and select the DataGrid control from the list of controls. The control will be selected.

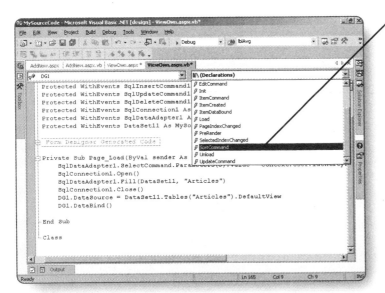

3. From the list of events supported by the control, select SortCommand. An event handler will be generated for the SortCommand event of the DataGrid control.

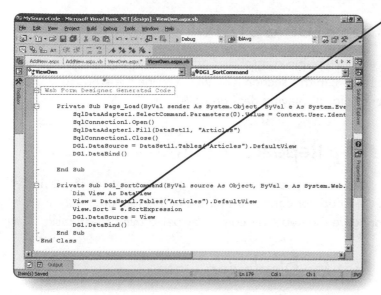

4. The SortExpression property specifies how the data in the DataGrid control should be sorted. You can use the SortExpression property to sort the data in a DataView object and associate the object with the DataGrid control, as shown here.

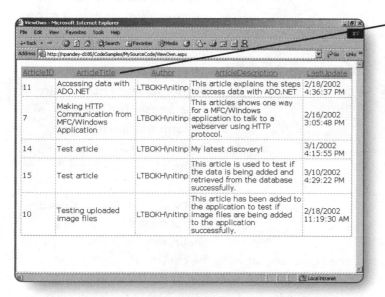

After you write the code for sorting data, run the application. You will notice that the header rows of the DataGrid are rendered as hyperlinks. When you click on a hyperlink, the data in the DataGrid control will be sorted by the column you selected.

Using the Repeater Control

The Repeater control is a customizable control that offers a high degree of flexibility for data presentation. In this section, you will examine the steps to configure a Repeater control for displaying data on a Web site.

Displaying Data in a Repeater Control

To display data in a Repeater control, you need to define the format for displaying data and then populate the Repeater control with data. In this section, I will describe the steps to configure the Repeater control by performing these tasks.

Defining the Format for Displaying Data

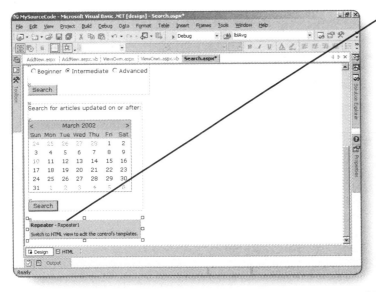

To add a Repeater control to a form, drag the control from the Toolbox to the form. In the form shown here, I have dragged the Repeater control to the Search.aspx form, which allows the user to search a database for an article. The structure of this form was discussed in Chapter 6, "Adding Server Controls to a Web Form."

As you can see, the Repeater control does not provide a default way to present data. You need to configure how data should be displayed in the control. However, the Repeater control does provide templates that specify how data should be displayed by the control. At run time, when a data view is bound to the Repeater control, the template is used to determine how each record in the data view should be displayed on the form.

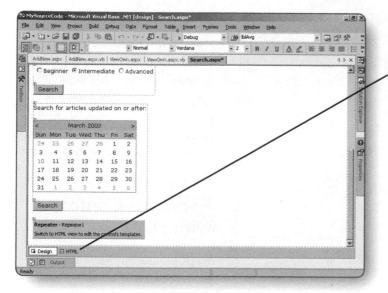

The steps to configure the Repeater control follow.

1. Click on the HTML tab to open the HTML view of the Web form.

2. Locate the HTML code that corresponds to the Repeater control.

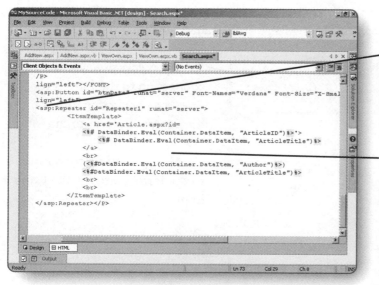

TIP

The code for the Repeater control begins with the <asp:Repeater declaration.

3. Add the definition of the ItemTemplate template. The ItemTemplate specifies how each item in the Repeater control should be formatted. I have used the data binding syntax to bind the ArticleID, ArticleTitle, and Author fields of the data source to the ItemTemplate.

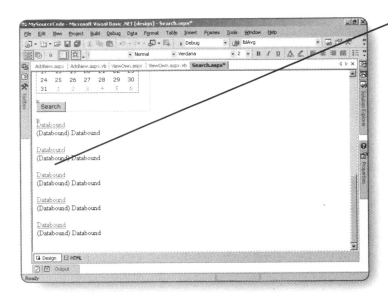

4. Switch back to the Design view of the form. The Databound fields that you created in the HTML view are displayed here. Data will be populated in these fields at run time.

Populating a Repeater Control with Data

To populate the Repeater control with data, I used a simple logic. First, I added a connection to the form. The connection can be opened whenever data needs to be retrieved from the data source. Next, I used the SqlCommand object to configure the search queries for different search parameters. Finally, I passed the SqlCommand object to a function that executes the command by using the connection and displays the result in the Repeater control. These steps are detailed below.

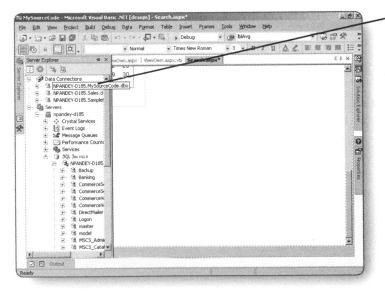

1. The quickest way to add a connection to the form is to drag the connection object from the Server Explorer to the form.

2. After you add a connection to the form, switch to the Code Editor.

3. Create a SqlCommand object for each search parameter and execute the query to retrieve the result in an SqlDataReader object.

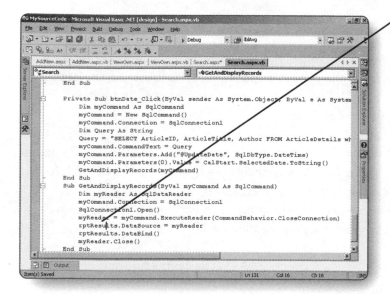

4. Bind the SqlDataReader object to the Repeater control.

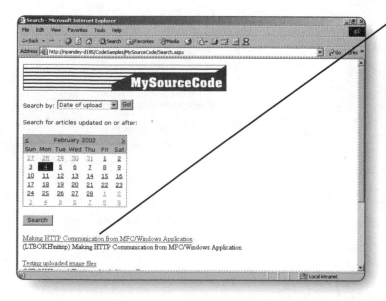

After you write the code to bind the Repeater control to the SqlDataReader object, run the application and navigate to the form to which you have added the Repeater control. An output similar to the output shown here will appear when you run a query on the form.

Customizing the Repeater Control

You can customize the Repeater control the same way you customize other data binding server controls. Since the output is specified in HTML format, the output entirely depends upon the HTML tags that you have used to configure the control. Thus, the output is already customized!

However, you can customize the output further by using the AlternatingItemTemplate template. The AlternatingItemTemplate specifies the formatting of alternate items in the Repeater control. Using this template improves the readability of data because it is often easier to read adjacent entries in a control when they follow different color patterns or when they are demarcated.

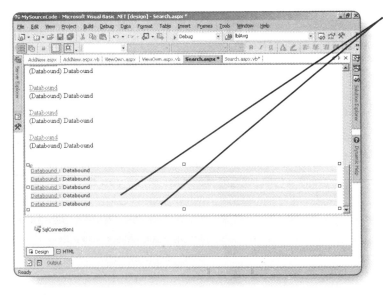

The syntax for using the AlternatingItemTemplate is the same as the syntax for using the ItemTemplate. Often, you just need to vary one or two elements of the Alternating ItemTemplate to make the alternating items appear distinct. For example, in the Repeater control displayed here, I have changed the back color of the AlternatingItemTemplate to make the background color of alternating items distinct from each other, although the distinction does not show up well in a one-color book!

Using the DataList Control

The DataList control is similar to the Repeater control. However, it is more flexible than the Repeater control because it enables you to add other controls to the ItemTemplate and respond to events generated by these controls.

In this section, I will configure a DataList control on the UserReviews.aspx page that enables users to submit their comments on articles in a Web application.

Designing the DataList Control

To design the DataList control, follow these steps.

1. Drag the DataList control from the Toolbox to the form.

2. Switch to the HTML view of the control and add the code for the HeaderTemplate and ItemTemplate of the control.

NOTE

The HeaderTemplate is used to display the header row in the DataList control.

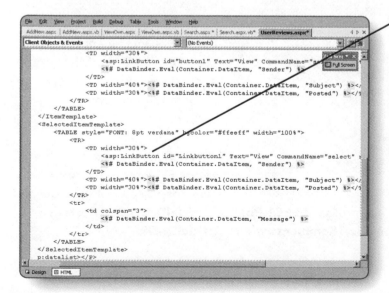

3. In the ItemTemplate of the DataList control, add a LinkButton control. When a user clicks on a command button in the DataList control, the DataList control can display the data in a SelectedItemTemplate template. So, you should specify a style for the SelectedItemTemplate.

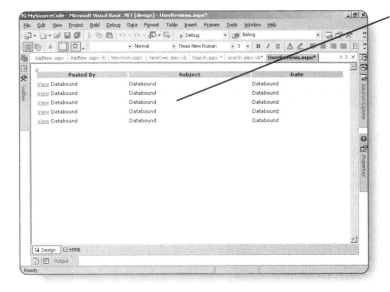

Switch back to the Design view, where you have the design of the DataList control ready. Next, you need to implement the logic to display data in the DataList control.

Implementing the Programming Logic

The programming logic of the application involves retrieving data from the data source and displaying it in the DataList control.

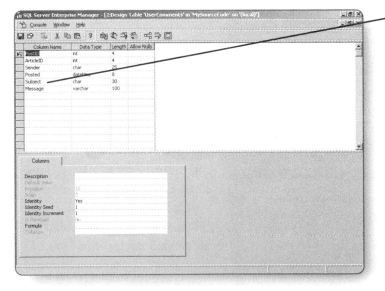

The data pertaining to user reviews is stored in the UserComments table of the MySourceCode database. The structure of this table is shown here.

Before you implement the programming logic of the application, add the SqlDataAdapter1 and SqlConnection1 controls to the form by dragging the UserComments table from the Server Explorer to the form. Type the SelectCommand query of the SqlDataAdapter1 control as **SELECT PostID, ArticleID, Sender, Posted, Subject, Message FROM UserComments where ArticleID=@id**.

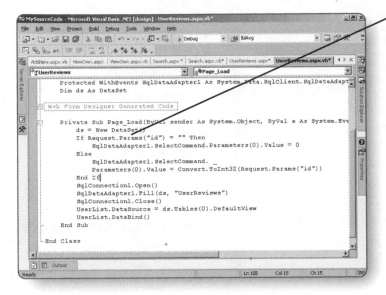

After you have added the SqlDataAdapter1 control to the form, switch to the Code Editor and write the code for the Load event of the form. First, determine whether the query string contains an article ID. If the query string does not specify an ID, specify the article ID as 0, which is reserved for the Default page of the Web application. Next, retrieve records from the database that match the article ID supplied by the user and display the records in the DataList control.

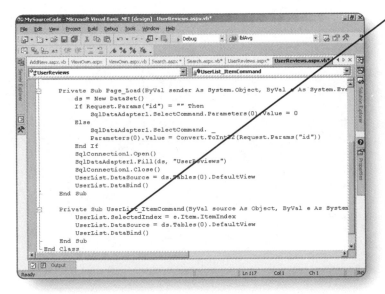

When the user clicks on the View button in the DataList control, the ItemCommand event of the form is fired. When the event is fired, you need to change the SelectedIndex property of the DataList control to the index of the option selected by the user.

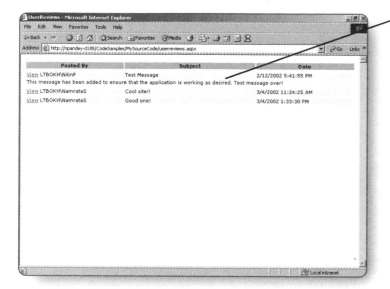

After you have configured the DataList control, run the form. The output of the control, with one user comment option selected, is shown here.

This completes the discussion of displaying data in data binding server controls. In the next chapter, you will learn how to convert a Web form into a user control and use the control on a number of Web forms.

12

Creating a User Control in ASP.NET

Often you need to replicate the same functionality on more than one Web form. For example, a set of controls might be used to rate a Web form. Instead of adding the same controls to each form one by one, you can create a user control and add it to all of the Web forms that require the functionality.

This chapter discusses the steps to create a user control and use the control on a Web form. In this chapter, you'll learn how to:

- Convert a Web form into a user control
- Add a user control to a Web form

Converting a Web Form into a User Control

To create a user control in ASP.NET, you need to create a Web form and then convert it into a user control. In this section, I will demonstrate the steps to convert the UserReviews.aspx form into a user control. See Chapter 11, "Displaying Data Using Data Binding Server Controls," for more information on the UserReviews.aspx form.

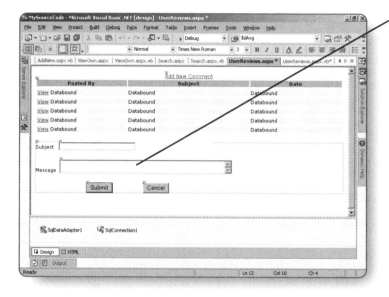

You will notice that I have made a slight change to the UserReviews.aspx form from the previous chapter. I have added the functionality to add a record to the UserComments table. You can refer back to Chapter 10, "Managing Data from ASP.NET Applications," for a review of how to add a record to a database. However, the change that I made will not affect your learning in this chapter.

Removing HTML Tags

The first step to convert a Web form into a user control is to remove the <HTML>, <BODY>, and <FORM> tags from the Web form. The tags are not required in the user control because the Web form to which you will add your user control will already have these tags, and duplicating tags on a Web form will lead to errors.

To remove the <HTML>, <BODY>, and <FORM> tags from the Web form, follow these steps.

1. Open the form that you want to convert to a user control.

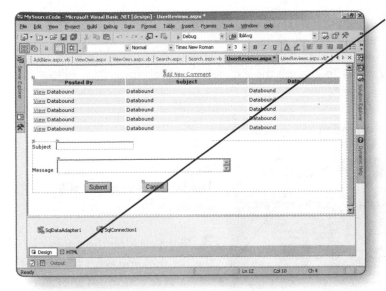

2. Click on the HTML tab to switch to the HTML view of the form.

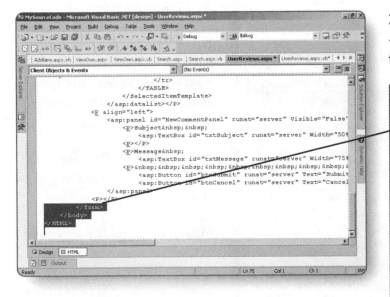

3. Delete the <HTML>, <BODY>, and <FORM> tags from the form.

TIP

When you delete the <HTML>, <BODY>, and <FORM> tags from the Web form, make sure that you delete the closing tags as well. For example, when you delete the <HTML> tag, make sure to delete the </HTML> tag as well.

After you delete the tags, you need to change the file extensions and page directives. Read on to find out how to change these items.

Renaming Web Form Files

User controls have a default extension of .ascx. You need to rename the Web form files from .aspx to .ascx. To change the extension of Web form files, follow these steps.

1. Click on View. The View menu will appear.

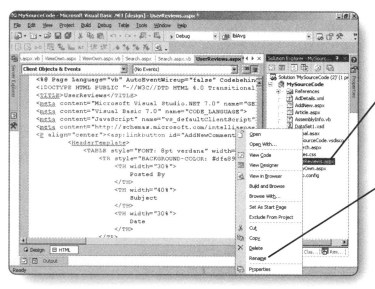

2. Click on Solution Explorer. The Solution Explorer will appear.

3. Right-click on the name of the file that you want to convert into a user control. A shortcut menu will appear.

4. Click on Rename.

5. Change the extension of the file from .aspx to .ascx. A message will appear, notifying you that the file might become unusable.

6. Click on Yes. The extension of the file will change from .aspx to .ascx.

After you change the extension of the file to .ascx, it is a user control. Therefore, from this point forward, I will refer to it as a user control, not a Web form!

Changing Page Directives

A Web form is derived from the System.Web.UI.Page class. However, a user control needs to derive from the System.Web.UI.UserControl class. You also need to change the @ Page directive on the page to @ Control. The following steps accomplish these tasks.

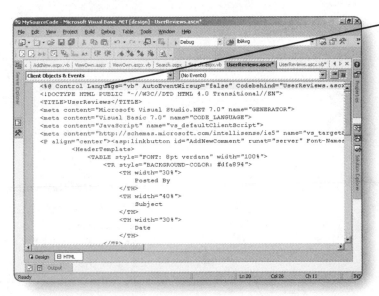

1. Set the @ Page directive in the HTML view of the Web form to @ Control. Also, change the extension of the code-behind file from .aspx to .ascx.

2. Switch to the Design view of the form and double-click on the form. The code-behind file for the control will open.

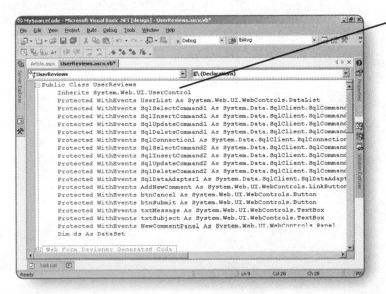

3. Locate the class declaration and change the base class to System.Web.UI.UserControl.

You have completed the steps to create a user control. Now it's time to add this control to a Web form and see how it works.

Adding a User Control to a Web Form

Adding a user control to a Web form and instantiating it is an extremely simple task. In this section, I will instantiate the user control that was created in the previous section to a Web form and test the control by running the form.

Instantiating the Control

To instantiate a user control on a Web form, follow these steps.

1. Open the Solution Explorer.

2. Double-click on the form to which you want to add the user control. The form will open in Design view.

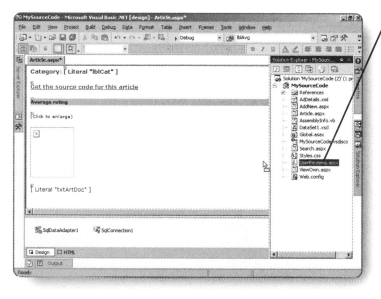

3. Click on the control that you want to add to the form. The control will be selected.

4. Press and hold the mouse button and drag the control to the location on the form where you want to place it.

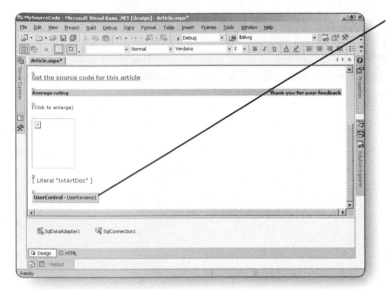

The control will be added to the form. The HTML tags required to instantiate the control automatically will be added to the form. You can switch to the HTML view if you want to view the HTML definition of the user control. Notice that the Form Designer does not enable you to view the structure of the control. The structure can only be viewed by opening the related .ascx files. After you add the control to the form, you can test the form to ensure that the output runs as desired.

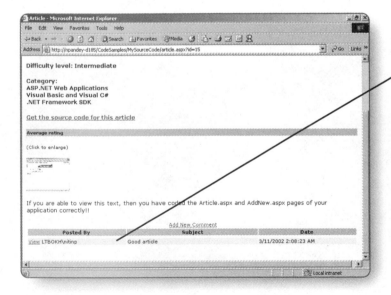

Testing the Application

After you add the user control to a form, run the application and navigate to the form on which you added the user control. The form should display the control. Notice that the final output of the application is the same when you are using user controls as when you are using a Web form.

This completes the discussion on creating user controls. In the next chapter, you will learn how to create composite controls. Although the end objectives of the two types of controls are similar—replicating functionality on a number of controls—they differ significantly in the manner in which they are created and used on a form.

13

Creating a Composite Control in ASP.NET

In Chapter 12, "Creating a User Control in ASP.NET," you learned how to create user controls in ASP.NET. Composite controls are another category of controls in ASP.NET; they are a combination of one or more controls that are compiled into a DLL (*Dynamic Link Library*) file. Composite controls can be used like the other controls that are available in Visual Studio .NET.

To create and use composite controls in Visual Studio .NET, you need to create a class library and import it into your ASP.NET application. This chapter describes the steps to do so in detail. In this chapter, you'll learn how to:

- Create a composite control
- Add the composite control to a Web form

Creating a Composite Control

To create a composite control, you need to create a class library project and code the functions of the composite control.

Creating a Class Library Project

To create a new class library project, launch Visual Studio .NET and follow these steps.

1. Click on File. The File menu will appear.

2. Move the mouse pointer to New. The New submenu will appear.

3. Click on Project. The New Project dialog box will open.

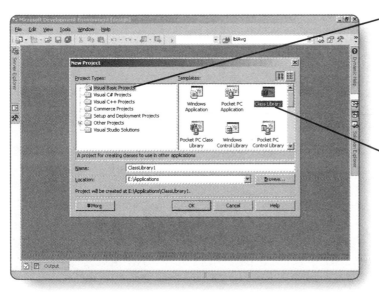

4. Click on the Visual Basic Projects folder in the Project Types pane. The project templates available in Visual Basic .NET will be listed in the Templates pane.

5. Click on Class Library. The option will be selected.

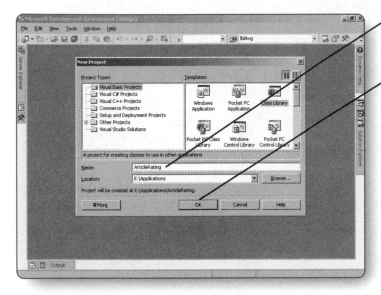

6. Type a name for the project in the Name text box.

7. Click on OK. Visual Studio .NET will create a class library project and add a module file to it.

Renaming the Module Files and the Class

After you create a new project, you should rename the module files and the default class name generated by the wizard so you can easily identify the control.

1. Right-click on the name of module file in the Solution Explorer. A shortcut menu will appear.

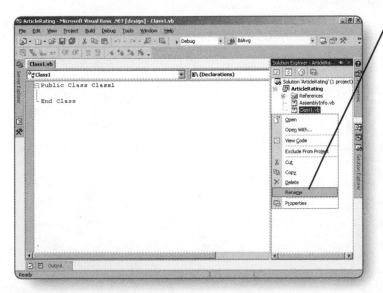

2. Click on Rename. The name of the module file will be highlighted.

3. Type a new name for the file.

TIP

When you rename the module file, make sure that you retain the default .vb file extension.

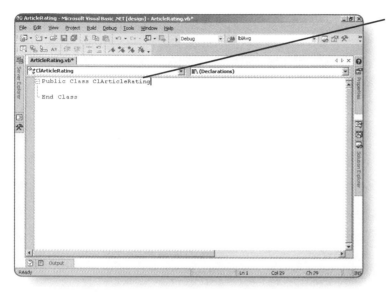

4. To change the name of the class in which the control will be defined, select the name of the class and type the new name.

Now you can use the class library project to create the composite control.

Coding the Functionality of the Control

To create a composite control, you need to derive the class used for implementing the control from the Control class and then implement the INamingContainer interface. You also need to override the CreateChildControls function of the Control class. The CreateChildControls function defines the controls that need to be rendered by the composite control.

When you create a composite control, you need to import the required namespaces into your application.

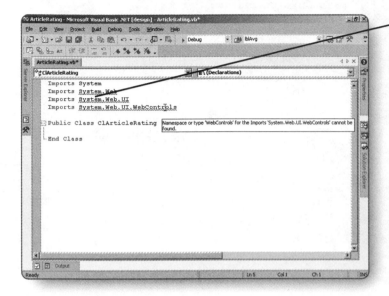

1. Type the statements to import the namespaces that need to be used by the control. Notice that when you import System.Web and its associated namespaces into your application, the application will display a notification that the namespace cannot be found. This notification is displayed because the System.Web.dll file, which contains the definition of the System.Web namespace, has not been referenced by the application.

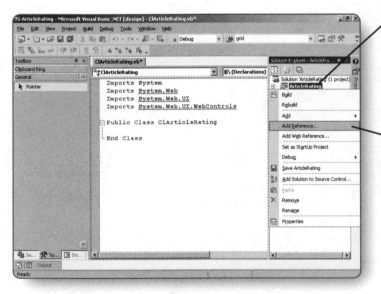

2. To add a reference to the System.Web.dll file, right-click on the name of the solution in the Solution Explorer. A shortcut menu will appear.

3. Click on Add Reference. The Add Reference dialog box will open.

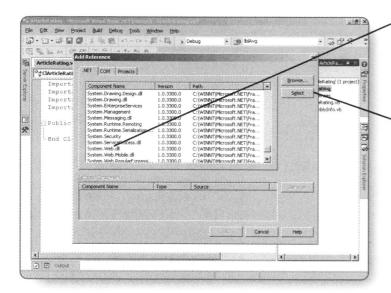

4. Scroll down the Component Name list and click on the System.Web.dll file. The file will be selected.

5. Click on Select. The file will be added to the Selected Components list.

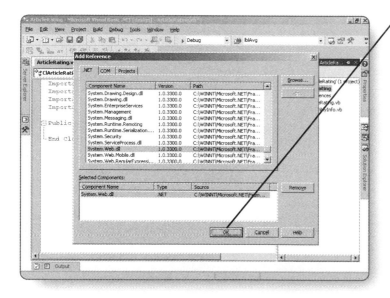

6. Click on OK. A reference will be added to the System.Web.dll file.

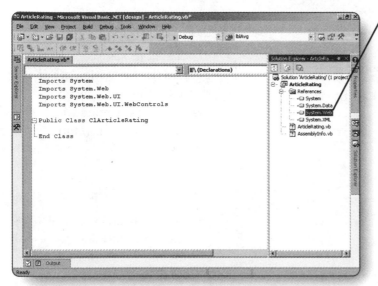

After you add a reference to the System.Web.dll file, the reference will appear in the References section of the Solution Explorer.

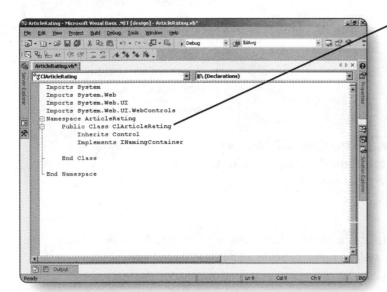

The next step in creating the composite control is to inherit the composite control class from the Control class and implement the INamingContainer interface. In the code shown here, I have inherited the ClArticleRating class from the Control class and implemented the INamingContainer interface. I have also defined the ArticleRating namespace for the class.

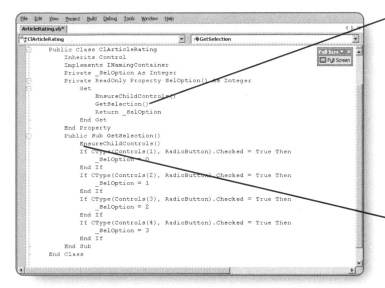

```
File Edit View Project Build Debug Tools Window Help
ArticleRating.vb*
ClArticleRating                                              GetSelection
        Public Class ClArticleRating
            Inherits Control
            Implements INamingContainer
            Private _SelOption As Integer
            Private ReadOnly Property SelOption() As Integer
                Get
                    EnsureChildControls()
                    GetSelection()
                    Return _SelOption
                End Get
            End Property
        Public Sub GetSelection()
            EnsureChildControls()
            If CType(Controls(1), RadioButton).Checked = True Then
                _SelOption = 0
            End If
            If CType(Controls(2), RadioButton).Checked = True Then
                _SelOption = 1
            End If
            If CType(Controls(3), RadioButton).Checked = True Then
                _SelOption = 2
            End If
            If CType(Controls(4), RadioButton).Checked = True Then
                _SelOption = 3
            End If
        End Sub
    End Class
```

Next, you need to define the properties that the control will expose. For example, I have defined the SelOption property that uses the GetSelection method to determine which option has been selected in the control.

NOTE

The EnsureChildControls function determines whether the child controls in the composite control have been instantiated. If the child controls have not been instantiated, the EnsureChildControls function will call the CreateChildControls function to instantiate the child controls.

Finally, you need to override the CreateChildControls function to render the child controls for the composite control. In the code for the composite control, I have added a Rate this Article label and added four RadioButton controls to enable users to rate the article.

After you create the composite control, build the application. A .dll file will be created for the control, which can be used in an ASP.NET application.

Adding the Composite Control to a Web Form

After you create the composite control, you can add a reference to the control and use it in an ASP.NET application. In this section, I will examine the steps to use a composite control on a Web form.

Creating a Reference to the Control

To create a reference to the composite control, open the ASP.NET application to which you want to add the reference and follow these steps.

1. Right-click on the name of the solution in the Solution Explorer. A shortcut menu will appear.

2. Click on Add Reference. The Add Reference dialog box will open.

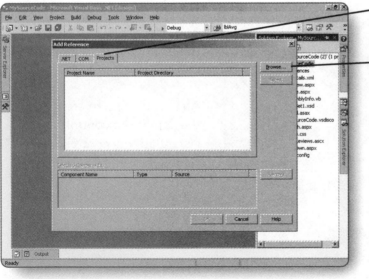

3. Click on the Projects tab. The tab will move to the front.

4. Click on the Browse button. The Select Component dialog box will open.

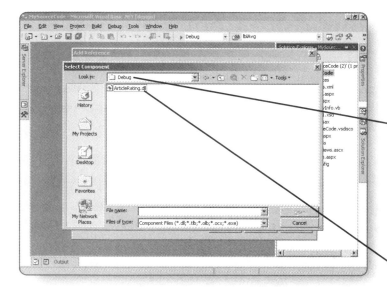

5. Navigate to the location of the .dll file for the composite control.

TIP

The .dll file for the component can be found in the Debug or Release subfolder of the Bin folder in the control's root folder.

6. Click on the .dll file and click on Open. The file will be added to the Selected Components list of the Add Reference dialog box.

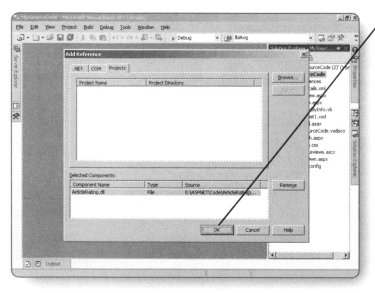

7. Click on OK. A reference to the composite control will be added to your project.

After you add a reference to the composite control, you can instantiate the control on a Web form.

Instantiating the Control

To instantiate a control on a Web form, you need to register the control by using the @ Register directive.

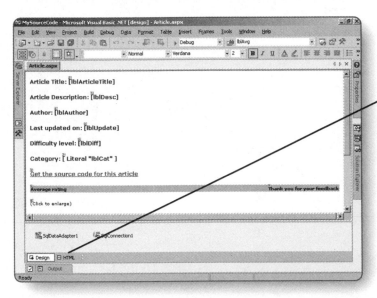

1. Open the Web form on which you want to instantiate the control.

2. Click on the HTML tab to switch to the HTML view of the form. The Web form will open in HTML view.

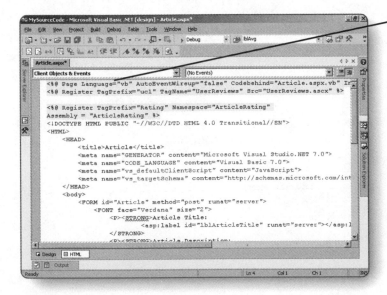

3. Add this directive to the Web form. The composite control will be registered on the Web form.

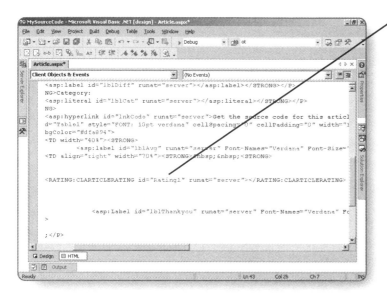

4. Instantiate the control on the form the same way you would instantiate any other server control.

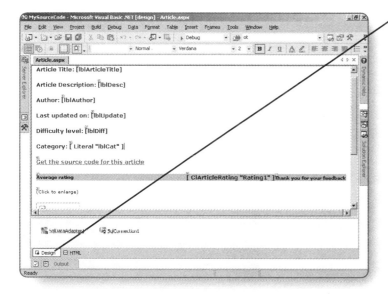

5. Click on the Design tab to switch to the Design view of the form. The control will be visible in the Design view of the form.

After you add the composite control to the form, you can change its properties using the Properties window, the same way you would change the properties for any other server control.

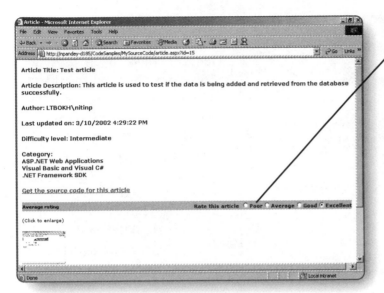

Testing the Control

The easiest way to test a control is to run the application and navigate to the Web form on which you have included the control. If you have coded the control correctly, it will display on the form.

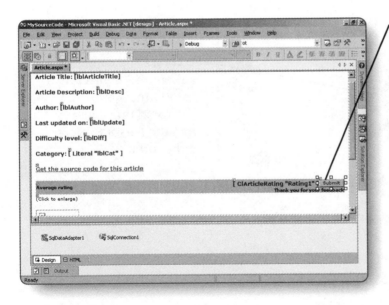

Although the control is functional, it is of little use unless you add functionality to it. Add a Submit button to the form to allow users to submit the rating of an article.

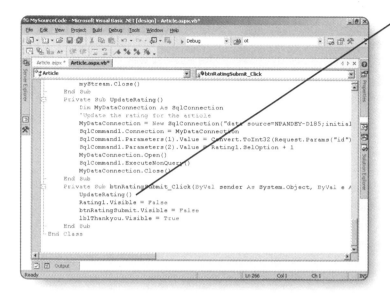

The Click event of the Submit button calls the UpdateRating function, which in turn uses the SqlCommand object to call a stored procedure that updates the rating of the article. (See Chapter 10, "Managing Data from ASP.NET Applications," for more information on the stored procedure used in the form.) The stored procedure, in turn, updates the rating of the article in the MySourceCode database.

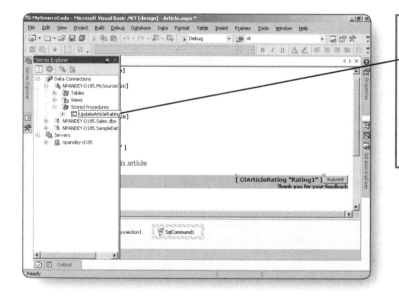

TIP

To create and configure a SqlCommand object for a stored procedure, drag the stored procedure from the Server Explorer to the form.

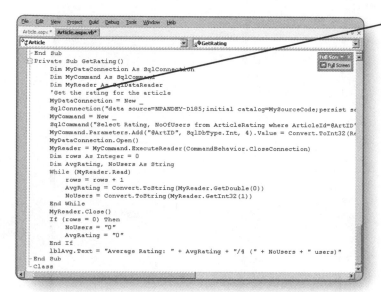

After you add the rating of an article to the database, you can retrieve the rating using the GetRating function. Make a call to this function in the Load event of the form and in the Click event of the Submit button.

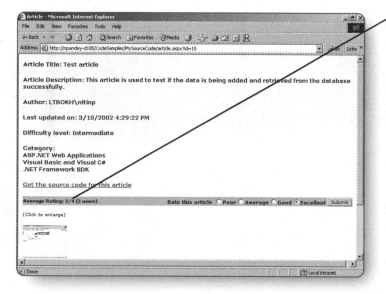

After you make these changes to the form, you can run the form and rate articles using the composite control.

This completes the discussion on creating and utilizing composite controls on a Web form. In the next chapter, you will be introduced to the concept of Web services, which form an integral part of ASP.NET and are one of the key components of the .NET initiative.

14

Getting Started with ASP.NET Web Services

In today's business world, people rely on the Web to access data and transfer it between Web sites and databases which is an example of distributed applications. However, consider a scenario in which you need to access data from a data source that is not compatible with ASP.NET. The easiest way to make this data available to a Web application is to use XML, a platform-independent industry standard that can be used for exchanging data between applications.

ASP.NET enables you to create XML Web services that can exchange data between applications in XML format. This chapter introduces you to XML Web services and provides you with the basic information to begin creating Web services in ASP.NET. In this chapter, you'll learn how to:

- Define Web services
- Create Web services in the .NET Framework

Defining Web Services

Consider a scenario in which you want to buy CDs on the Internet. When you place an order for a CD, you also need to specify your credit card details. These details are then validated against a database that stores the credit card details, such as the number, the card's validity, your credit limit, and so on. A similar validation is required when you order other products on the Internet, such as books or garments. To validate credit card information, you can implement the validation code in a Web service that can be used by different Web sites.

Web service providers can host a Web service on the Internet. Applications can then communicate with the Web service by using the Web service's URL. Applications that utilize a Web service by calling its functions are called *Web service clients*. A Web site that provides data to users is an example of a Web service client.

Web services use Internet protocols and standards, such as XML and HTTP. Internet standards enable you to create a platform-independent infrastructure that can be used for the effective integration of applications. Web services use the XML messaging technology to access or implement the code written to provide the required functionality. Therefore, the Web service provider application and the Web service client application can be integrated to provide a complete business solution even if they are running on different platforms. Web services are also referred to as *XML Web services* because they use XML for data exchange.

XML Web services offer significant advantages. For example, you don't need to worry about the database schema, which defines the relationships between tables in a database, or the internal implementation of business logic at the data source. Since the data is transferred in XML format, it can easily integrate with the existing line-of-business applications of an organization. In addition, you can automate some of the common business processes that involve data transfer between organizations.

In this section, I will describe the architecture of Web services and then explain how they work. Finally, I will describe some of the common technologies that are associated with XML Web services to help you understand the concept.

Understanding the Architecture of Web Services

A Web service is made up of four layers—the data layer, the data access layer, the business layer, and the listener layer. These layers work together to allow a Web service client to interact with a Web service. Table 14.1 explains the layers in the Web service architecture.

TABLE 14.1 Web Service Architecture Layers

Layer	Description
Data layer	The data layer contains data that can be accessed by a Web service. It includes a database or another data source that can be accessed by the Web service to manage information.
Data access layer	The data access layer is an intermediate layer between the data layer and the business layer. It is responsible for interacting with the data layer to retrieve data and make it available for the Web service. The data access layer also updates the data source after a business transaction. Finally, it maintains the integrity of data by validating changes that are made to the data with the business logic of the application.
Business layer	The business layer implements the business logic of the application and provides accessibility to the Web service. To do this, the business layer is internally divided into two layers—the business logic layer and the business façade layer. The business façade layer is an interface that provides access to the services provided by the business logic layer.
Listener layer	The listener layer is the uppermost layer in the Web service architecture; it is also the closest to the client application. The listener layer listens for requests that are made by Web service clients and converts the requests to forms that can be deciphered by the Web service. The business façade layer processes the request and sends the result back to the listener layer. The listener layer then forwards the result to the Web service client in the form of an XML message.

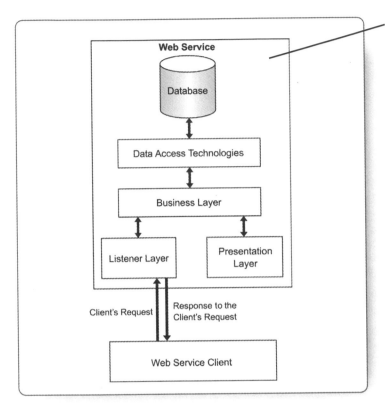

The .NET Web services architecture is very similar to the generic Web services architecture. Therefore, it is easy to create Web services in the .NET Framework. Move on to the next section to learn more about the workings of Web services.

Understanding the Workings of Web Services

A Web service exposes one or more Web methods. Web service clients can use these Web methods to interact with a Web service. A Web service client calls one or more Web methods of a Web service by using its URL. The request for the Web service is received and interpreted by the listener layer. The request sent to the listener layer is in the form of an XML message and is transferred using an Internet transfer protocol such as HTTP. (You will learn more about XML and HTTP later in this chapter.)

The request is interpreted by the listener layer and forwarded to the business layer, which performs the necessary business processes to process the request. While processing the request, the business layer might interact with the underlying data layer.

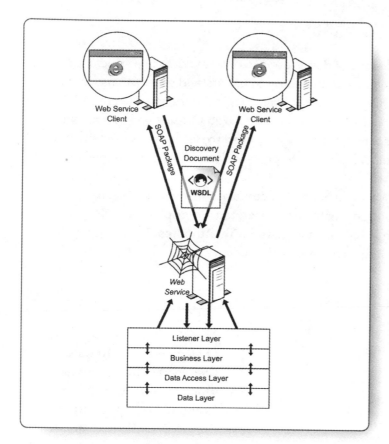

When the request is processed, the result is sent back to the Web service client following the same path that was used to route the request to the Web service. The result for the request is transported as a SOAP (*Simple Object Access Protocol*) package, which I will discuss in the following section.

The interaction of a Web service client with a Web service is a straightforward procedure. However, it involves a number of technologies, such as XML, SOAP, WSDL (*Web Services Description Language*), and UDDI (*Universal Description Discovery and Integration*). In the next section, I will discuss these technologies briefly.

Web Service Technologies

As I discussed earlier, Web services support Internet standards and technologies, such as HTTP and XML. Read on to learn more about these standards and technologies.

HTTP

You need a common set of rules or protocols to facilitate the transfer of data on the Internet. HTTP is the network protocol that is used for transferring data on the Internet; It defines the procedure for transfer of data over the network. In addition, HTTP provides a framework for displaying data on a Web page in a Web browser. Data that is transferred using HTTP includes requests, responses, HTML pages or files, and Web application data.

XML

XML is a meta-markup language that is used to describe data in a structured format. A meta-markup language uses easy to understand descriptions for data, which makes it possible for users to determine what data is stored in the XML document. XML is defined by W3C (*World Wide Web Consortium*) as a means to store, transport, and display data. It is widely used to display data over the Internet because it provides a standard format to present data across applications.

XML data is stored in XML documents that contain XML tags. In addition to the tags present in XML, you can create customized tags to display data. XML tags contain elements, which in turn are associated with attributes. To understand the tags used in XML, you should create an XML document.

CREATING AN XML DOCUMENT

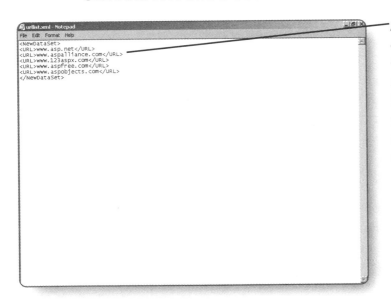

An XML document is composed of elements and attributes. Creating an XML document is as simple as writing data in a Notepad file and saving the file with an extension of .xml. A sample XML document is displayed here.

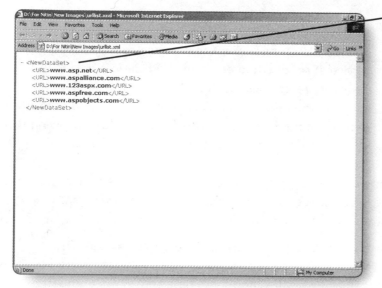

After you create an XML document, you can open it in Internet Explorer. Notice that Internet Explorer represents an XML document hierarchically, by grouping each element and its attributes.

The urllist.xml file declares a tag named NewDataSet containing an element called URL. The URL element stores five Web addresses: www.asp.net, www.aspalliance.com, www.123aspx.com, www.aspfree.com, and www.aspobjects.com.

Now that you've looked at an XML document, take a look at how XML encompasses the concept of Web services.

THE ROLE OF XML IN WEB SERVICES

XML is a platform-independent format for porting data. Data in XML format can be accessed by any XML-enabled application. Because the data is easily accessible, Web applications are able to communicate effectively with Web services.

Web services should be available to devices and Web browsers running on any operating system. XML makes this possible by presenting the text from a Web service in plain text that is easily understood by all devices.

SOAP

As I discussed earlier, when a request for a Web service is made, the request is packaged as a SOAP package. SOAP is a lightweight protocol based on XML that is used to transfer data from a Web service client application to a Web service provider application and vice versa. The support for XML and HTTP makes SOAP a platform-independent transfer protocol.

> **NOTE**
>
> SOAP also supports transport protocols such as FTP (*File Transfer Protocol*) and SMTP (*Simple Mail Transfer Protocol*).

When a Web service client communicates with a Web service, it sends a request to the Web service as a SOAP message, which includes the call to the Web service. In addition, the result of the Web service is sent as a SOAP package in the form of an XML document. The following list presents the components of a SOAP package.

- A SOAP package contains an envelope that encapsulates the data that is communicated from a Web service client to a Web service and vice versa. The envelope is a mandatory component of the SOAP package.

- When data is transferred over a network, a transport protocol is used. This protocol defines a set of rules to encode or decode data that is transferred over the network. This helps to maintain the integrity of data and allows a smooth transfer of data over the network. This component is also mandatory.

- In addition to the previously listed components, a SOAP package includes two optional components—a message pattern and the binding between SOAP and HTTP.

Although SOAP is a protocol, it does not define any syntax for the transfer of data. Instead, SOAP defines the mechanism of data transfer across multiple applications. SOAP does not require any additional hardware or software investments and can be accessed by any device that supports basic Internet standards.

WSDL

Similar to XML, WSDL is also a markup language that defines data in a Web service. WSDL is used to generate a discovery document for a Web service. A discovery document is an XML file that contains information about the Web services, such as the parameters passed to the Web service call statement, a SOAP message, and the exchange mechanism used to transfer data.

A discovery document also specifies the mechanism used by the Web service client applications to communicate with the Web service. The discovery document has a .wsdl file extension and can be accessed using the Web Services Discovery tool. This tool is an executable file, Disco.exe, that generates files with extensions such as .disco, .wsdl, .discomap, and .xsd.

UDDI

A Web service can be accessed by several Web service clients. However, to make Web service clients aware of your Web service, you need to register it with a directory called a *UDDI directory*. A UDDI directory is like a Yellow Pages that contains a list of all the Web services created by users across the network. To register the Web service with a UDDI directory, you use UDDI. UDDI is a mechanism that is employed by a Web service client to discover a Web service using the service's discovery document.

After you create a Web service, you register it with a UDDI directory. Interested users can use the Web service by customizing it to fit their needs.

A UDDI directory contains a pointer to all of the Web services registered with the UDDI directory in an XML file maintained by the directory.

NOTE

The pointer to the Web service contains information about the WSDL document of the Web service. Therefore, you first need to create a WSDL document for your Web service.

Searching for information about Web services is similar to searching for data on a Web site. A developer can type the search criteria for the required Web service in the UDDI directory, and the directory will return a list of matching Web services. The user can then use the required Web service.

Now that you know more about the Web service technologies, move on to the next section to explore the creation of Web services in the .NET Framework.

Creating Web Services in the .NET Framework

The .NET Framework provides complete support for creating, deploying, and maintaining Web services. Web services in the .NET Framework are created using ASP.NET. To create a Web service in ASP.NET, you can use the ASP.NET Web Service template provided by Visual Studio .NET. To access the template, open Visual Studio .NET and perform the following steps.

1. Click on File. The File menu will appear.

2. Move the mouse pointer to New and click on Project. The New Project dialog box will open.

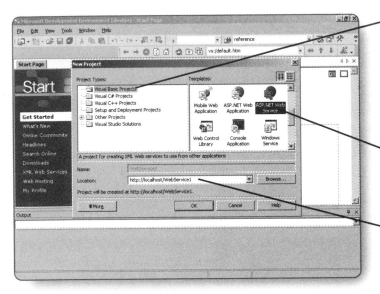

3. In the Project Types pane, select the Visual Basic Projects option. The templates available for creating Visual Basic .NET projects will appear in the Templates pane.

4. In the Templates pane, select the ASP.NET Web Service option.

5. In the Location text box, type the address of the server on which you want to develop the Web service.

TIP

If the development server is the same as the local machine, type the address of the development server as http://localhost/WebService1. You can also specify a different name for your Web service in the Location text box. For example, to name the Web service that you create MyWebService, type http://localhost/MyWebService in the Location text box.

---

6. Click on OK. Visual Studio .NET will create a new Web service on the server.

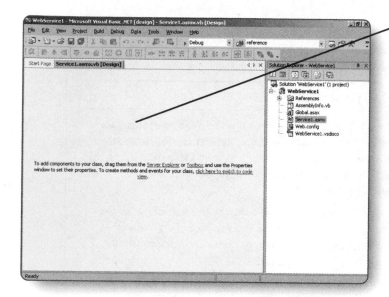

Visual Studio .NET will create a blank page with the name Service1.asmx.vb and open it in the Design view. This view is called the Component Designer view of the WebService1 Web service.

NOTE

If a Web service already exists with the name that you have specified in the Location text box, Visual Studio .NET will prompt you to specify another name. A new Web service will then be created at the specified location with the name that you choose.

Understanding Default Files Created for Web Services

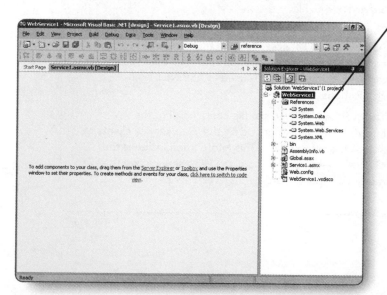

If you view the Solution Explorer, you will notice that Visual Studio .NET creates some default files and adds Web references for your Web service.

Table 14.2 discusses the files created by Visual Studio .NET in detail.

TABLE 14.2 Web Service Project Files Created by Visual Studio .NET

File	Description
References	The References folder contains the Web references for WebService1. By default, the References folder contains references to the System.dll, System.Data.dll, System.Web.dll, System.Web.Services.dll, and System.XML.dll files.
AssemblyInfo.vb	The AssemblyInfo.vb file contains the metadata for the assemblies required for a Web service. This metadata includes information such as name and version of the assembly for a Web service.
Global.asax	The Global.asax file contains the code for events generated in the WebService1 project. In addition, the Global.asax file defines variables with application level scope and manages application and session state.
Service1.asmx	The Service1.asmx file is used to implement the functionality of the Web service. A Web service has a proxy class that handles the transfer of SOAP messages over a network. The proxy class is created using the Wsdl.exe tool and uses HTTP to transfer SOAP messages. The information about this proxy class is stored in the Service1.asmx file.
Web.config	The Web.config file contains the configuration settings for ASP.NET Web services. You can make changes to the configuration settings, if required. This file is the same as the Web.config file that is used in ASP.NET Web applications.
WebService1.vsdisco	The WebService1.vsdisco file contains all of the information that is required by the Web service clients to access the Web service. This information includes the discovery information about the Web service and the Web methods implemented by the Web service.

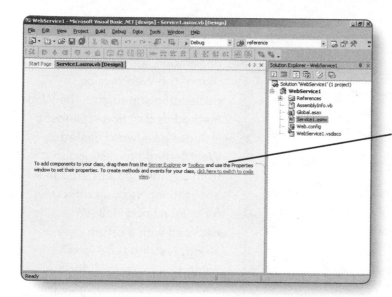

Understanding the Default Code Generated for Web Services

In addition to the default files, Visual Studio .NET generates default code for Web services. To view the default code, press the F7 key in the Component Designer view. You can also view the code by clicking on the Click Here to Switch to Code View link in the Component Designer view of the Service1.asmx.vb file.

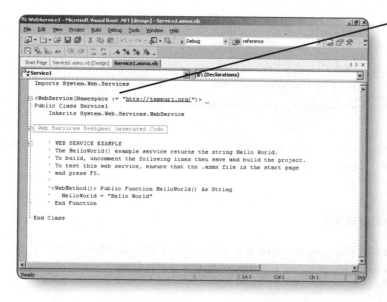

I will now discuss the template-generated code in detail. The code for the Web service includes an Imports directive to include the System.Web.Services namespace into your Web service. Next, the code contains a declaration statement for the Web service. This statement indicates to the server that the application is a Web service. The Web service declaration statement includes the name of the default namespace used by the Web service. In this case, the namespace is http://tempuri.org.

In addition, a public class with the name Service1 that is inherited from the System.Web.Services.WebService class is created. The Service1 class also contains a default Web method, HelloWorld().

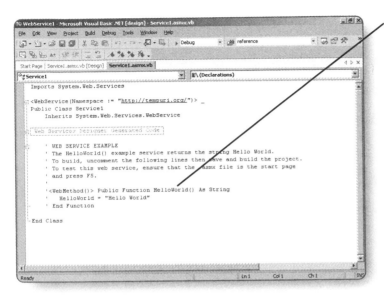

The HelloWorld() Web method includes a Web method declaration statement similar to that of the Web service declaration statement. The Web method declaration statement includes a keyword named WebMethod() to distinguish it from any method declared in an application. Next, a public function named HelloWorld() is declared with a return type as string. A string type variable named HelloWorld is declared and initialized to the value Hello World, which is returned by the Web method.

NOTE

The functionality in a Web service is provided by the Web methods that you create in the Web service.

The HelloWorld() Web method is enclosed within comment entries by default. To run the Web service, remove the comment entries.

Testing Web Services

After you create a Web service, you need to test it to ensure that it works correctly. Before testing and debugging a project, you need to set the Service1.asmx page as the start page.

1. Right-click on the Service1.asmx file in the Solution Explorer. A shortcut menu will appear.

2. Click on the Set As Start Page option.

3. Once you have created the Web service, you can test it on a Web browser, such as Internet Explorer. Click on Debug. The Debug menu will appear.

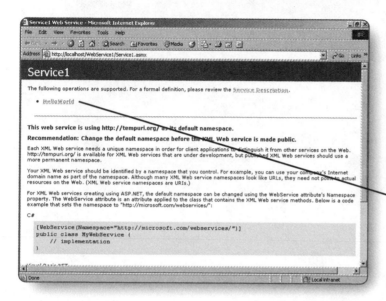

4. Click on Start. The Web service will be launched in Internet Explorer.

When you run the project, the Service1.asmx page will be displayed in the Internet Explorer browser window.

The Service1.asmx page contains a link to the HelloWorld() Web method. To invoke the method, click on the HelloWorld link.

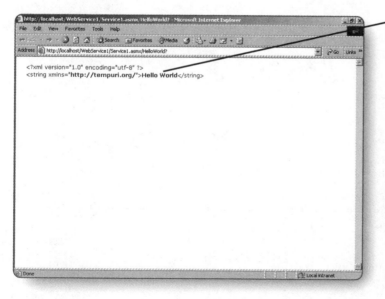

The HelloWorld() Web method returns a string, Hello World, that is embedded in an XML file.

This completes the discussion on Web services. In the next chapter, I will continue with the MySourceCode application, and you will learn to create a Web service for the application. The Web service accesses XML data and displays the data using a Web service client.

15

Building ASP.NET Web Services

The last chapter introduced the concept of Web services. ASP.NET Web services can interact with other applications using XML. Since XML is a platform-independent format for transferring data, you can create a Web service on one platform and implement it on another.

ASP.NET provides inherent support for XML Web services. When you create an ASP.NET Web service in Visual Studio .NET, you don't need to worry about implementing the programming logic to make data accessible in XML format to a Web service client. Instead, you can concentrate on coding the business logic of the Web service; the development environment takes care of the rest.

This chapter provides you with the skills to create an ASP.NET Web service. In this chapter, you'll learn how to:

● Create an ASP.NET Web service

● Access a Web service from a Web service client

Creating a Web Service

The ASP.NET Web Service project template is used to create ASP.NET Web services. You can create a new project by using the template and adding Web methods to the project. In this section, I will explain the steps to create a Web service using the ASP.NET Web Service template.

Creating an ASP.NET Web Service Project

To create an ASP.NET Web service project, launch Visual Studio .NET and follow these steps.

1. Click on File. The File menu will appear.

2. Move the mouse pointer to New. The New submenu will appear.

3. Click on Project. The New Project dialog box will open.

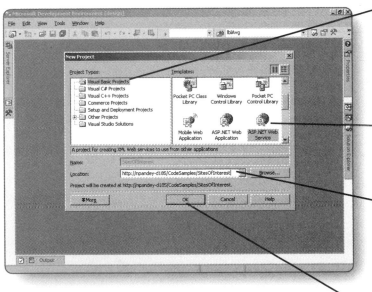

4. Click on the Visual Basic Projects folder in the Project Types pane. The available Visual Basic .NET templates will be listed in the Templates pane.

5. Click on ASP.NET Web Service. The option will be selected.

6. Change the name of the Web service by appending the name of the Web service to the location displayed in the Location text box.

7. Click on OK.

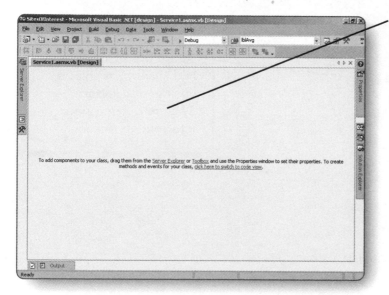

A new Web service will be created for you. By default, the Service1.asmx page will be added to the Web service. The page will open in Design view.

Adding Web Methods to the Web Service

After you create the new Web service, you will need to add Web methods to it. You add Web methods to the Web service using the Code Editor.

1. Double-click on the Service1.asmx.vb page in the Design view. The form will open in the Code Editor.

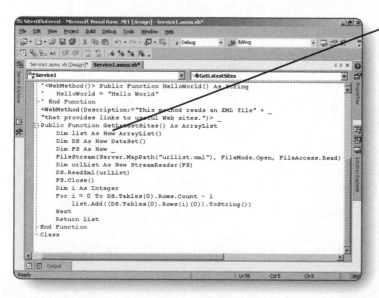

2. Type the definition of the Web method as shown here. In this definition, I have used a FileStream object to open the urllist.xml file from the Web server. The FileStream object is used to initialize a StreamReader object. The StreamReader object is used as a data source by a DataSet object, which reads XML data from the urllist.xml file. The data read by the DataSet object is stored in an ArrayList object, which is returned by the Web method.

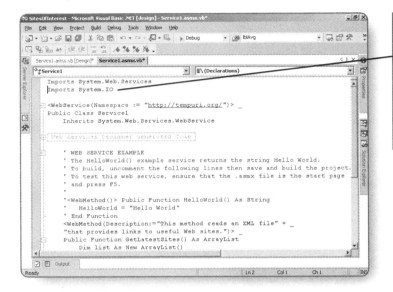

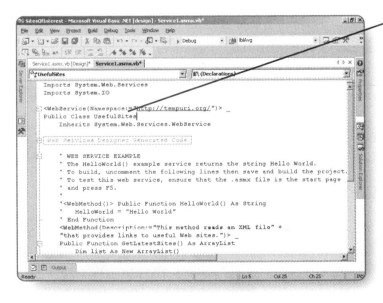

3. Change the name of the Web service class from Service1 to a name that can be associated with the Web service.

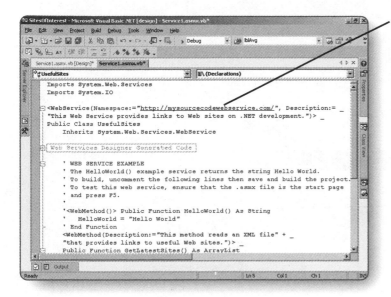

4. Change the default namespace of the Web service and add a description to the service using the WebService attribute.

After you make these changes, your Web service will be ready.

Testing the Web Service

After you create a Web service, you should test it. You can test a Web service without creating a Web service client. All you need to do is to run the Web service and use the HTML interface that is provided by Visual Studio .NET to retrieve data from Web methods that are defined in the Web service.

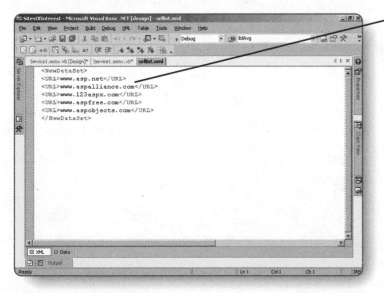

To test the Web service that you created in the last section, first make sure that you have added the urllist.xml file to the root directory of the Web service project. The structure of the urllist.xml file is shown here.

After you add the XML file to the root directory of the Web service project, follow these steps to test the Web service.

1. Click on Debug. The Debug menu will appear.

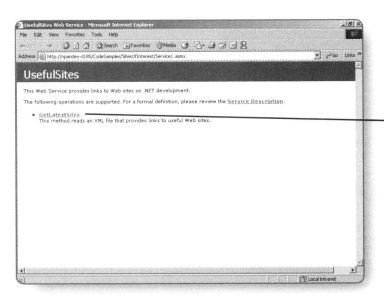

2. Click on Start. Visual Studio .NET will compile and run the Web service, and the UsefulSites page will appear.

3. The UsefulSites page provides a list of Web methods implemented by the Web service client as hyperlinks. To test the Web method that you added to the site, click on the GetLatestSites link. The GetLatestSites page will appear.

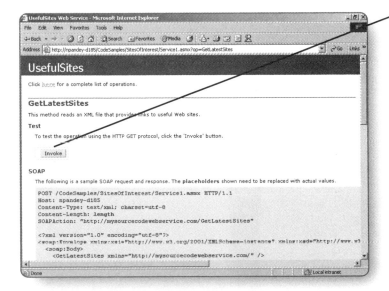

4. The GetLatestSites Web method does not require any parameters; therefore, the Web service does not prompt you to specify any. Click on Invoke to test the Web method. Data from urllist.xml will be retrieved and displayed on the Web page.

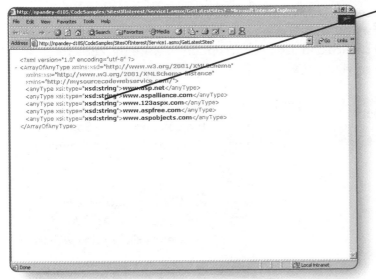

When a Web service is run successfully, you can see the output of the Web service in XML format, as shown here. Notice that the data has been retrieved from the urllist.xml file.

Accessing a Web Service

A Web service does not display information directly to users. Instead, a Web service is often associated with one or more Web service clients that can display data. In this section, I will use a Web service client to access data from the Web service created in the preceding section.

Adding a Web Reference

Often, an ASP.NET Web service client is an ASP.NET Web application. Visual Studio .NET enables you to easily implement the functionality of a Web service in an ASP.NET Web application.

The Web service client that I will use to connect to the Web service is the MySourceCode application that was discussed in the last few chapters. As you'll recall, MySourceCode is an ASP.NET Web application.

Consider that the MySourceCode application needs to display a list of useful Web sites on its home page. If the Web application does not have direct access to this information, it can connect to the Web service created in the preceding section and utilize its Web methods to display data.

To connect to the Web service and utilize its Web methods, you need to add a Web reference to the Web service. A Web reference enables you to download the description of the Web service and use the description to write the code for implementing the Web service.

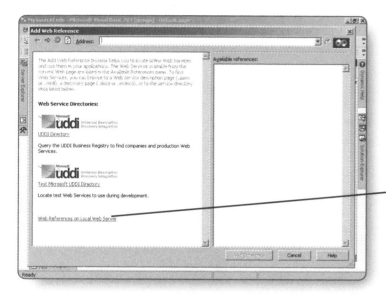

1. Right-click on the name of the solution in the Solution Explorer. A shortcut menu will appear.

2. Click on Add Web Reference. The Add Web Reference dialog box will open.

3. Click on the Web References on Local Web Server link. A list of Web services available on the local computer will appear.

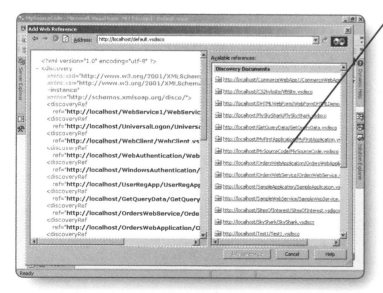

4. Click on the link for the Web service that you want to implement. Links to the contractual information and the documentation of the Web service will be displayed.

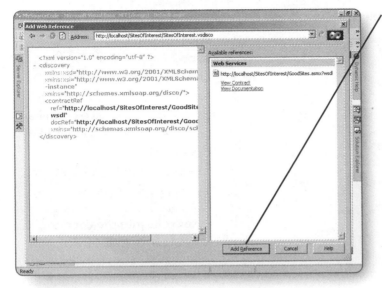

5. Click on Add Reference. A reference to the Web service will be added to the application.

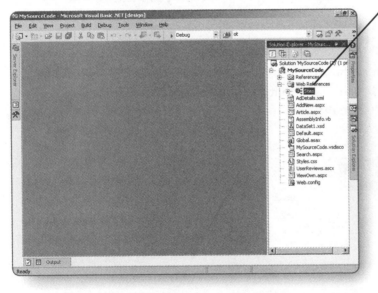

After you add a reference to the Web service, notice that the reference appears in the Web References section of the Solution Explorer. You can change the name used to refer to the Web service from localhost to a name of your choice. For example, I have changed the name of the reference to Sites.

Implementing the Web Service

After you add a Web reference to the Web service, you need to write the code to use the Web methods of the Web service in your application.

1. Open the form in which you want to implement the Web reference in the Code Editor.

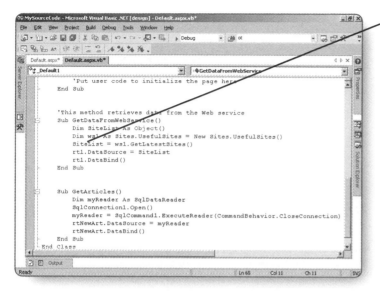

2. Type the code to retrieve data from the Web service, as shown here. In the GetDataFromWebService function, I have retrieved data from the Web service using its GetLatestSites Web method. I have displayed the data retrieved from the Web service by using a Repeater control.

After you write the code to implement a Web service, you can test the Web application to determine whether the output is what you want.

Testing the Output of a Web Service

You can test the output of the Web service by running the ASP.NET Web application in which you have implemented the Web service. When you run the application, it will connect to the Web service, retrieve data using its Web methods, and display data on a Web form.

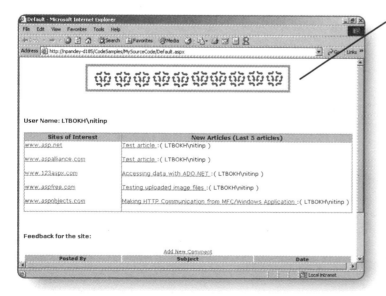

The output of the Web service that I have implemented in the MySourceCode application is displayed here. Notice that the final output does not depend on whether the data has been retrieved from a Web application or a Web service.

This completes the discussion on creating and implementing ASP.NET Web services. In the next chapter, you will learn how to create applications that can be accessed from mobile devices.

16

Building Mobile Web Applications

Mobile Web applications enable you to access a Web application using a WAP (*Wireless Access Protocol*)-enabled device, such as a cell phone or a personal digital assistant.

Microsoft has provided a Mobile Internet Toolkit that enables you to create mobile applications using Visual Studio .NET. This chapter describes the procedure for creating mobile applications using Visual Studio .NET. In this chapter, you'll learn how to:

- Install prerequisite software for creating mobile applications
- Create a mobile application in Visual Studio .NET

Overview of Mobile Web Applications

Before the advent of Visual Studio .NET, it was difficult to create mobile applications. The reasons why were attributed in part to the lack of a suitable technology that could cater to the needs of a mobile application developer and in part to the limited capabilities of mobile devices.

While mobile device manufacturers have done their bit to improve the performance of mobile devices, Microsoft has introduced the Mobile Internet Toolkit, which can be integrated with Visual Studio .NET to create mobile applications.

The Mobile Internet Toolkit provides all the necessary tools, mobile Web forms, mobile Web controls, and extensive documentation that are required to create mobile applications.

The applications that you create using the Mobile Internet Toolkit are executed in the .NET Framework environment. Therefore, you can use the class library of the .NET Framework in mobile applications.

One important component of the Mobile Internet Toolkit is mobile Web forms, which can be used to design the interface of a Web application as it should appear on the mobile device. A mobile Web form can contain several forms that can be displayed on the mobile device one at a time. The advantage to displaying information on multiple forms is that you can account for the limited display area of the mobile device.

You will learn more about creating mobile applications later in this chapter. First, I will explain the steps to install prerequisite software for creating mobile applications.

Installing Prerequisite Software

To create mobile Web applications, you need to install the Microsoft Mobile Internet Toolkit. The toolkit can be downloaded for free from http://msdn.microsoft.com/vstudio/device/mitdefault.asp.

After you install the Microsoft Mobile Internet Toolkit, you should install Microsoft Mobile Explorer, which emulates a mobile device and can be used for testing the output of a mobile application. The Microsoft Mobile Explorer Toolkit can be downloaded from http://msdn.microsoft.com/vstudio/device/mitdefault.asp.

In this section, I will explain the steps to install the Mobile Internet Toolkit and the Microsoft Mobile Explorer Toolkit.

Installing the Mobile Internet Toolkit

After you download the Mobile Internet Toolkit, follow these steps to install it.

1. Double-click on the installation file. The Welcome screen of the wizard will appear.

2. Click on Next. The License Agreement screen will appear.

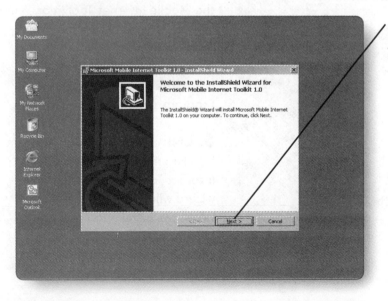

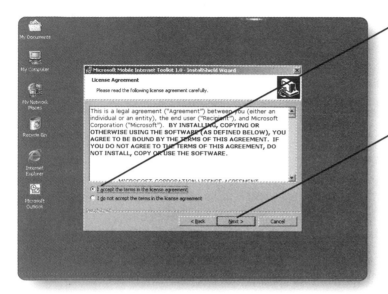

3. Click on the I Accept the Terms in the License Agreement option. The option will be selected, and the Next button will be enabled.

4. Click on Next. The Setup Type screen will appear.

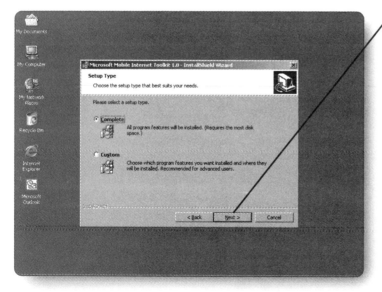

5. On the Setup Type screen, you can specify whether you want to install all components of the Mobile Internet Toolkit or only specific components. To install all components, retain the default option and click on Next. The Ready to Install the Program screen will appear.

6. Click on Next to begin the installation of the Mobile Internet Toolkit. The setup wizard will install the toolkit. When the installation is complete, the InstallShield Wizard Completed screen will appear.

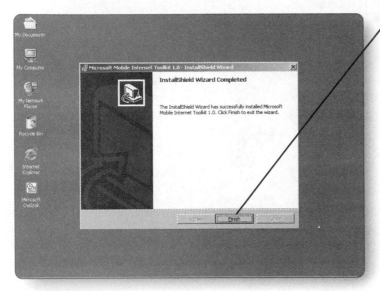

7. Click on Finish to exit the wizard.

After you complete the installation, you can create mobile applications in Visual Studio .NET.

Installing the Microsoft Mobile Emulator

The Microsoft Mobile Emulator enables you to test the output of your application as it would appear on a mobile device. To install the Microsoft Mobile Emulator, download the Microsoft Mobile Explorer Toolkit installation file and follow these steps.

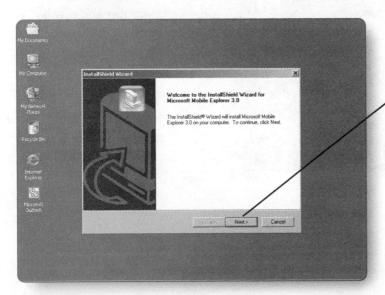

1. Double-click on the installation file. The Welcome screen of the wizard will appear.

2. Click on Next. The License Agreement screen will appear.

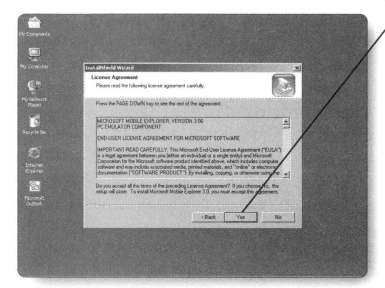

3. Click on Yes to accept the license agreement. The Select Components screen of the wizard will appear.

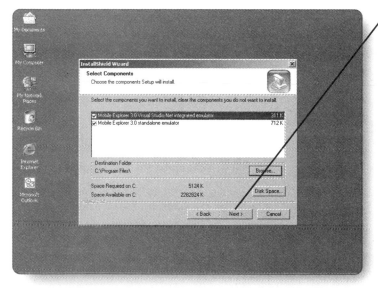

4. Retain the default options to install all the components of Microsoft Mobile Explorer and click on Next. The wizard will install Microsoft Mobile Explorer on your computer and display the Microsoft Mobile Explorer - Readme screen.

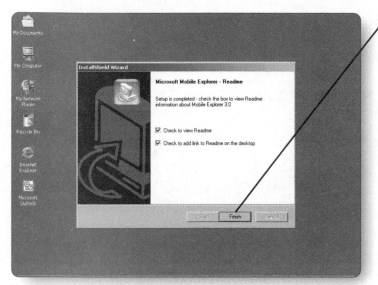

5. Click on Finish to exit the wizard.

Creating a Mobile Web Application

To create a mobile Web application, you can use the Mobile Web Application template, which is installed when you install the Mobile Internet Toolkit. However, you can also add mobile Web forms to your existing application to make them mobile-device enabled.

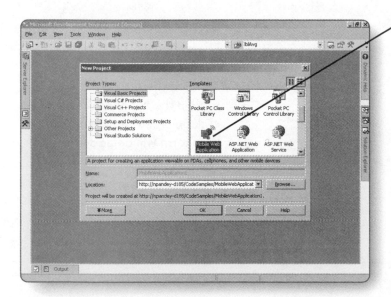

The tasks involved in creating a mobile application are similar whether you use a Mobile Web Application template or add mobile Web forms to your existing application. In this section, I will explain the steps to create a mobile application by adding mobile Web forms to your existing application.

Adding a Mobile Web Form to a Project

To add a mobile Web form to your application, follow these steps.

1. Right-click on the solution to which you want to add the mobile Web form. A shortcut menu will appear.

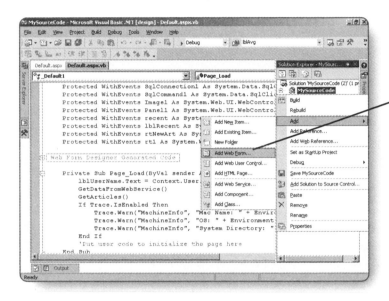

2. Move the mouse pointer to Add. The Add submenu will appear.

3. Click on Add Web Form. The Add New Item dialog box will open.

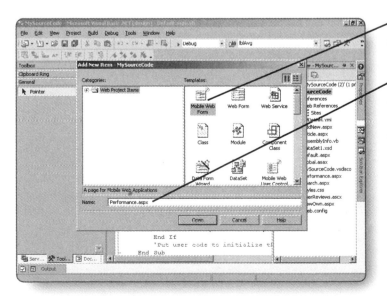

4. Click on Mobile Web Form. The option will be selected.

5. Type the name of the Web form in the Name text box and click on Open. A new mobile Web form will be added to the application.

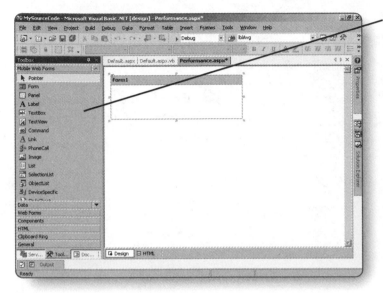

When you add a mobile Web form to your application, a number of mobile Web controls appear in the Toolbox. You can use these controls to add functionality and design the Web forms for your mobile application.

Designing Forms for a Mobile Application

To design the forms for a mobile application, you can use the mobile controls available in the Toolbox. If you view the list of mobile controls available in the Toolbox, you will notice that the list includes a Form control.

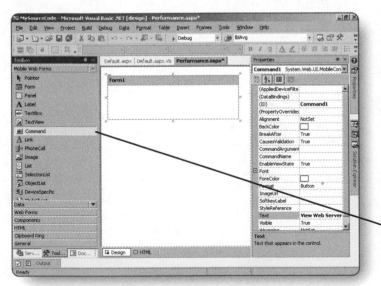

The Form control is used to display a different screen on the same Web form. This control has been included in the Mobile Internet Toolkit to account for the smaller display area on mobile devices.

To design forms for a mobile application, follow these steps.

1. Click on the Command control in the Toolbox. The control will be selected.

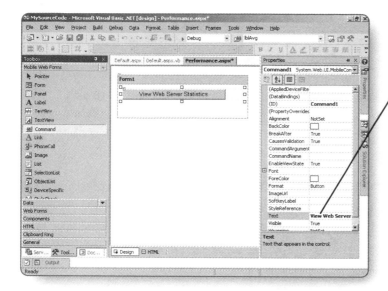

2. Press and hold the mouse button and drag the control to the form.

3. Change the Text property of the control to View Web Server Statistics.

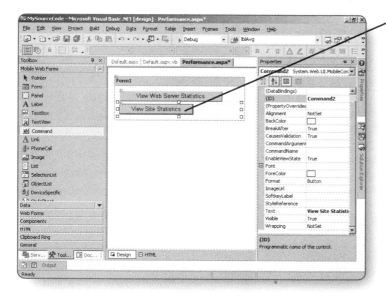

4. Add another Command control to the form and change its Text property to View Site Statistics.

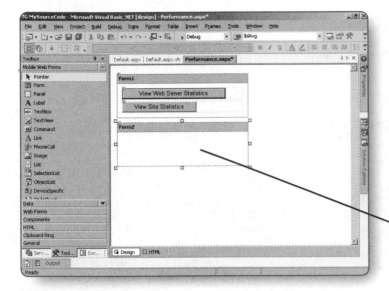

This completes the design of the first form. However, to display data pertaining to the performance of the Web server and Web application, you need to add another form to the application.

1. Click on the Form control in the Toolbox.

2. Press and hold the mouse button and drag the control to the form. A new form will be placed on the Web form.

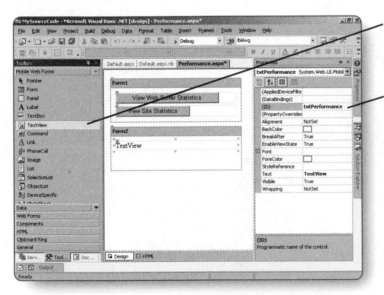

3. Add a TextView control to the form. The control will appear on the form.

4. Change the ID property of the TextView control to txtPerformance.

Writing the Code for the Form

After you design the form, you need to write the code for it.

1. Double-click on the View Web Server Statistics button to open the Code Editor.

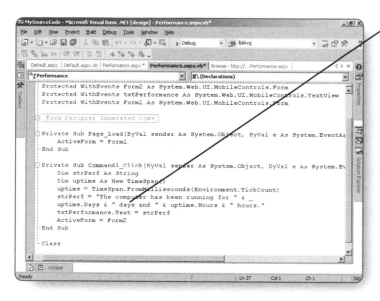

2. Type the code shown here in the Click event of the control. In this code, I have determined the amount of time the computer has been running. This value, retrieved by the Environment.TickCount property, has been assigned to an object of the TimeSpan class. The object of the TimeSpan class is then used to display the time on the second form in the Web form. To switch to the second form, I have used the ActiveForm property of the mobile Web form.

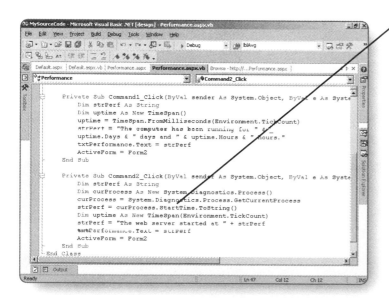

3. Repeat steps 1 and 2 to write the code for the Click event of the View Site Statistics button. In this code, I have used the GetCurrentProcess method of the Process class to create an object that represents the application the user is accessing. Then, I used the StartTime property of the application to determine when the application was started. This information is displayed to the user in the second form.

Testing a Mobile Application

You can test a mobile application using the Microsoft Mobile Emulator. When you install the emulator on your computer, two versions of it are installed—the stand-alone version, which operates as a stand-alone application, and the integrated version, which integrates with the Visual Studio .NET development environment.

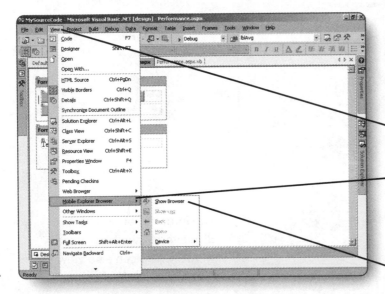

You can use either of the two versions to test your application. To test the application using the integrated version of the emulator, follow these steps.

1. Click on View. The View menu will appear.

2. Move the mouse pointer to Mobile Explorer Browser. The Mobile Explorer Browser submenu will appear.

3. Click on Show Browser. The MME Emulator window will appear.

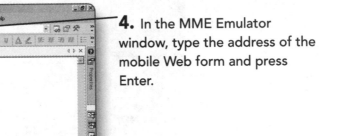

4. In the MME Emulator window, type the address of the mobile Web form and press Enter.

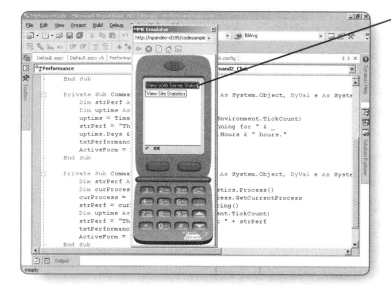

5. The mobile Web form will appear in the emulator window. Click on the first button to obtain information about the duration of time for which your computer has been on.

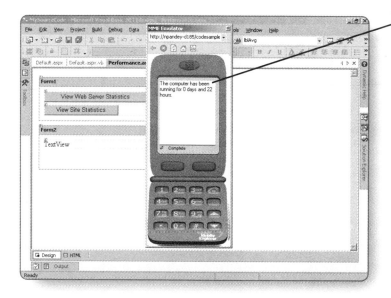

The information will be displayed in the emulator window. You can also view the time when the Web server was started by clicking on the View Site Statistics button.

You have now successfully created a mobile Web application. The application can be accessed on any WAP-enabled mobile device. As you probably noticed, the steps to create the application are quite similar to the steps to create other Web applications.

17

Managing State in ASP.NET Applications

HTTP is a stateless protocol. Thus, when a user sends a request to the server, the request is processed and the data that was involved in processing the request is cleared. By simply using the HTTP protocol, there is no way in which the server can determine whether a subsequent request is from the same user. However, it is often necessary to track the users who are visiting your Web application. For example, to determine which shopping cart needs to be displayed to a user, you need to know the credentials of the user who is logged on to the Web application.

ASP.NET allows you to track visitors to your Web site by implementing state management. State management is a procedure by which a unique session is generated for every user who visits your Web site. Whenever the user sends a request to the Web application, the session data is used to retrieve the identity of the user and process the request.

ASP.NET provides client-side and server-side state management capabilities. In this chapter, you'll learn how to:

- Implement client-side state management
- Implement server-side state management

Implementing Client-Side State Management

For client-side state management, ASP.NET provides cookies, query strings, and hidden fields. Each of these options stores data that pertains to the state of the user at the client end. Therefore, these mechanisms are referred to as *client-side state management*. In this section, I will explore these three mechanisms for client-side state management.

Using Cookies

A *cookie* is a token that is used by a Web server to identify the client of a Web application. When you enable forms authentication on a Web application, the application uses client-side cookies to authenticate a user and process user requests.

Cookies can be either temporary or persistent. Temporary cookies are stored in the client's browser. These cookies are removed when the browser session with the Web application ends. Persistent cookies, on the other hand, are stored on the hard disk of the client computer as a text file. These cookies can be retrieved by the Web application when the client establishes another session with it.

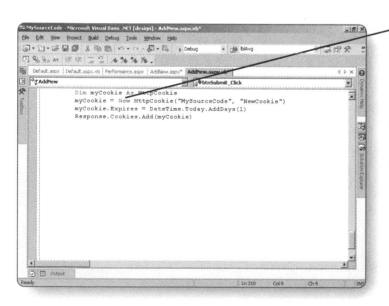

To generate a cookie, you need to use the HttpCookie class. In the code snippet displayed here, I have used the HttpCookie class to add a cookie to the application. I have also specified the expiration date of the cookie using the Expires property of the HttpCookie class.

```
Dim myCookie As HttpCookie
myCookie = New HttpCookie("MySourceCode", "NewCookie")
myCookie.Expires = DateTime.Today.AddDays(1)
Response.Cookies.Add(myCookie)
```

Using Query Strings

Query strings are used to pass values from one Web form to another. The value that must be passed from the first form is added to the address of the second form.

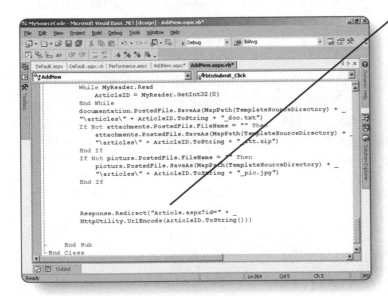

Chapter 10, "Managing Data from ASP.NET Applications," demonstrated the implementation of query strings. Here, the ID of the article that a user has added to a form is passed from the AddNew.aspx form of the application to the Article.aspx form, where the ID is used to retrieve article details and display them on the form.

Using Hidden Fields

Hidden fields are used by ASP.NET to handle postbacks from a form. Whenever a Web form submits data to a Web application, the data on the form is processed and the same form might need to be reloaded. For example, when a user submits a registration form after filling in all the data fields, the form should be redisplayed to the user if the data in one or more fields is not valid.

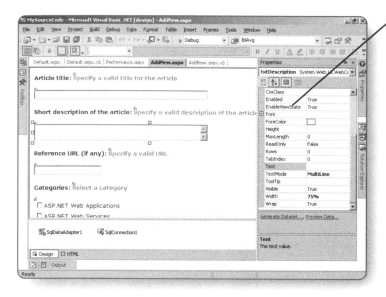

When a form is redisplayed to a user, the data that the user has entered should not be lost. If you specify the EnableViewState property of a control on the form as True, then the state of the control will be retained on the form in hidden fields. The hidden fields store data on the client side. When the form is reloaded, the data is retrieved from the hidden fields and displayed to the users. Therefore, users can view the data they had specified on the form before posting it to the server.

Implementing Server-Side State Management

Server-side state management is implemented in ASP.NET by the Session and Application state objects. Although the implementation of these objects is quite similar, their purposes are different. The Application object is used to initialize a set of variables when the application is first started. The Session object is used to initialize a set of variables every time a client starts a new session.

In this section, I will examine the steps to configure the Session and Application state objects for an application.

Implementing Session State Management

The Session object manages the session state. You can use the Start and End events of the Session object to configure the session state. The Start and End events are always coded in the global.asax file of the application. The global.asax file defines application level variables, which can be accessed by all files in the application.

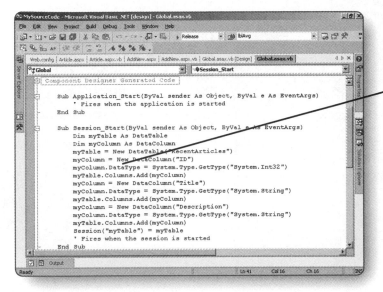

Take a look at an example of the implementation of the Session state object.

In the code shown here, I have used the Start event to create a DataTable object that has three columns—ID, Title, and Description. The table is created whenever a client starts a new browser session.

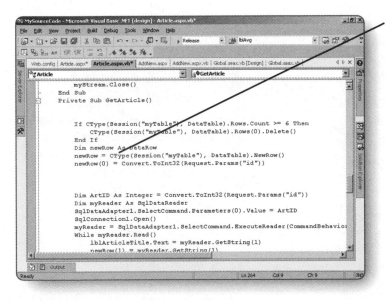

Whenever the user browses the Article.aspx page of the Web application, I add the details of the article to the DataTable object, which is a session variable.

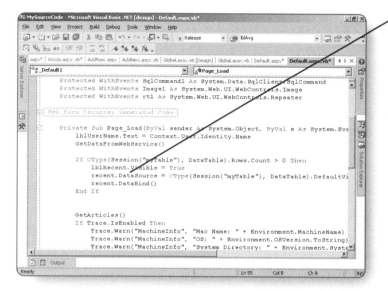

The data added to the DataTable object is retrieved on the Default.aspx page of the application, and a list of recently viewed articles is generated.

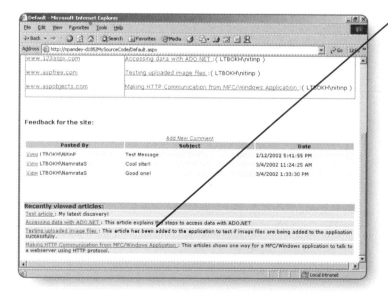

When the application is run, a DataTable object is created for the user whose session has started. The DataTable is populated whenever the user browses the Article.aspx page. When the user returns to the home page of the Web site, the article that the user had initially browsed is displayed in the Recently Viewed Articles list.

Implementing Application State Management

Application state is configured in the same way as the Session state object. Application state is configured in the Start and End events of the Application object. However, the code in these events is executed only once; the code for the Start event is executed when the application is started, and the code for the End event is executed when the application is terminated.

Variables that need to be accessed from a number of pages in the Web application are configured in the Application state. For example, you might store the database connection strings in an XML file. In the Start event of the Application object, you can retrieve the connection strings and store them in global variables. These variables can be used throughout the application to connect to the data source and retrieve data.

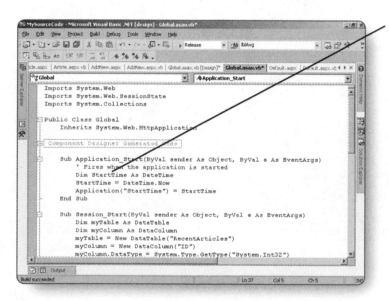

In the code snippet shown here, I have used the Application object to assign the current date and time to the StartTime variable. Any page of the Web application can access this variable to determine when the application was started.

This completes the discussion on the implementation of state management in ASP.NET. In the next chapter, you will learn about implementing caching in ASP.NET applications, which enables you to store frequently used data within the application to improve the application's performance.

18

Caching in ASP.NET Applications

Data-intensive applications often require frequent access to the data source. When many users access an enterprise application, the load on the database might increase substantially, leading to a decline in performance. You can reduce the load factor on Web servers and database servers by implementing caching on a Web application. Caching enables you to store data at temporary locations. When a user requests data that is cached, the data is retrieved from the cache instead of the original data source, thus reducing the load on the data source.

ASP.NET provides three types of caching—page-output caching, page-fragment caching, and page-data caching. Page-output caching and page-fragment caching are used to cache an entire Web form as it appears on the screen. However, page-data caching is used to cache specific elements of a Web form, but not its complete interface. In this chapter, you'll learn how to:

- Implement page-output caching
- Implement page-fragment caching
- Implement page-data caching

Implementing Page-Output Caching

In page-output caching, when the page is requested for the first time, a page-level cache is created to cache the contents of a Web form. When subsequent requests are made to the Web form, the data is retrieved from the cache, which reduces the load on the Web server.

To implement page-output caching, you need to use the @ OutputCache directive. The @ OutputCache directive includes a number of attributes that are used to configure the cache. These attributes include

- **Duration**. The Duration attribute determines the number of seconds for which a cache is valid. For example, if you specify a duration of 60, the cache will be valid for one minute. After that time, the cache will be recreated.

- **Location**. The Location attribute specifies the location of a cache. ASP.NET applications are capable of caching content on any cache-enabled device, such as the client computer that has requested the Web form or the proxy server that is used to access the Web application. By default, the value of the Location attribute is set to Any, which enables ASP.NET applications to cache data on any client-enabled device. However, if you want to use a specific device for caching data, you can specify Client, Downstream, or Server. If you do not want caching enabled for a Web form, you can specify the value None.

- **VaryByParam**. Consider a scenario in which you have enabled caching for a Web form, Article.aspx. The Web form accepts the article ID from the query string and retrieves data for the article. When the page is requested for the first time, the article with ID=1 is loaded. This page will be cached. If another user requests the same form with article ID=2, the cached page will not be loaded because the cache represents the article with ID=1.

  To avoid loading cached data when the value passed in the query string is different, you can specify the query string key in the VaryByParam attribute. Therefore, in this case, you should specify ArticleID for the VaryByParam attribute.

To implement page-output caching, use the Article.aspx page of the MySourceCode application. See Chapter 10, "Managing Data from ASP.NET Applications," for more information on how the Article.aspx page was created.

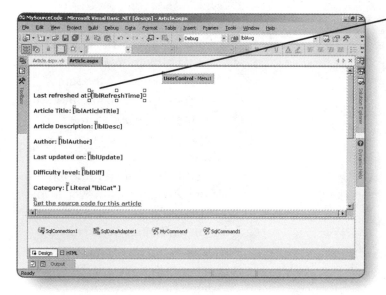

On the Article.aspx page, I have added a lblRefreshTime label. This label displays the time when the page was last loaded. The label has been added only to test whether the page is being cached successfully. After caching has been implemented, I will delete the label.

In the Load event of the form, specify the following line of code to show the current time in the lblRefreshTime label.

```
lblRefreshTime.Text = DateTime.Now.ToShortTimeString()
```

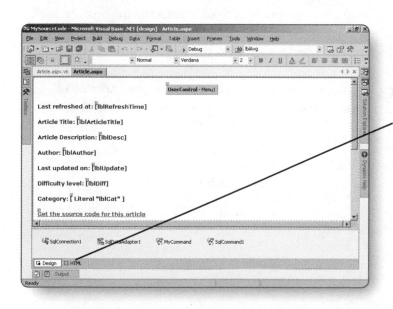

After you add the label, you need to add the @ OutputCache directive to the Article.aspx form.

1. Click on the HTML tab to switch to the HTML view of the Article.aspx form.

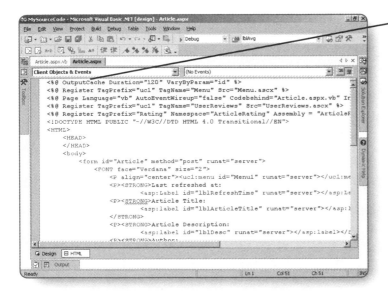

2. Add the @ OutputCache directive, as shown here. The Article.aspx form will be cached for two minutes. If the same article is loaded before the two minutes has elapsed, the time displayed in the lblRefreshTime label will remain the same, implying that the data is retrieved from the cache. However, if you load a different article, the time in the lblRefreshTime label will be updated, implying that the data has been queried from the database.

Implementing Page-Fragment Caching

Page-fragment caching is not much different than page-output caching, except that one or more components of the Web form are cached, instead of the complete Web form. In page-fragment caching, you can typically cache the data of a user control, which is rendered from the cache each time the page is requested.

You can implement page-fragment caching for specific components on a Web page. For example, you can cache the output of a user control by implementing page-fragment caching.

For page-fragment caching, you need to specify the @ OutputCache directive for the user control in which you want to implement caching.

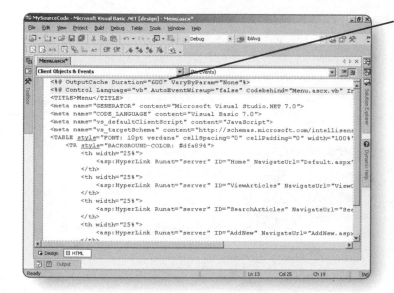

Here you can see the implementation of page-fragment caching in the Menu.ascx user control. This control is used to render the menu options on each Web form. Since the menu does not depend on the query string parameters that are passed to the Web form, the value of the VaryByParam attribute is set to None.

Implementing Page-Data Caching

In page-data caching, the data of a page is cached, instead of the complete page. This method is very useful in a dynamic page that is changed often, when you want to cache only the components that are relatively static.

To implement page-data caching, you need to use the Cache class of the System.Web.Caching namespace. One object of the Cache class is created for every application. You can use this object to cache and retrieve frequently accessed data.

To cache data using the Cache class, you need to use key and value pairs. For every value that you add to the cache, you need to specify a key. The key can be used to access the value that you add to the cache.

In this section, I will explain the steps to implement page-data caching in an ASP.NET application. I will also explain how you can generate dependencies to invalidate the cache when elements that are associated with it are updated.

Adding Items to the Cache

To add items to the cache, you can access the Cache object from the Page object. (See Chapter 3, "Exploring the New Features of ASP.NET," for more information on the Page object.) In this section, I will use the Cache object to cache the data that is retrieved from a Web service.

Since the data retrieved from the Web service is relatively static, you need to make a call to the Web service frequently. This will significantly improve the performance of your Web application. In Chapter 15, "Building ASP.NET Web Services," I retrieved data from an XML file and exposed the data using a Web service. The data, once retrieved from the Web service, can be cached to avoid unnecessary calls to the Web service.

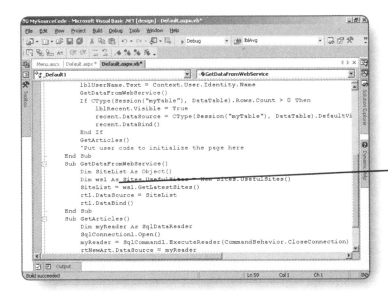

To implement page-data caching, modify the GetDataFromWebService() function that calls the GetLatestSites() function to retrieve the list of sites from an XML file.

The existing definition of the GetDataFromWebService() function is shown here. In this definition, the SiteList variable stores the data that is retrieved from the Web service. When the data is retrieved the first time, you can cache the data. Subsequent requests can be retrieved from the cache, thus avoiding unnecessary calls to the Web service.

In the modified definition, the application first checks whether the UsefulSites key in the Cache object has stored any data. If no data is available in the cache, the data is retrieved from the Web service and stored in the cache for subsequent requests.

Creating Cache Dependencies

In many cases you might need to reconstruct the cache to retrieve updated data from the data source. When you cache data, you can establish dependencies on resources. Every time the resource is updated, the cache is cleared and the updated data is reloaded. This way, data in the cache is always up to date.

To ensure that data in a cache is always updated, you can create dependencies on files. For example, if the Sales report for a department is always obtained in an XML document, you can create a dependency to the document. Whenever the document is updated, the cache is recreated and the updated report is reflected on the Web site. Similarly, in the preceding example, a dependency on the urllist.xml file can be created.

As you create dependencies on files, you can also create a dependency on time. For example, if you want to reconstruct the cache every 5 minutes, you can use the time-dependency method.

To create dependencies, you need to create an object of the CacheDependency class. The CacheDependency class tracks dependencies of cache data. The dependency can be to files, directories, or keys for other objects in the cache. After you create the object of the CacheDependency class, you can assign it to the Insert method of the Cache class.

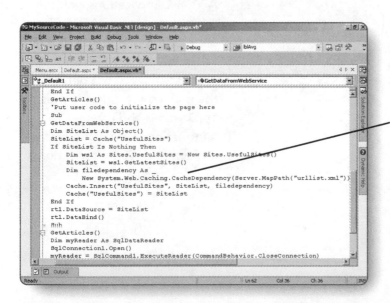

I will now implement file dependency for the page-data caching that was configured in the preceding section.

To add a dependency to the urllist.xml file, create an object of the CacheDependency class, supplying the path to the file as a parameter to the constructor of the class. Then, assign the dependency object to the Insert method of the Cache class.

Caching in Web Services

Caching in Web services is different than the caching that is implemented in ASP.NET applications. In Web services, you need to use the CacheDuration property of the WebMethod attribute to implement caching.

The CacheDuration property is similar to the Duration property of the @ OutputCache directive. It specifies the number of seconds for which the Web method should cache its output before invalidating the cache. Once the cache is invalidated, it is reconstructed on the next request.

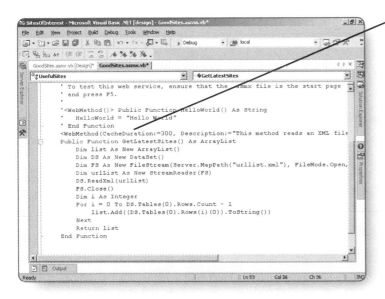

Use the CacheDuration property in the WebMethod attribute, as shown in the form here. Notice that I have specified 300 as the CacheDuration property. This implies that the Web method will cache its output for five minutes.

Now that you have learned how to implement caching in ASP.NET applications, you can move on to tracing ASP.NET applications in the next chapter. When you trace ASP.NET applications, you can determine the path of execution of your applications and use the information to eliminate errors and optimize your application.

19

Tracing ASP.NET Applications

Tracing is a method of tracking the path of execution of a Web form or an application. When you enable tracing for a Web application, you are able to gather information on how a Web form was loaded after the client requested the form. You can also insert custom statements in your code to examine the state of the application. For example, you might insert tracing statements to generate a warning whenever a variable has not been initialized.

When you enable tracing for a Web application, the trace output is appended to the output of Web forms. Thus, you can examine how each page of your Web application has been executed. In this chapter, you'll learn how to:

- Enable page-level tracing
- Enable application-level tracing

Enabling Page-Level Tracing

If you want to trace the execution of only a few Web forms in an application, you can enable tracing for each page of the application separately. You can also add custom output to the trace messages that are generated on a page. In this section, I will explain the steps to trace Web forms in ASP.NET applications.

Generating Trace Output

Tracing can be enabled on Web forms by changing the Trace attribute of the page directive to true. When you set this value to true, you can also specify a value for the TraceMode attribute. The TraceMode attribute determines how trace messages are displayed on the Web form when tracing is enabled. Trace messages can be sorted either by category or by time. By default, they are sorted by time.

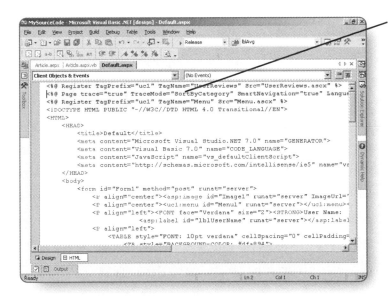

In this Web form, I have enabled tracing by changing the value of the Trace attribute. I have also used the TraceMode attribute to sort trace output by category.

When you run this form, the trace output is appended to the output of the page. Notice that the trace information is available in a number of tables. Each table has specific information about the application. The information that is displayed in the tables is explained in this section.

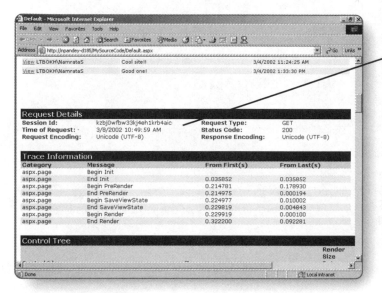

Request Details

The Request Details table specifies the session ID, the time when the request was made, the character encoding that was used for the request and the response, and the status code associated with the response.

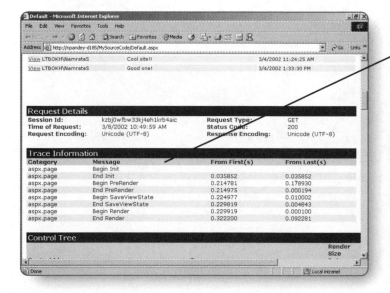

Trace Information

The Trace Information table displays all of the messages that are generated by the trace output. By default, an ASP.NET page generates some messages when the page is being initialized. These messages are displayed in the Trace Information table. As you will see in the "Adding Custom Data to Trace Output" section later in this chapter, custom messages that you add to the trace output are displayed in Trace Information table.

Status Codes Associated with Responses

When you enable tracing for an application, the trace output displays the status code of the request. The status code is derived from the W3C (*World Wide Web Consortium*) standards on HTTP 1.1 standards.

The status code that is returned by a Web request is a three-digit number. The first digit can be 1, 2, 3, 4, or 5; the representations of these numbers follow.

1. The digit 1 means that the request has been received and is being processed.

2. The digit 2 means that the request was successfully executed.

3. The digit 3 means that the request was redirected to another location and has not been completed.

4. The digit 4 means that the request is not correctly formed or points to an invalid resource.

5. The digit 5 means that an error occurred at the server end, although the request might have been valid.

You might have encountered the 404 - Not Found error when you requested a Web page that does not exist. Now you can determine that the error was in the request that was sent by the client, because the first digit of the status code is 4. Similarly, the 500 - Internal Server Error occurs when the server is unable to process information because of an internal error.

You can find detailed information on the HTTP protocol and the status codes for HTTP requests on the W3C Web site at http://www.w3.org/Protocols/rfc2616/rfc2616-sec6.html.

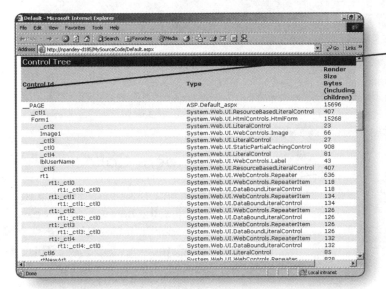

Control Tree

The Control Tree table shows a list of controls that have been loaded on the form. If you have specified an ID for your controls, this ID is used for writing the output to the Control Tree. However, you might not have specified the ID property for some controls. For example, if you used the FlowLayout to design your form, you might have typed the label for each control directly onto the form.

When you do not specify the ID property of a control, the control is automatically assigned a unique ID by ASP.NET. Therefore, some controls that appear in the Control Tree table might have IDs that you do not recognize because they were generated by ASP.NET.

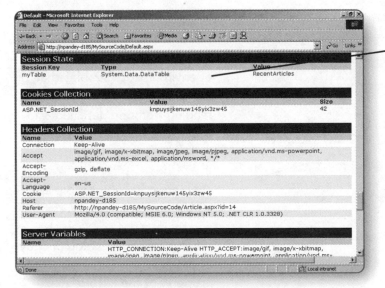

Session State

The Session State table identifies the data that is stored in the Session object. Data is always stored in the Session object by key-value pairs. The Session State table lists the keys, as well as the data types and values stored in the keys, for each session variable.

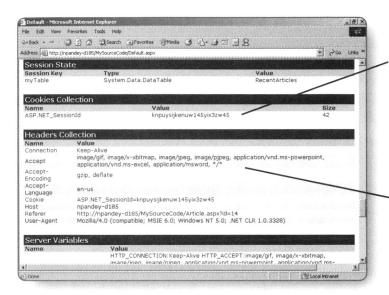

Cookies Collection

The Cookies Collection table stores the name, value, and the size of the cookie that has been issued to a user.

Headers Collection

The Headers Collection table specifies the names and values of header variables that are associated with a request. This table identifies whether the connection is kept alive after the request is processed. It also includes details of the host computer and the browser that were involved in processing the request.

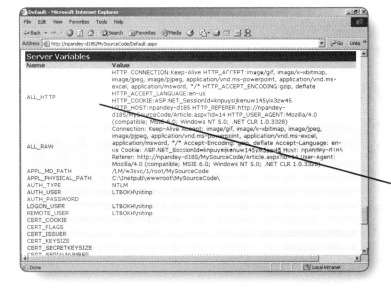

Server Variables

Server variables are a collection of environment variables that contain a host of information, ranging from the details of the request to the user who is currently logged on.

The Server Variables table lists all of the environment variables and their values. You can also retrieve this information directly from the ServerVariables property of the HttpRequest class.

Adding Custom Data to Trace Output

The TraceContext object generates the trace output that is displayed on a Web form. Any information that you add to this object will automatically appear in the trace output.

To display custom tracing information, you need to use the Write and Warn methods of the Trace class. Both the methods are used to write to the trace output. The only difference is that when the Warn method is used, the text displayed in the trace output is red. The Write and Warn methods can accept the message to be displayed in the trace output as a string parameter, or they can accept both the category and the message that need to be displayed.

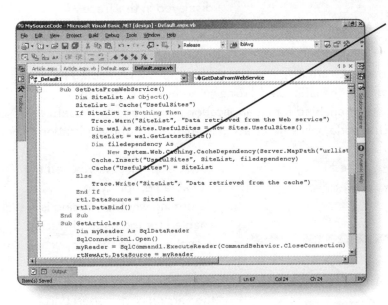

In this form, I have used the Write and Warn methods to determine whether data is being retrieved from the Web service or the cache. When the data is retrieved from the Web service, I have used the Warn method to emphasize that the data is retrieved from the Web service.

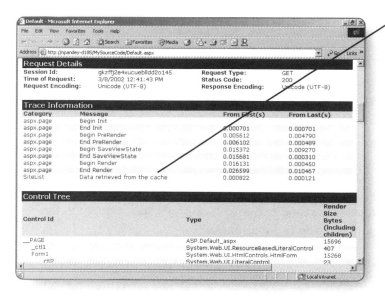

When you run this form, the data is retrieved from the Web service when the form is loaded for the first time. Therefore, the "Data retrieved from the Web service" message is displayed. However, on subsequent requests, data is retrieved from the cache, and the "Data retrieved from the cache" message is displayed. Notice that all custom messages are displayed in the Trace Information table.

Even though all trace messages are displayed only when tracing is enabled on a Web application, you can use the IsEnabled property of the Trace class to determine whether tracing is enabled for an application. This property is useful when you want to execute code only when tracing is enabled for the application.

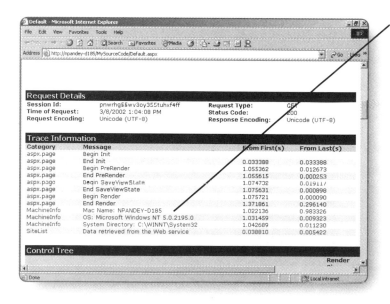

In this example, I have used the IsEnabled property to determine whether tracing is enabled for the page. If tracing is enabled, I use the properties of the Environment class to determine the machine name, the version of the operating system, and the Windows directory for the application.

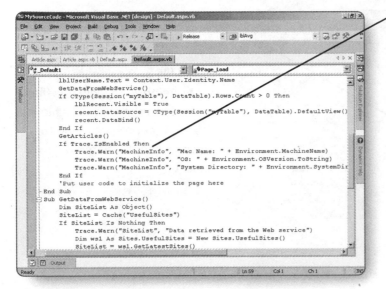

When you run the application, the system information is generated in the trace output.

Enabling Application-Level Tracing

Instead of enabling tracing for each Web form individually, you can enable tracing for an entire application. When you enable tracing for the application, the trace output for all pages is generated. In this section, I will explain the steps to enabling tracing for an ASP.NET application.

Configuring the Trace Service

To enable tracing for an application, you need to change the properties of the <trace> element in the Web.config file. Change the value of the enabled attribute of the <trace> element from false to true.

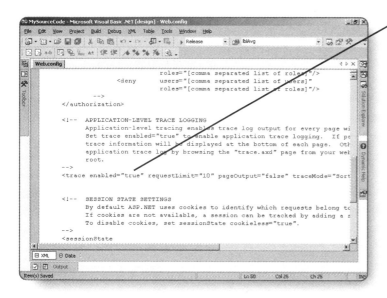

When you enable tracing for an application, the application logs all tracing output to an XML-based file in the application's root directory. To view this file, navigate to the trace.axd file in the application's root directory when the application is executing.

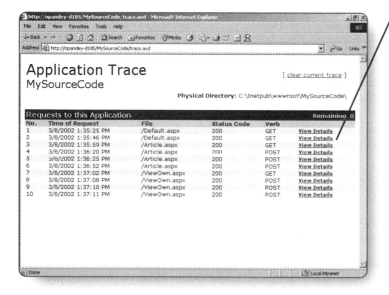

The tracing information that was displayed on the Web form is now displayed on a separate page. A link to the trace output of each page is provided on the trace.axd page. To view the trace output of each Web form, click on the View Details link.

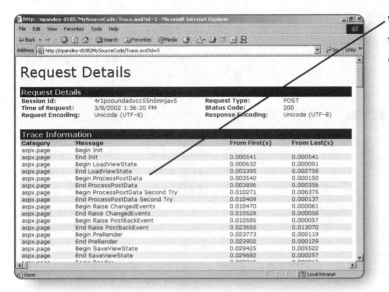

When you click on the link, the trace output for the page is displayed.

Changing Properties of the Trace Output

The <trace> element provides a number of attributes that can be configured to change the default tracing properties of the application. For example, in the default setting of the <trace> element, only the trace information for the last 10 pages is available on the trace.axd page.

Apart from the enabled attribute, the trace property provides four other attributes that can be used to control the trace output of an application. These attributes are

- **requestLimit**. The requestLimit attribute specifies the maximum number of pages for which the trace output should be available at a given period of time. The default value is 10.

- **pageOutput**. If you want the trace information to be appended to every page, you need to change the value of the pageOutput attribute from false to true. By default, this value is false.

- **traceMode**. The traceMode property determines whether tracing information is sorted by time or by category. The default value is SortByTime.

- **localOnly**. The localOnly property determines whether tracing is enabled for local users only or also for remote users. By default, tracing information is available to only those users who are logged on to the local computer.

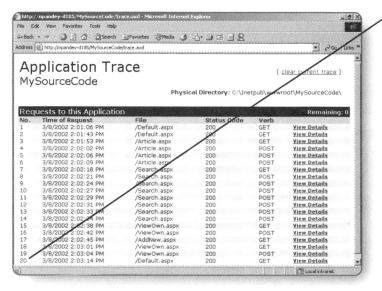

In this application, I have specified the requestLimit as 20. Therefore, the trace output for the first 20 Web requests on the Web application is available on the trace.axd page.

You should now have a good basic understanding of tracing ASP.NET applications. In the next chapter, you will learn how to debug ASP.NET applications using the debugging tools that are available in Visual Studio .NET.

20

Debugging ASP.NET Applications

The advantage of creating ASP.NET applications in Visual Studio .NET is that you can use the debugging features of Visual Studio .NET to debug the applications. Visual Studio .NET provides many debugging tools that can be used to eliminate errors in applications.

This chapter introduces you to all of the debugging tools that are provided by Visual Studio .NET. It also provides a step-by-step procedure for debugging ASP.NET applications. In this chapter, you'll learn how to:

- Identify debugging tools that are provided by Visual Studio .NET
- Debug applications in Visual Studio .NET

Debugging Tools in Visual Studio .NET

Visual Studio .NET provides a number of debugging windows that can be used to debug applications. In this section, I will discuss each debugging window in detail.

Using the Breakpoints Window

When you code your application, you might not be sure of the output of some lines in the code. You can add breakpoints to these lines of code and examine the state of the application when it is at the breakpoint.

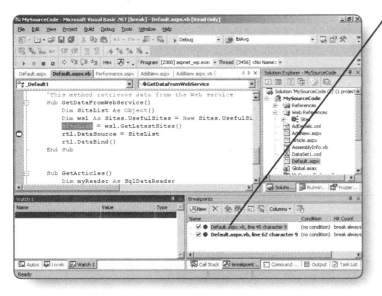

All breakpoints that you add to your application are listed in the Breakpoints window. When the code of your application is executing, you can view the Breakpoints window and determine whether the application has encountered the breakpoint in the code that has executed up to that point.

Using the Watch Window

You can use the Watch window to monitor the values of variables. You can type the name of a variable in the Watch window and press Enter to display the current value of the variable in the Watch window.

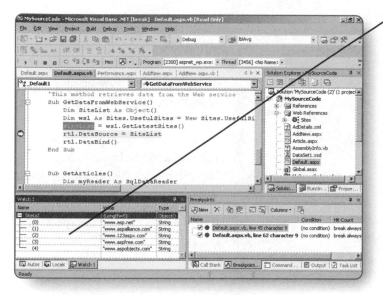

A useful implementation of the Watch window is to keep adding variables to the window at design time and simultaneously add breakpoints to the application for each variable. Then, every time your application encounters a breakpoint, it will enter a suspended mode, and you will be able to view the value of the variable in the Watch window.

Using the Autos Window

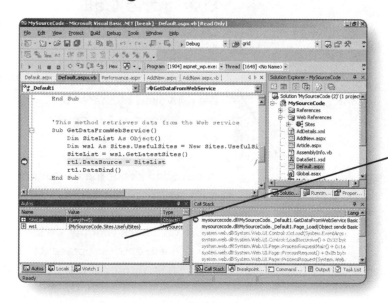

The Autos window is similar to the Watch window. It displays the names and values of all variables that are involved in the execution of the current and previous lines of code.

When the executing line of code is a function, the Autos window displays the name of the function and the value returned by the function.

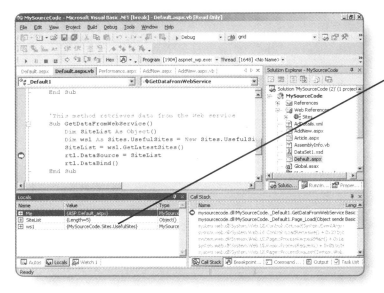

Using the Locals Window

The Locals window displays the values of all variables that are executing within the local scope of the application. For example, all variables defined in a function on a Web form are local to the function and will be displayed in the Locals window.

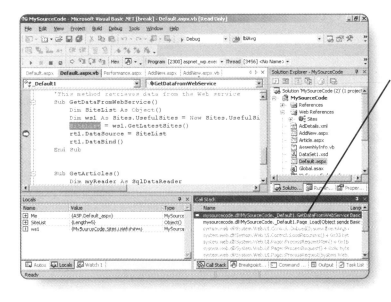

Using the Call Stack Window

The Call Stack window displays a list of all functions that have been invoked by the Web application up to the point of execution of the code. This window provides important information about the execution path taken by your application. Notice that the first two entries in the Call Stack window are in bold. These entries represent the GetDataFromWebService and Form_Load methods. The GetDataFromWebService method was invoked from the Form_Load method. Both the methods are active and are therefore displayed in bold.

Using the Command Window

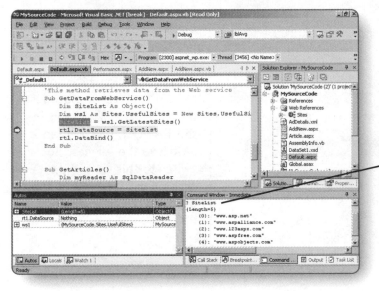

You can use the Command window to determine the output of a given expression. This window probably gets its name from the Command Prompt, where every command must be typed.

To use the Command window, type **?** followed by the expression that needs to be checked. The output of the expression that you type will be listed immediately below your command.

Using the Task List Window

The Task List window is a useful tool for recording the pending work in an application. It provides a number of useful features. For example, all of the build errors that occur in your application are automatically recorded in the Task List window. In addition, all comments that you add to your code using the 'TODO keyword are also automatically added to the Task List.

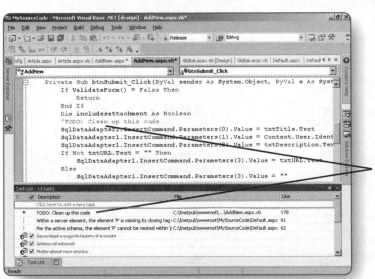

In this form, I have used the 'TODO keyword to add comments to the Task List. I have also typed some comments directly into the Task List.

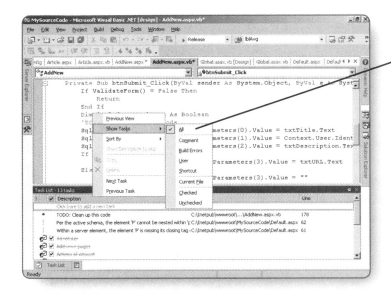

Debugging Applications

To debug applications in Visual Studio .NET, you need to insert breakpoints in your application and run it. When your application encounters a breakpoint, it enters a suspended mode. You can debug the application in suspended mode and resume the execution of your application.

In this section, I will examine the steps to debug an application using the debugging tools that were discussed in the previous section.

Using the Debugging Tools in Visual Studio .NET

To use the debugging tools, first insert a breakpoint in the application.

1. Click on the line of code to which you want to add a breakpoint.

2. Click on Debug. The Debug menu will appear.

3. Click on New Breakpoint. The New Breakpoint dialog box will open.

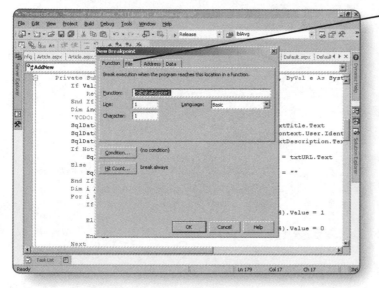

4. In the New Breakpoint dialog box, you can specify breakpoints either at the definition of a function or at a specific line in the code. To specify a breakpoint at a specific line of code, click on the File tab. The File tab will move to the front.

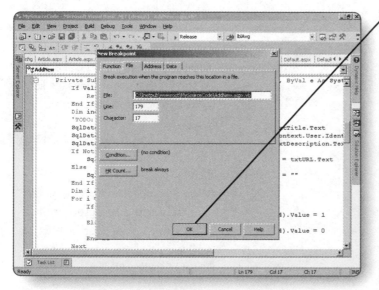

5. Notice that the location of the file you had selected is already specified. Click on OK. A breakpoint will be inserted in your application.

After you insert the breakpoint, you can run the application. When the application encounters the breakpoint, it will temporarily suspend execution, and you can use the debugging windows to debug your application.

Attaching a Debugger to an External Application

The Visual Studio .NET debugger enables you to debug even those applications which have not been created in Visual Studio .NET. Each application that executes on your computer is represented by a process. You can attach the Visual Studio .NET debugger to a running process and debug it.

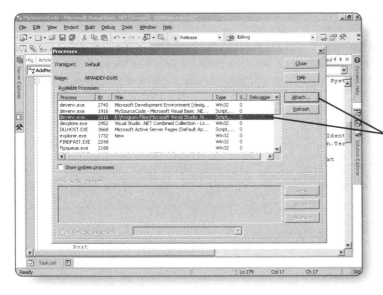

1. Click on Debug. The Debug menu will appear.

2. Click on Processes. The Processes dialog box will open.

3. Select the process that you want to debug and click on Attach. The Attach to Process dialog box will open.

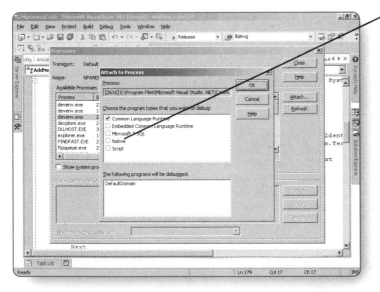

4. Select the component of the application that you want to debug and click on OK. The process you selected will appear in the Debugged Processes list of the Processes dialog box.

5. Click on Break to debug the process.

When you click on Break, you can debug the selected application using Visual Studio .NET, as you would debug any other Visual Studio .NET application.

This completes the discussion on debugging ASP.NET applications. Even after you have debugged your application and ensured that it is error free, users might encounter certain types of errors. For example, if a user requests a Web form that does not even exist, the application will display an error message. Similarly, if the .NET Framework is not installed correctly, your application might display an error even if it is developed correctly. To account for such anomalies, the .NET Framework allows you to add exception-handling code and create error pages. In fact, that is your next destination.

21

Handling Exceptions in ASP.NET Applications

There might be instances when your application encounters unexpected conditions. For example, if you are using a database to retrieve information, there might be times when the database is not accessible. In such a scenario, your application might terminate abnormally.

To prevent your application from terminating abnormally, you can use the exception-handling capabilities of ASP.NET. Whenever an abnormal condition is generated in the application, an exception is thrown. You can catch the exception to determine the cause of error and take corrective action. In the case of database connectivity failure, corrective action might be to connect to an alternate data source.

This chapter will introduce you to exception handling in ASP.NET. In this chapter, you'll learn how to:

- Implement structured exception handling
- Add error pages to an ASP.NET application

Implementing Structured Exception Handling

To implement structured exception handling, you can either use try-catch-finally statements or you can redirect the user to an error page when your application generates an error. In this section, I will examine the steps to accomplish both tasks.

Using Try-Catch-Finally Statements

Try-catch-finally statements enable you to catch exceptions generated in your application. Whenever statements in the try block generate an exception, the control of the program moves to the catch block.

All exceptions that are generated by an application are objects of a class that is derived from the Exception class. You can determine the type of exception generated to determine where the error occurred and take corrective action accordingly.

The set of statements in the finally block are optional. These statements are executed regardless of whether an exception was generated. You should use the finally block to write those statements that should always be executed. For example, you might use the finally block to close the connection to a data source.

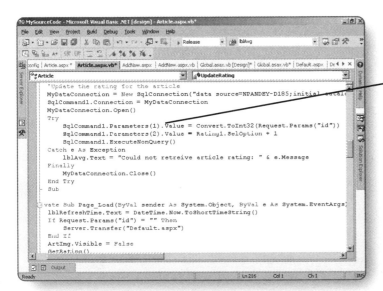

In the set of statements shown here, I have used the try block to assign values to parameters of the sqlCommand1 object. These statements might generate an error if the ID of the article that is passed in the query string is not of the Integer data type.

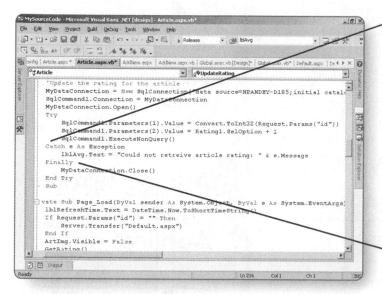

If the statements generate an error, the control of the program passes to the catch block. In the catch block, I have created an error message for the user, signifying that the details of the article could not be retrieved. I have displayed the error message generated by the application using the Message property of the Exception class.

In the finally block, I have closed the connection to the data source. This statement is executed regardless of whether an exception was generated in the try block.

Redirecting Users to Error Pages

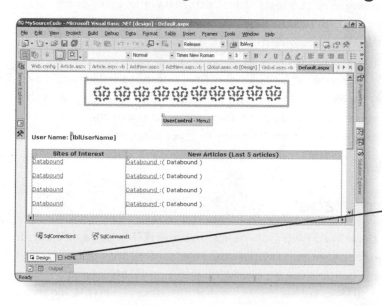

Instead of defining multiple try and catch blocks for a Web form, you can specify an error page to which the user is directed if a Web page throws an exception.

1. Open the file for which you want to specify an error page.

2. Click on the HTML tab. The HTML view of the file will be displayed.

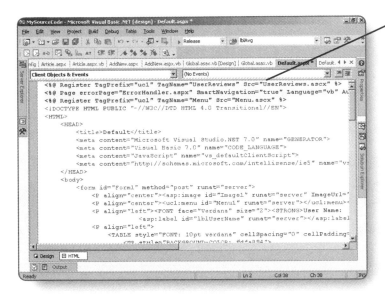

3. Specify the errorPage attribute in the @ Page directive. The user will be redirected to the error page whenever an exception is generated on the Web form.

Adding Error Pages to an Application

Your application might sometimes generate errors that are not linked to exceptions in the application. For example, if the user requests a Web form that does not exist, an error message stating that the resource could not be found will be displayed, although your application will not generate an error.

This error message is associated with the HTTP errors that can be encountered by applications while processing Web requests. These errors have an error code associated with them that determines the cause of an error. For example, the error code 500 signifies that the Web server encountered an error.

Whenever an HTTP error is generated by an application, Internet Explorer displays a default error page. You can change the default error page that is displayed for an HTTP error by creating your own error pages and assigning them to the application. In this section, I will examine the steps to create an error page and modify the Web.config file to assign the error page to the application.

Creating an Error Page

You can create an error page in ASP.NET, or you can use any HTML page as an error page. I prefer creating error pages in HTML because the content that I display on error pages is static. Static content can be displayed easily on HTML pages. Moreover, the stress on the Web server is less when it processes an HTML file than when it processes an .aspx file.

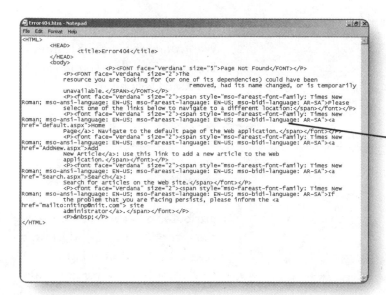

To create an HTML error page, follow these steps.

1. Create a new file in Notepad.

2. Type the code to create the HTML interface of the application in the file.

> **TIP**
>
> You can also create the HTML page in an HTML editor, such as Microsoft FrontPage 2000.

3. Save the file in the root folder of the Web application.

The design of the form created in the preceding steps is shown here. Now you can add this form as an error page for the application.

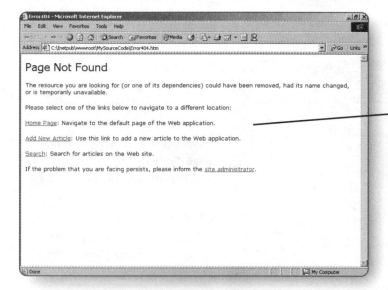

Modifying the Web.Config File

To add an error page to an application, you need to change the customErrors element in the Web.config file. The customErrors element includes an error sub-element that maps error codes generated by the application to the HTML pages that should be displayed for the error codes. To modify the Web.config file, follow these steps.

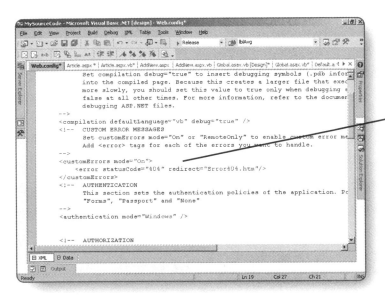

1. Double-click on the Web.config file in the Solution Explorer. The file will open in the XML Designer.

2. Locate the customErrors element of the Web.config file and change the element, as shown here. In this example, I have changed the mode attribute to On and associated the Error404.htm file, which was created in the preceding section, with the error code 404.

3. Save and run the application.

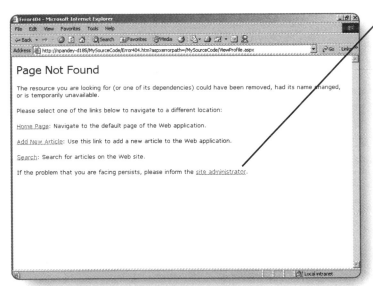

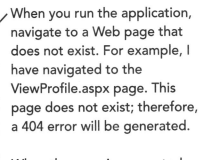

When you run the application, navigate to a Web page that does not exist. For example, I have navigated to the ViewProfile.aspx page. This page does not exist; therefore, a 404 error will be generated.

When the error is generated, the application displays the customized error page instead of displaying the standard "Page Not Found" error message.

This completes the discussion on error pages. It also brings you to the most important element in developing an ASP.NET application—the security of the application. In the next chapter, you'll learn how to secure ASP.NET applications and implement different types of authentication provided by ASP.NET.

22

Securing ASP.NET Applications

The need to secure ASP.NET Web applications can never be overstated. You frequently encounter or read about the security of Web sites being breached or about unauthorized users uploading malicious content on a Web site. After you create an ASP.NET Web application, it becomes imperative that you secure the application. ASP.NET offers a robust security mechanism. It enables you to implement security at two levels on a Web site. You can secure a Web application by implementing security mechanisms at IIS (*Internet Information Server*), and you can also use the Web.config file to secure an ASP.NET application internally.

This chapter describes some of the important methods for securing a Web application. In this chapter, you'll learn how to:

● Implement security at IIS

● Implement authentication in ASP.NET

Implementing Security at IIS

Every application created in ASP.NET has a virtual directory associated with it. IIS provides an MMC (*Microsoft Management Console*)-based interface, Internet Services Manager, which can be used to manage virtual directories and configure directory security and authentication for a Web site.

In this section, I will describe the steps to secure a Web application using Internet Services Manager. I will also describe the steps to implement Windows authentication for an ASP.NET Web application.

Securing a Virtual Directory

Internet Services Manager provides many options that can be configured to secure the virtual directory of a Web application. For example, you can grant or deny access to specific machines or you can restrict the permissions of users for the virtual directory. You can also configure authentication on a Web application using Internet Services Manager.

Before you proceed to secure a virtual directory, I will explain the authentication methods that are available in IIS. IIS provides three types of authentication methods:

- **Basic authentication**. In basic authentication, the log-on name and password specified by a user are used to authenticate the user before processing a request. This method has one drawback—the user name and password become vulnerable to hacking because they are sent from the client to the server in an unencrypted form.

- **Digest authentication**. The digest authentication method is similar to the basic authentication method. However, this method is more secure than basic authentication because it sends the user credentials for validation in an encrypted form.

- **Integrated Windows authentication**. The integrated Windows authentication method uses the account credentials of a user in the Windows 2000 domain to authenticate a user.

In addition to the three authentication methods described, IIS also provides an anonymous authentication method. In anonymous authentication, IIS uses a built-in user account to request resources from the Web server. This method is also referred to as *impersonation* because IIS requests resources on behalf of the user.

When you want to implement authentication on your Web site, you need to disable anonymous authentication so that the user's credentials are used to request resources.

To secure a virtual directory and implement authentication, you first need to invoke Internet Services Manager.

1. Click on the Start menu. The Start menu will appear.

2. Move the mouse pointer to Programs. The Programs menu will appear.

3. Move the mouse pointer to Administrative Tools. The Administrative Tools submenu will appear.

4. Click on Internet Services Manager. The Internet Information Services window will appear.

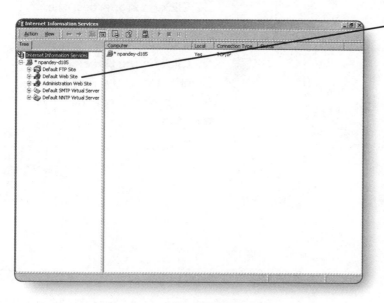

The Internet Information Services window displays a list of Web sites and virtual directories installed on the computer. You can either change the configuration of a Web site or change the configuration of each virtual directory on a Web site separately. However, if you apply changes to the configuration at the Web-site level, all virtual directories on the Web site will be affected.

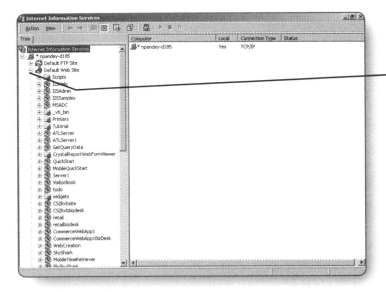

To configure a virtual directory, follow these steps.

1. Click on the plus sign next to the Default Web Site option in the Internet Information Services window. The virtual directories that are installed on the default Web site will appear.

2. Right-click on the virtual directory for the Web site that you want to configure. For example, if you want to configure the virtual directory for the MySourceCode application that has been created in this book, right-click on the MySourceCode option. A shortcut menu will appear.

3. Click on Properties. The Properties dialog box will open.

4. Click on the Directory Security tab of the Properties dialog box. The tab will move to the front.

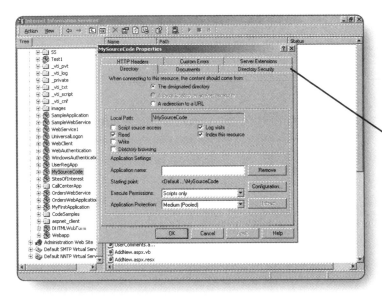

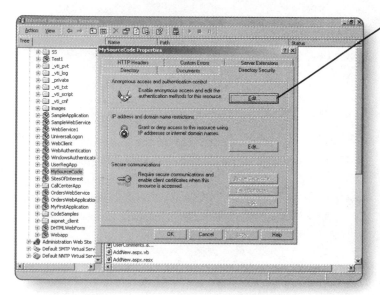

5. The Directory Security tab allows you to configure authentication for a Web site and grant or restrict permissions to specific computers accessing the Web site. To configure authentication for the Web application, click on Edit in the Anonymous Access and Authentication Control group. The Authentication Methods dialog box will open.

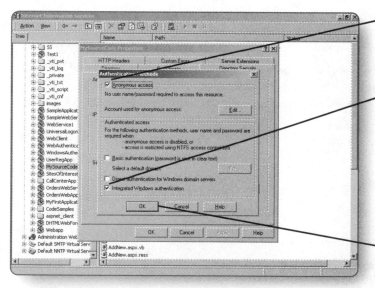

6. Click on the Anonymous Access check box to clear it. The option will be deselected.

7. To implement integrated Windows authentication, click on the Integrated Windows Authentication check box if the option is not already selected. A check mark will be placed in the check box.

8. Click on OK. The Authentication Methods dialog box will close.

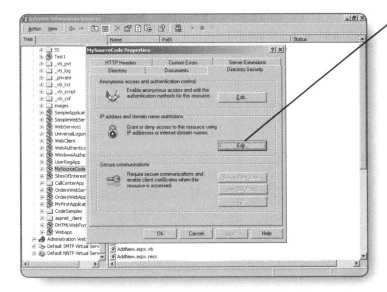

9. Next, you can enable or restrict access to the application by applying IP address and domain name restrictions. To restrict access to the Web application, click on the Edit button in the IP Address and Domain Name Restrictions group. The IP Address and Domain Name Restrictions dialog box will open.

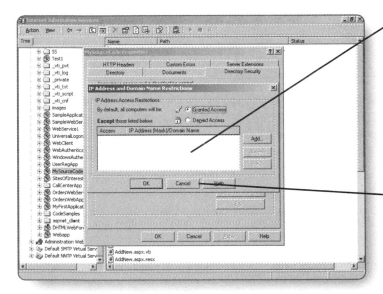

10. In this dialog box, you can specify which computers are allowed to access the Web application. However, do not change any settings in this dialog box if you want your application to be accessible from all remote computers.

11. Click on Cancel. The IP Address and Domain Name Restrictions dialog box will close, and the Properties dialog box will become active.

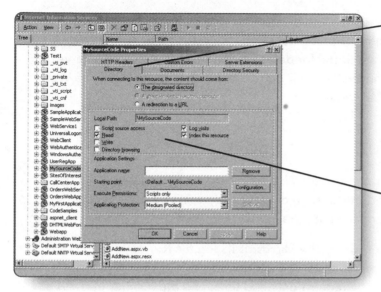

12. You can also restrict permissions of users on the Web site directory. For example, you can restrict users from viewing the contents of a directory. To restrict permissions to the directory, click on the Directory tab in the Properties dialog box.

13. Select the appropriate permissions that you want to grant for the Web application directory. The permissions that you can grant are

- **Script Source Access**. When you check this option, users are able to browse the code for the application.

- **Read**. When you check this option, users can browse and download Web pages from the virtual directory of the application. You need to check this option to allow users to browse your Web application.

- **Write**. When you check this option, users are able to upload files to the physical directory that corresponds to the virtual directory of the Web application.

- **Directory Browsing**. When you check this option, users are able to view the contents of a directory if they type the path of the directory instead of the path of a Web form.

- **Log Visits**. When you check this option, the Web server logs details of all requests that it processes.

- **Index This Resource**. When you check this option, the Microsoft Indexing Services index the Web pages in the virtual directory.

14. Click on Apply. Your changes will be applied to the Web site configuration.

15. Click on OK. The Properties dialog box will close.

Now that you have secured the virtual directory of the application, you can configure Web server log files to log details of requests that are processed by the Web server. These logs are useful for determining the load on the Web server or problems that it might encounter. I will now explain the steps to configure Web server log files on the Web server.

Configuring Web Server Log Files

IIS provides a number of formats for Web server log files. You can specify the format, the duration, and the location of log files by using Internet Services Manager. The log file formats that are supported by IIS are

- **Microsoft IIS log file format**. The Microsoft IIS log file format records basic information about Web requests. The information includes the IP address of the client, the user name, the request date and time, and the number of bytes of data exchanged while processing the request.

- **NCSA common log file format**. The NCSA common log file format also records details of requests processed by the Web server. However, the details recorded for each request are not as comprehensive as the details that are recorded by the Microsoft IIS log file format.

- **ODBC logging**. The ODBC logging format records Web server activity in an ODBC-compliant database, such as Microsoft Access or Microsoft SQL Server.

- **W3C extended log file format**. The W3C extended log file format is the default format that is used by IIS. This format records the most detailed description of a Web request and can be customized to record only data that is relevant to analysis.

Now that you have examined the log file formats, I will describe the steps to select one of these formats using Internet Services Manager. Open Internet Services Manager and follow these steps to configure the log file format, the frequency of logging, and the location of log files.

1. Right-click on Default Web Site in Internet Services Manager. A shortcut menu will appear.

2. Click on Properties. The Default Web Site Properties dialog box will open. Make sure that the Web Site tab of the dialog box is selected.

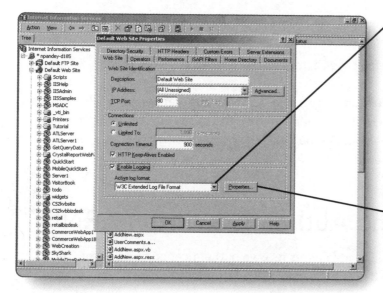

3. Click on the Active Log Format drop-down list. The items of the list will be displayed.

4. Select a logging format. The format that you select will become the active logging format.

5. To specify the location and frequency for log files, click on Properties. The Extended Logging Properties dialog box will open.

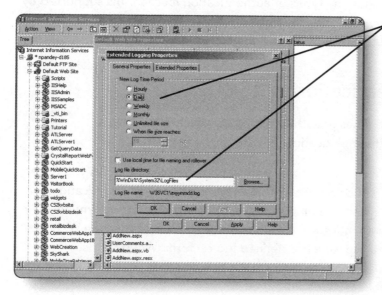

6. Select a log time period from the New Log Time Period group and specify the location of log files in the Log File Directory field.

NOTE

The default location for log files is in the C:\Winnt\System32\ LogFiles directory.

7. Click on OK. The Extended Logging Properties dialog box will close, and the Default Web Site Properties dialog box will reappear.

8. Click on Apply. The changes that you made will be applied.

9. Click on OK. The Default Web Site Properties dialog box will close.

This completes the discussion on securing ASP.NET applications using IIS. However, ASP.NET also includes a robust authentication mechanism that can provide even greater security for a Web site. In the next section, I will examine the implementation of authentication in ASP.NET.

Implementing Authentication in ASP.NET

In addition to IIS, ASP.NET implements its own authentication mechanism. This mechanism is based on the XML-based configuration of the application in the Web.config file.

In this section, I will describe the types of authentication mechanisms supported by ASP.NET. Then, I'll examine the steps to implement two authentication mechanisms—Forms authentication and Windows authentication.

Types of Authentication in ASP.NET

ASP.NET supports three types of authentication mechanisms—Forms authentication, Passport authentication, and Windows authentication.

- **Forms authentication.** The Forms authentication mechanism enables you to use a log-on form to authenticate users before they access the Web application. When users request a resource on the Web site, the application determines whether the user is authenticated. If the user is not authenticated, the Web application directs the user to a pre-defined log-on form. When the user successfully logs on using the log-on form, he or she is redirected to the resource that was initially requested.

- **Passport authentication.** The Passport authentication mechanism is based on the Microsoft Passport authentication service. The Microsoft Passport authentication service enables you to authenticate users against their accounts with the service. See Chapter 1, "Introducing the .NET Initiative," for more information on Passport authentication.

- **Windows authentication**. The Windows authentication mechanism utilizes the user's account in the Windows 2000 domain for authentication. This type of mechanism is typically used for a corporate intranet, where each user who needs to access the Web site has a user account in the Windows 2000 domain.

Now that you have examined the types of authentication mechanisms, you should learn how to implement Forms authentication and Windows authentication in a Web application.

Implementing Forms Authentication

In ASP.NET, the Web.config file is primarily responsible for implementing authentication on a Web site. This XML-based file includes two elements that are involved in authentication—<authentication> and <authorization>. In addition, when you use Forms authentication, you also need to use the <forms> element.

Before I explain how to implement Forms authentication on a Web application, think for a moment about these elements.

- **<authentication>**. The <authentication> element is used to configure the mode of authentication on a Web site. It includes an attribute called *mode* that specifies the type of authentication implemented on a Web site. The mode attribute can have four values: Windows, Passport, Forms, or None.

- **<authorization>**. The <authorization> element specifies the list of users who are allowed to access a Web application. This element includes two sub-elements— <allow> and <deny>. You can specify the list of users who are allowed to access the Web site in the <allow> tag and the list of users who are not allowed to access the site in the <deny> tag. The <allow> and <deny> tags also accept the wildcard entries ? and *. The ? symbol represents anonymous users who access the Web site, and the * symbol represents all users who access the Web site.

- **<forms>**. The <forms> element is a sub-element of the <authentication> element. When you implement Forms authentication, the <forms> tag specifies the default extension of the cookie that is generated for authenticated users with the name attribute. You can also specify the name of the form to which an unauthenticated user is redirected by using the loginUrl attribute. Finally, you can specify the amount of time, in minutes, for which a user session is valid by using the timeout attribute.

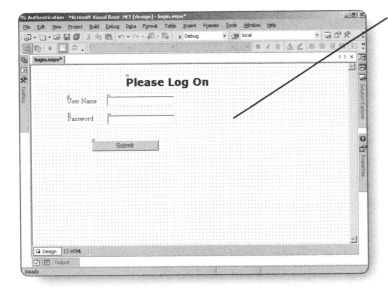

To illustrate Forms authentication, I have created an ASP.NET Web application called Authentication. I have added two Web forms to the application—default.aspx and login.aspx. The login.aspx form is displayed to a user who is not authenticated. To implement Forms authentication in an ASP.NET Web application, follow these steps.

1. Double-click on the Web.config file in the Solution Explorer. The file will open in the XML Designer.

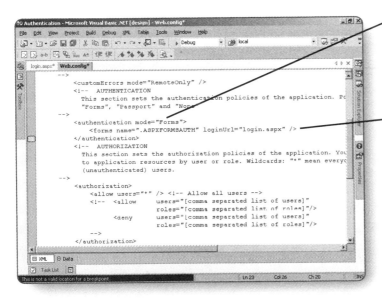

2. Locate the <authentication> element in the Web.config file. Change the value of mode from Windows to Forms.

3. Add a forms sub-element to the <authentication> element. Specify the value of the loginUrl attribute as login.aspx and the name as .ASPXFORMSAUTH, which is the default extension of cookies that are generated by ASP.NET applications.

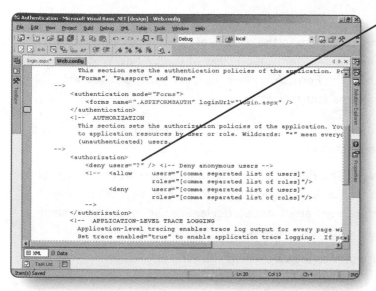

4. Next, restrict anonymous access to the Web application by using the <deny> sub-element of the <authorization> element. This will ensure that users who have not been authenticated by the Web application cannot access any page except the login.aspx page.

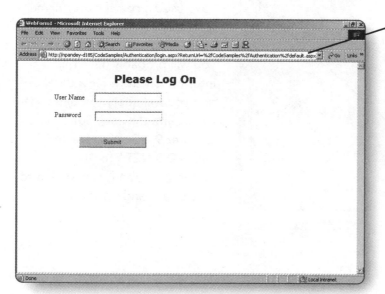

5. Run the application. You will notice that when you request the default.aspx page, you are redirected to the login.aspx page. The address of the default.aspx page is passed as a query string to the login.aspx page.

Now, you need to write the code for the Click event of the Submit button to authenticate users and redirect them to the default.aspx page. To authenticate a user, you need to use the FormsAuthentication class of the System.Web.Security namespace. The methods of the FormsAuthentication class that provide the required functionality of Forms authentication are

- **Authenticate**. The Authenticate method is used to validate the user name and password against a data source.

- **RedirectFromLoginPage**. The RedirectFromLoginPage method is used to send the page that the user had initially requested to the log-in page in the query string. The RedirectFromLoginPage function declares a user as authentic and redirects the user to the originally requested page.

- **SignOut**. The SignOut function logs a user off the Web application.

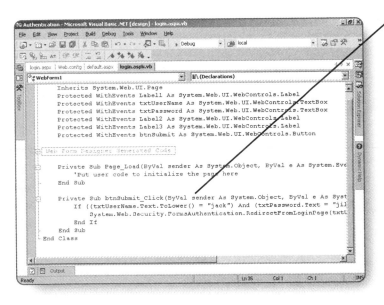

The code for the Submit button is shown here. Notice that I have used a specific user name and password to validate the user. In a real-world application, you will probably have this information stored in a database and you will query the database to validate the user. See Chapter 9, "Getting Started with ADO.NET," for more information about connecting to a database and retrieving information.

Implementing Windows Authentication

Implementation of Windows authentication is straightforward. First, you need to disable anonymous access on IIS. The steps to disable anonymous access were described in the "Securing a Virtual Directory" section earlier in this chapter.

After you disable anonymous authentication at IIS, you can change the settings of the Web.config file to enable Windows authentication on the Web site. In this section, I will implement Windows authentication on the authentication application that you created in the previous section.

To implement Windows authentication in an application, open the application and follow these steps.

1. Double-click on the Web.config file in the Solution Explorer. The file will open in the XML Designer.

2. Change the value of the mode attribute of the <authentication> element to enable Windows authentication.

3. Specify the list of users who are allowed to access the Web site using the <allow> element.

4. Deny access to all other users by using the <deny> element.

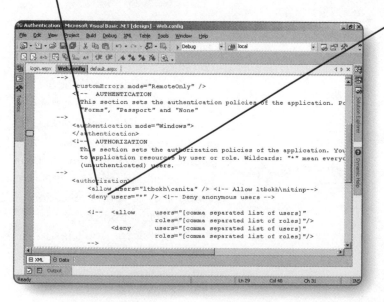

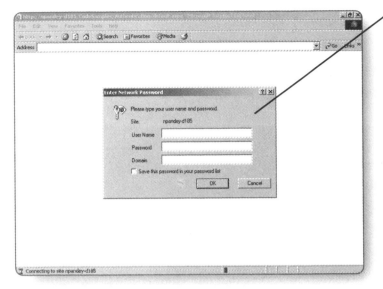

When a user who is not on the list of users to whom you have granted access tries to access the Web application, the Enter Network Password dialog box will open. The user must specify the log-on credentials of a user who is allowed to access the Web application to proceed.

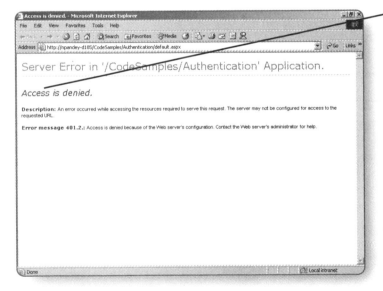

If the user is unable to specify the log-on credentials of a user who is allowed to access the Web application, the Access is Denied screen will appear.

With the implementation of Windows authentication, I have completed my discussion on securing ASP.NET Web applications. This completes the development of a Web application. To distribute your application, you should create a deployment project that allows you to install the Web forms of your application on the destination computer. In the next chapter, you'll learn how to deploy your Web application by creating a deployment project in Visual Studio .NET.

23

Deploying ASP.NET Applications

Deploying ASP.NET applications can be as simple as creating a virtual directory on the destination computer and copying the .aspx files to the directory. Though this is an easy way to deploy applications, it is not an efficient one. What if the computer on which you want to deploy the application is not accessible on the local network? Or what if you do not know the configuration of that computer? In such a scenario, how would you ensure that the installation process is efficient and error free?

You have greater control over the deployment of ASP.NET applications if you create a deployment package in Visual Studio .NET and use the package to deploy your applications. For example, you can ensure that the destination computer fulfills the minimum hardware requirements before the application is installed. You can also ensure that the .NET Framework run-time files are available on the destination computer, and so on. In this chapter, you'll learn how to:

● Configure a deployment project to deploy a solution

● Deploy an application using a deployment project

Configuring a Deployment Project

A solution can include a number of projects. When you create an ASP.NET application, Visual Studio .NET creates a solution and adds a project for your application by default. When you want to deploy the application, you need to add a deployment project to the same solution and configure the deployment project.

In this section, you will learn how to add a deployment project to the MySourceCode application. Then, you will configure the deployment project to customize it for your application's needs.

Adding a Deployment Project

To add a deployment project to an ASP.NET solution, follow these steps.

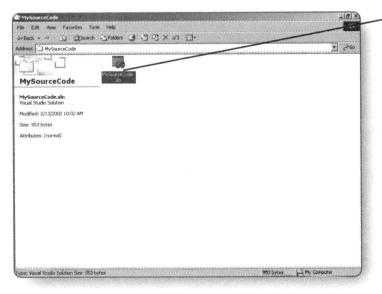

1. Double-click on the solution file to which you want to add a deployment project. (The solution file has the .sln extension.) The solution will open in Visual Studio .NET.

2. Right-click on the name of the solution in the Solution Explorer. A shortcut menu will appear.

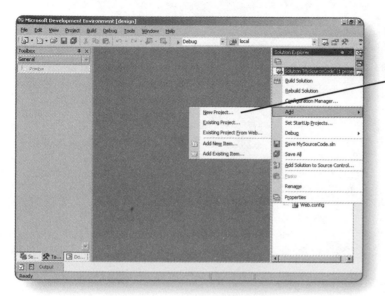

3. Move the mouse pointer to Add. A submenu will appear.

4. Click on New Project. The Add New Project dialog box will open.

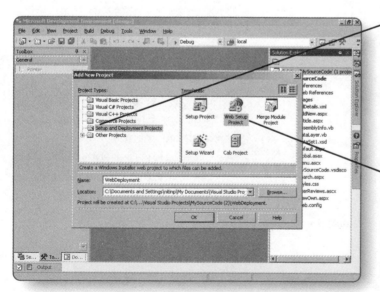

5. Click on the Setup and Deployment Projects option in the Project Types list. The project templates available in the Setup and Deployment Projects option will appear in the Templates list.

6. Click on Web Setup Project. The option will be selected.

NOTE

The Web Setup Project option is used to deploy ASP.NET Web applications and Web services. You can select other options to deploy Windows applications and components.

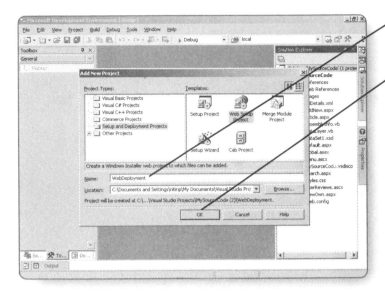

7. Type the name of the project in the Name text box.

8. Click on OK to add the Web Setup Project to the solution. The project will appear in the Solution Explorer.

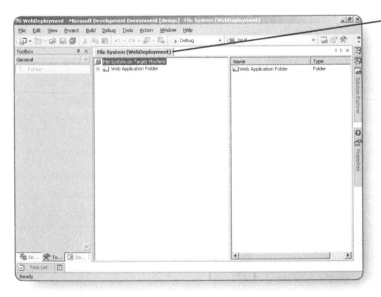

When you add a deployment project to your solution, a deployment editor will open. This deployment editor is called the File System editor. Visual Studio .NET provides a number of deployment editors to help you deploy your application. You will learn more about each of these editors in the next section.

Understanding the Deployment Editors

If you click on the View menu and move the mouse pointer to Editor, you will see the deployment editors available in Visual Studio .NET.

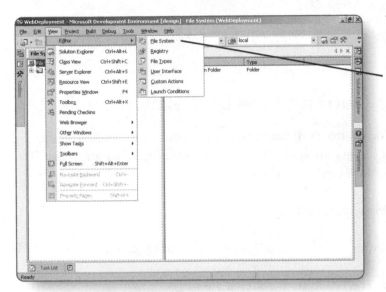

The editors that are available for deploying Web applications are

- **File System**. The File System editor simulates the directory structure that would be created on the destination computer. Use this editor to configure the directory structure and add project files to the deployment project.

- **Registry**. Occasionally, you might need to store information, such as the configuration of the application, in a Windows registry. You can specify key and value pairs for such information in the Registry editor.

- **File Types**. When you need to associate specific file types with your application, you can use the File Types editor. Although you might use this editor more often in Windows applications, it comes in handy for Web applications as well, because you can associate application configuration files or other data files with your Web application.

- **User Interface**. The deployment package created in Visual Studio .NET has an interface that allows users to select a number of options, such as the destination directory or the type of installation. You can use the User Interface editor to customize the interface of your application.

- **Custom Actions**. Often, you need to execute specific tasks to complete the installation and configuration of your application. For example, you might need to install a database and run a custom script to populate it, so the database can be used by your ASP.NET application. Such tasks, which are not associated directly with the application, are known as *custom tasks*. You can use the Custom Actions editor to perform these tasks.

- **Launch Conditions**. The Launch Conditions editor ensures that the software and hardware requirements on the destination computer are fulfilled before a user can install an application. For example, when a user installs your ASP.NET application, the Launch Conditions editor can ensure the availability of IIS and the .NET Framework run-time files.

In most of this chapter, you will use these deployment editors to configure your deployment project.

Adding Project Output to the Deployment Project

To install your application on the destination computer, you need to add project files to the deployment project using the File System editor. Make sure that the File System editor is open before you begin these steps.

1. Click on View. The View menu will appear.

2. Move the mouse pointer to Editor. The Editor submenu will appear.

3. Click on File System. The File System editor will open.

4. Click on Project. The Project menu will appear.

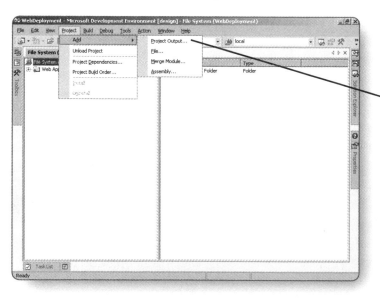

5. Move the mouse pointer to Add. The Add submenu will appear.

6. Click on Project Output. The Add Project Output Group dialog box will open.

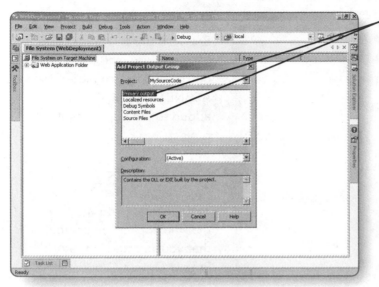

7. Press and hold the Ctrl key and click on Primary Output and Source Files. The Primary Output and Source Files options will be selected.

TIP

In the Add Project Output Group dialog box, you can select the components of an ASP.NET project that you want to add to the deployment project. For example, if you want to distribute the primary output of your project, you should select the Primary Output option. Similarly, if you want to distribute the source files, you should select the Source Files option.

8a. Choose Release .NET from the Configuration list. The active configuration of the project will be set to Release.

OR

8b. Choose Debug .NET from the Configuration list. The active configuration of the project will be set to Debug.

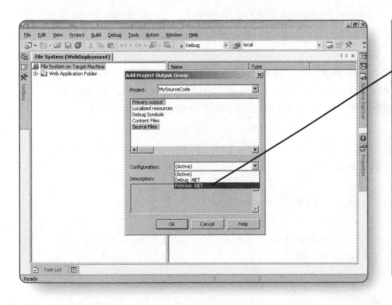

TIP

When you distribute your application, you should select the Release .NET project configuration, which optimizes your application for speed and performance. You can change the project configuration by clicking on the Solution Configurations drop-down list on the Standard toolbar.

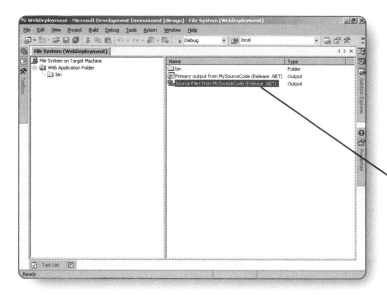

9. Click on OK. The Add Project Output Group dialog box will close, and the primary output and source files of the ASP.NET application will be added to the deployment project.

If you click on the Web Application Folder in the File System editor, you will notice that the application components that you selected in the Add Project Output Group dialog box have been added to the folder.

Adding a License Agreement to the Deployment Project

Commercial software usually includes a license agreement that the user needs to accept before proceeding with the installation. When you package your application, you can include a license agreement as specified by your organization, so that a user agrees to the terms and conditions before using the application.

To add a license agreement to the deployment project, you need to use the File System and User Interface editors. Before you use these editors, you need to create an RTF (*Rich Text Format*) file that specifies the license agreement.

Save your license agreement in RTF format, and then follow these steps to add the agreement to your application.

1. Click on Project. The Project menu will appear.

2. Move the mouse pointer to Add and select File. The Add Files dialog box will open.

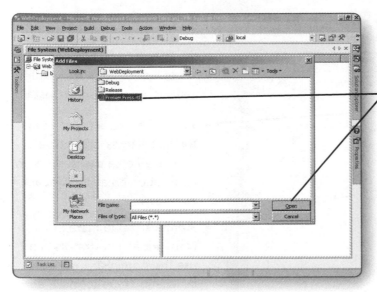

3. Navigate to the license agreement file in the Add Files dialog box.

4. Select the license agreement file and click on Open. The license agreement file will be imported into the deployment project and will appear in the Web Application Folder.

5. In the Web Application Folder, click and hold the license agreement file and drag it to the Bin folder. The license agreement file will be placed in the Bin folder.

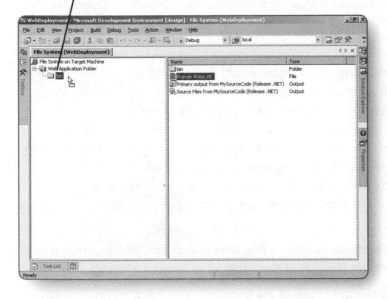

TIP

All data files pertaining to an application are usually stored in the Bin folder. Therefore, it is a good idea to store the license agreement in the Bin folder.

6. Click on View. The View menu will appear.

7. Move the mouse pointer to Editor and select User Interface. The User Interface editor will open.

Understanding the Installation Types

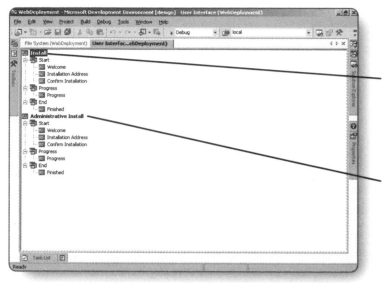

In the User Interface editor, two types of installations are visible: Install and Administrative Install.

- **Install**. The screens listed in the Install installation type appear when a user installs an application on an individual computer.

- **Administrative Install**. Network administrators can use the Administrative Install installation type to make an application available for installation over a network.

Every installation type has three stages—Start, Progress, and End. These stages denote the stages of installation that an application undergoes. Each stage has one or more dialog boxes associated with it.

- **Start**. The Start stage is used for collecting information from a user about the location and the components of the application. By default, this stage includes three dialog boxes: Welcome, Installation Address, and Confirm Installation. These dialog boxes display a welcome note, prompt for the location of application files, and confirm that the user is ready to install the application, respectively. However, you can add more dialog boxes to the Start stage to customize the installation program. For example, you can add a License Agreement dialog box to display a license agreement, or you can add a Checkboxes dialog box to allow the user to select the components that should be installed.

- **Progress**. The Progress stage displays a Progress dialog box, which contains a progress bar to show what fraction of the application has been installed.

- **End**. The End stage is the last stage of the installation process. It is composed of only one dialog box—Finished. The screen notifies the user that the installation was completed successfully.

NOTE

If you remove all the dialog boxes from the User Interface editor, your installation program will have no interface. Thus, the program will have an unattended installation, in which the user need not intervene.

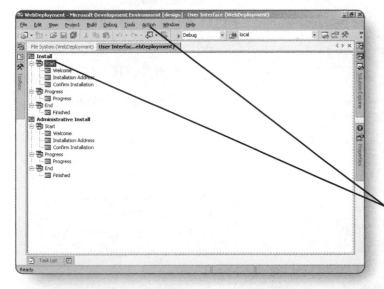

Adding the License Agreement to the Installation Program

To add a license agreement to the installation program, you add a License Agreement dialog box from the User Interface editor.

1. Click on the Start stage in the User Interface editor. The Start stage will be highlighted, and the Action menu option will appear on the menu bar.

2. Click on Action. The Action menu will appear.

3. Click on Add Dialog. The Add Dialog dialog box will open.

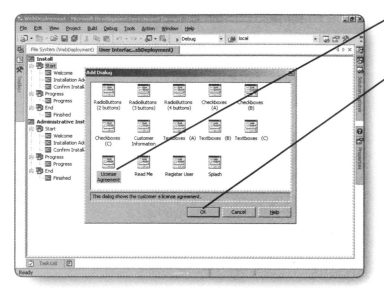

4. Click on License Agreement. The option will be selected.

5. Click on OK. The Add Dialog dialog box will close and the License Agreement dialog box will be added to the User Interface editor.

Moving the License Agreement

The license agreement should conventionally appear immediately after the Welcome screen, so that users proceed to the installation options only if they accept the license agreement. Follow these steps to change the placement of the license agreement.

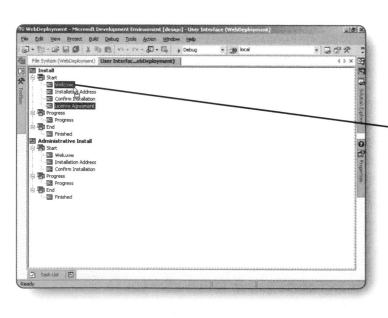

1. Click on License Agreement in the Start stage. The License Agreement dialog box will be selected.

2. Press and hold the mouse button and drag the License Agreement dialog box to the Welcome dialog box. The License Agreement dialog box will move below the Welcome dialog box. Next, you need to associate the License Agreement dialog box with the license agreement file that you imported in RTF format.

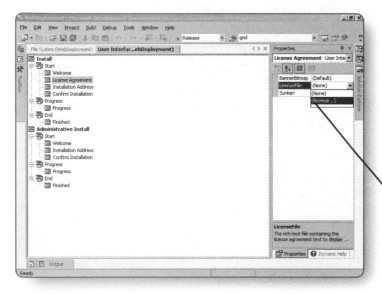

3. Right-click on License Agreement. The shortcut menu will appear.

4. Click on Properties Window° in the shortcut menu. The Properties window for License Agreement will appear.

5. Choose Browse from the LicenseFile list. The Select Item in Project dialog box will open.

6. Double-click on Web Application Folder. The contents of the folder will be listed in the Select Item in Project dialog box.

7. Double-click on Bin. The license agreement that you added to the Bin folder will be listed in the Select Item in Project dialog box.

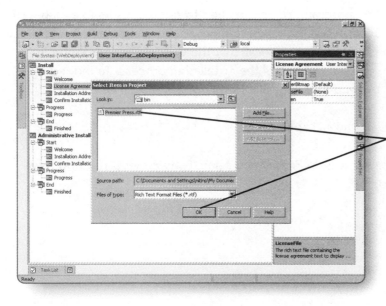

8. Select the license agreement and click on OK. The Select Item in Project dialog box will close, and the license agreement file will be associated with the License Agreement dialog box.

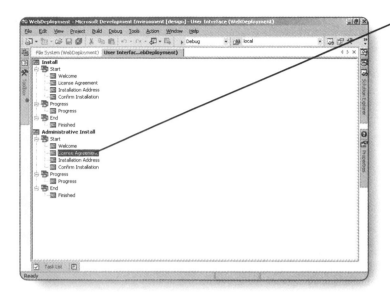

You have now added the license agreement to the Install installation type. In a similar manner, you can add the license agreement to the Administrative Install installation type.

Redirecting Users to a Web Site

At the end of an installation program, you often need to redirect users to a Web page where they can register the software. Such functionality can be achieved by using the Custom Actions editor. You will recall that the Custom Actions editor is used to perform custom tasks at the end of the installation process. To redirect users to a Web page at the end of the installation process, follow these steps.

1. Click on File. The File menu will appear.

2. Move the mouse pointer to Add Project and select New Project. The Add New Project dialog box will open.

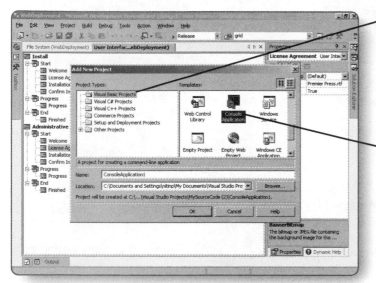

3. Click on Visual Basic Projects in the Project Types pane. The project templates available in the Visual Basic Projects category will appear in the Templates pane.

4. In the list of available templates, click on Console Application. The Console Application project type will be selected.

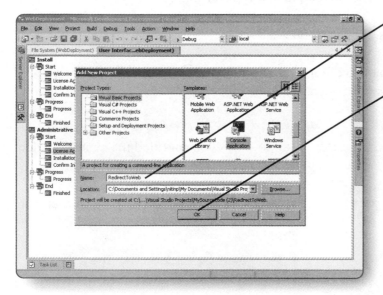

5. Specify the name of the console application in the Name text box.

6. Click on OK. The new project will be added to the deployment project, and the main() function of the application will be visible.

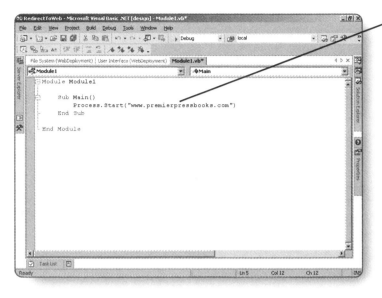

7. Code the Start function of the Process class to redirect the user to a Web site.

8. Click on the Save button to save the Module1.vb file.

9. Click on Close for the Module1.vb file. You will return to the screen on which you started the steps of this section.

You have successfully added to the solution a project that redirects the user to a Web site.

Now you need to add the output of the project to the deployment solution. To do so, switch to the File System editor and follow these steps.

1. Click on Project. The Project menu will appear.

2. Move the mouse pointer to Add and select Project Output. The Add Project Output Group dialog box will open.

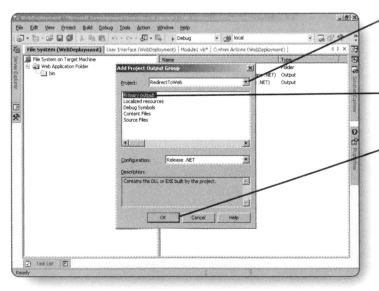

3. Choose the project in which you specified the main() function from the Project list.

4. Click on Primary Output. The option will be selected.

5. Click on OK. The Add Project Output dialog box will close, and the output of the project that you selected in Step 3 will be added to the deployment project.

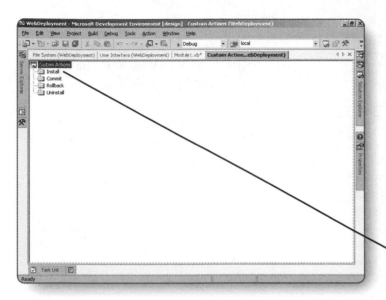

To add the custom action to your project, you need to use the Custom Actions editor.

1. Click on View. The View menu will appear.

2. Move the mouse pointer to Editor and click on Custom Actions. The Custom Actions editor will open.

3. Click on Install. The Install option will be selected.

TIP

In the Custom Actions editor, you can specify different actions for different stages of an application. For example, if you create databases in the Install stage, delete existing application databases in the uninstall stage. Similarly, in the Rollback stage, you can delete applications components that were not installed correctly.

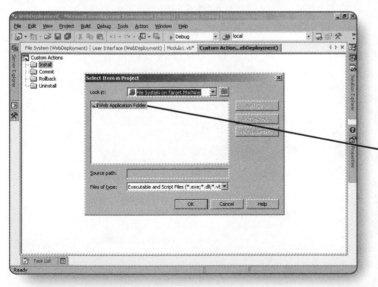

4. Click on Action. The Action menu will be selected.

5. Click on Add Custom Action. The Select Item in Project dialog box will open.

6. Double-click on Web Application Folder. The contents of the Web Application Folder will appear in the Select Item in Project dialog box.

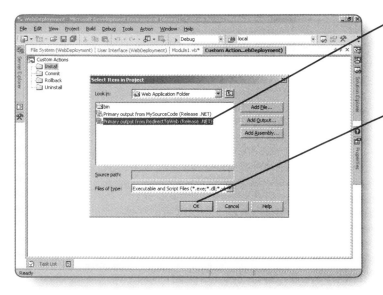

7. Click on the primary output for the project that redirects the user to a Web site. The option will be selected.

8. Click on OK. The custom action will be added to the deployment project.

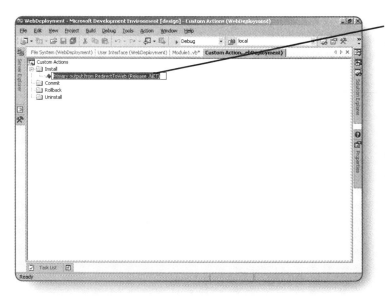

9. If you want, you can change the name of the custom action.

10. Click on View. The View menu will appear.

11. Click on Properties Window. The Properties window will appear.

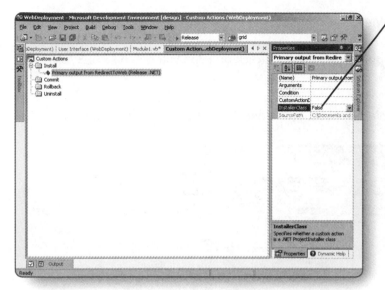

12. Double-click on InstallerClass in the Properties window for the custom action. The value of the InstallerClass property will change to False.

> **TIP**
>
> The InstallerClass property should be True only if the custom action is a .NET ProjectInstaller class.

You have studied all of the important concepts pertaining to deployment of ASP.NET applications. In the next section, you'll look at ways to optimize the installation program.

Optimizing the Installation Program

There are several ways to optimize an installation program. In this section, I will explain three aspects of optimizing an installation program—by changing the name of the virtual directory, adding bootstrapper files, and reducing the size of the program.

Changing the Name of the Virtual Directory

Often, you will want to use a particular name for the virtual directory of your ASP.NET application. Developers usually associate the name of the virtual directory with the name of their organization, so the Web application is easily accessible. To specify a name for the virtual directory, follow these steps.

> **NOTE**
>
> Even if you specify a name for the virtual directory, a user can change it when installing your application. However, the name that you specify is the default name that appears when the installation program is run.

1. Click on View. The View menu will appear.

2. Move the mouse pointer to Editor and click on File System. The File System editor will open.

3. Right-click on the Web Application Folder. A shortcut menu will appear.

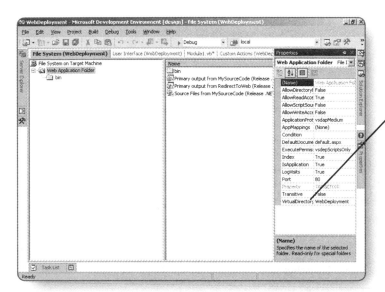

4. Click on Properties Window in the shortcut menu. The Properties window for the Web Application Folder will appear.

5. Double-click on VirtualDirectory. The name of the virtual directory will be selected.

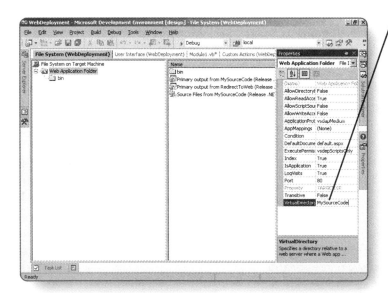

6. Type a new name for the virtual directory and press the Enter key.

After you change the name of the virtual directory, the new name will be the default name that appears when a user installs your application.

Adding Bootstrapper Files to the Deployment Project

Windows and Web application deployment projects that you create in Visual Studio .NET are compiled as MSI (*Microsoft Installer*) files. MSI files use the Microsoft Windows Installer Service to install applications on a computer.

TIP

The MSI technology optimizes application deployment by ensuring that any component that is accidentally deleted by a user can be automatically installed without adversely affecting the application's performance. The MSI technology also enables you to install only those components that you want to use, which optimizes the use of disk space.

To run MSI files created in Visual Studio .NET, a user must have Windows Installer 1.5 or later installed on his or her computer. The user will not be able to run the installation program if version 1.5 of Windows Installer is not available. However, Visual Studio .NET offers a solution to this problem by way of bootstrappers, which include the necessary files or links to Web sites for installing the latest version of Windows Installer. In Visual Studio .NET, you can include the Windows or Web bootstrapper in your application. The bootstrapper provides the necessary files to install Windows Installer 1.5 if it is not available on the destination computer. To include bootstrapper files in your application, follow these steps.

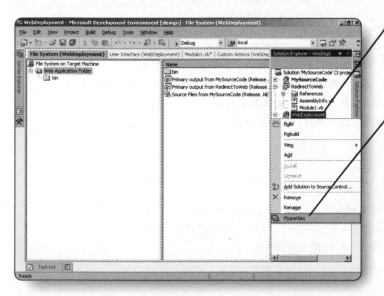

1. Right-click on the name of the project in the Solution Explorer. A shortcut menu will appear.

2. Click on Properties. The Property Pages dialog box for the deployment project will open.

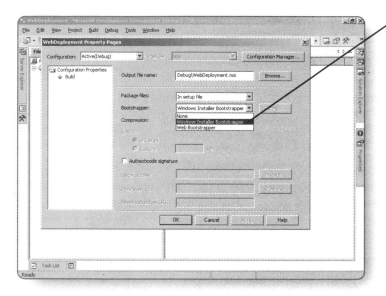

3. Choose Windows Installer Bootstrapper from the Bootstrapper drop-down menu. The option will be selected.

TIP

The Windows Installer Bootstrapper option packages the files required to run the Windows Installer service in the deployment project. You can also make these files available on a Web site and select the Web Bootstrapper option to direct users to a Web site if the files are not available on their computers.

---

4. Click on Apply. The changes that you made will be applied to the project.

5. Click on OK. The Property Pages dialog box will close.

Reducing the Size of the Deployment Project

If you create a deployment project in Visual Studio .NET by retaining most of the default options, the size of the deployment program will be anywhere from 16–20 MB. You might wonder whether there is a way to reduce the size of the deployment program. There is an easy solution—you need to exclude the .NET run-time files from the deployment project. This reduces the size of the deployment project considerably—by about 75 percent. To exclude the .NET run-time files, follow these steps.

CAUTION

If you exclude the .NET run-time files, be sure that these files are available on the destination computer. Otherwise, a user will not be able to run your application.

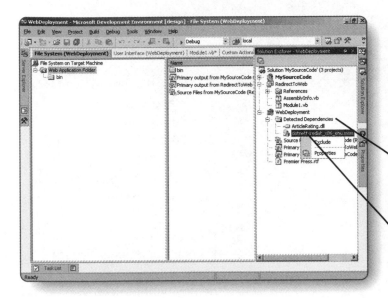

1. Click on View. The View menu will appear.

2. Click on Solution Explorer. The Solution Explorer will appear.

3. Locate the Detected Dependencies folder in the deployment project.

4. In the Detected Dependencies folder, right-click on dotnetfxredist_x86_enu.msm. A shortcut menu will appear.

NOTE

The dotnetfxredist_x86_enu.msm file is a merge module that contains the .NET run-time files. Merge modules are packaged components that can be included in other deployment projects.

---

5. Click on Exclude to exclude the .NET run-time files from your project. A check mark will appear next to the Exclude option to signify that the option is enabled, and the shortcut menu will disappear.

When you exclude the .NET run-time files from your project, the size of the project is typically reduced to 1–3 MB.

Checking for Availability of Prerequisite Software

ASP.NET applications can be installed only on IIS. Therefore, you should make sure that IIS is available on the destination computer before a user installs your application. Similarly, if you have excluded the .NET run-time files from your application, you should make sure that these files are available on the destination computer.

You can use the Launch Conditions editor to check for the presence of files, software, and hardware on the destination computer. To check for the presence of .NET run-time files, follow these steps.

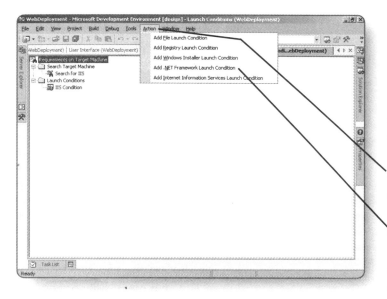

1. Click on View. The View menu will appear.

2. Move the mouse pointer to Editor and click on Launch Conditions. The Launch Conditions editor will open.

3. Click on Action. The Action menu will appear.

4. Select Add .NET Framework Launch Condition. A launch condition will be added to the deployment project.

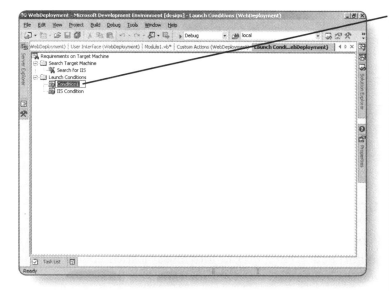

5. Type a new name for the condition, if you want.

TIP

When a launch condition is not fulfilled on the destination computer, the installation program displays an error message. You can customize this message by changing the value of the Message property for a launch condition. However, I suggest that you retain the default message that is specified by Visual Studio .NET because the default message can automatically change to different languages depending on the language that a user runs on the operating system.

NOTE

The launch condition for IIS is added by default to the deployment project.

Deploying an Application

In the final stages of deploying your application, compile the application and run the installation program to ensure that the application is deployed successfully. This section describes the procedure for compiling and testing your installation program.

Compiling the Deployment Project

You should always compile your application in the Release project configuration to optimize it. If you have not already changed the project configuration to Release, do it now by choosing Release from the Solution Configurations list on the toolbar. To compile your application, follow these steps.

1. Click on Build. The Build menu will appear.

2. Click on Build WebDeployment. (WebDeployment is the name of the project in this case. The name of this option will vary for you, depending on what you named the project.) The Output window will appear, and your solution will be compiled.

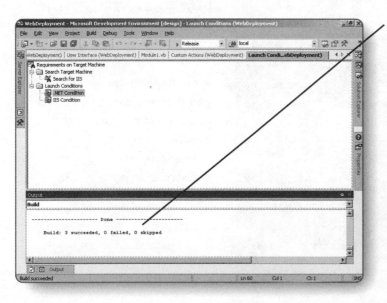

Errors, if any, will be displayed in the Output window. You should not encounter any errors in this case. However, in case you do encounter errors, it is helpful to know that some possible causes of errors are incorrect placement of dialog boxes on the User Interface editor or errors in applications that you are deploying. Correct any errors and build the solution again.

Running the Installation Program

After you compile your application successfully, an MSI file will be created in the Release subfolder of the deployment project's folder. You should test this deployment file for:

- All launch conditions that you have specified
- All custom actions that you have specified
- Successful installation of the application
- Successful uninstallation of the application

Checking for Launch Conditions

To check for the .NET run-time files launch condition, copy the deployment file (the file with the MSI extension) and its associated files (all of the files in the Release subfolder) to a computer that does not have the .NET run-time files installed. Then try to run the installation.

> **TIP**
>
> If you have trouble locating the MSI file for the deployment project, scroll up in the Output window to see the exact location of the file.

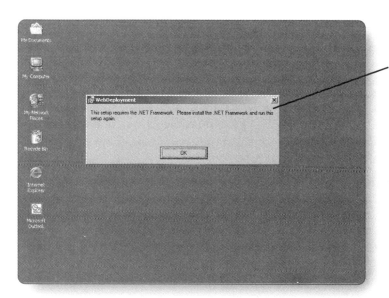

A message might appear to tell you that you cannot install the application because of the absence of the .NET Framework. You might also encounter an error message that informs you of the absence of IIS.

Installing and Uninstalling the Application

To install the application:

1. Double-click on the MSI file. The installation program will begin.

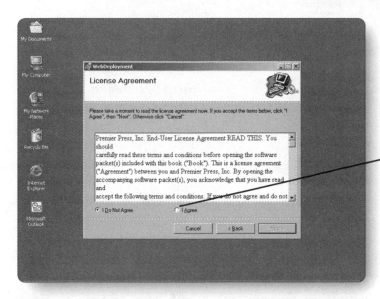

2. On the Welcome screen of the installation program, click on Next. The License Agreement screen will appear and will display the license agreement that you specified in the RTF file.

3. Click on I Agree. The Next option will be enabled.

4. Click on Next. The Select Installation Address screen will appear. Notice that the default name for the virtual directory you specified is displayed here.

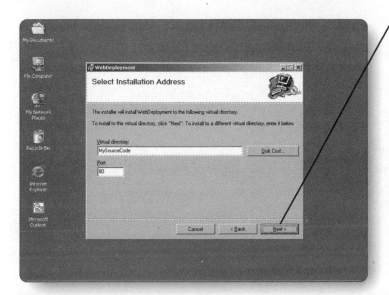

5. Click on Next. The Confirm Installation screen will appear.

6. Click on Next. A progress bar will indicate the progress of the installation. This will be followed by the Installation Complete screen. Simultaneously, Internet Explorer will launch and the Web site that you had specified for the custom action will open.

7. Close Internet Explorer.

8. Click on the Close button on the Installation Complete screen. The installation program will close.

After you successfully install your application, you should uninstall it to confirm that the uninstallation process operates smoothly. To uninstall an application, select the Add/Remove Programs option from the Control Panel and perform the uninstall steps as you would for any other Windows application.

You have now completed your learning of ASP.NET. Deploying is the last stage of an application's development. When you have successfully deployed your application, you can be sure that you have developed your application correctly!

As the next step, you can create your own ASP.NET application to master the concepts that you learned in the book. Before you do that, take a look at Appendix A, "Keyboard Shortcuts in Visual Studio .NET," which lists the commonly used shortcut keys in Visual Studio .NET. Those of you familiar with Visual C# can read Appendix B, "Developing ASP.NET Applications in Visual C#," to learn how ASP.NET applications can be created in Visual C#. If you have an ASP 3.0 application available, you should also read Appendix C, "Migrating from ASP 3.0 to ASP.NET," which describes the steps to migrate an ASP 3.0 application to ASP.NET. Finally, Appendix D, "Online Resources for ASP.NET," is a useful reference tool.

Happy coding!

A

Keyboard Shortcuts in Visual Studio .NET

It is often easier and quicker to perform tasks using the keyboard instead of the mouse. For example, instead of clicking on the View menu and then selecting Solution Explorer, you can press Ctrl+Alt+L.

In this appendix, I have provided a categorized list of useful keyboard shortcuts that you can use in Visual Studio .NET. With practice and experience, you will gradually become accustomed to using keyboard shortcuts more often than you use menu options.

Keyboard Shortcuts for the Code Editor

In the Code Editor, you can use keyboard shortcuts to move, copy, and delete text. Table A.1 lists the commonly used shortcut keys in the Code Editor.

Table A.1 Keyboard Shortcuts for the Code Editor

Task	Shortcut Key(s)
Copy selected text from the Code Editor	Ctrl+C and Ctrl+Insert
Cut selected text from the Code Editor	Ctrl+X and Shift+Delete
Cut one line of text from the Code Editor	Ctrl+L
Paste text at the insertion point	Ctrl+V and Shift+Insert
Move between text in the ClipboardRing	Ctrl+Shift+V and Ctrl+Shift+Insert
Undo the last change made	Ctrl+Z or Alt+Backspace
Redo the last change that was undone	Ctrl+Y or Ctrl+Alt+Backspace
Save the currently open file	Ctrl+S
Save all open files	Ctrl+Shift+S
Open the Code Editor window	F7
Transpose characters at the insertion point	Ctrl+T
Insert auto-complete entry	Tab
Format and indent code	Ctrl+K and then Ctrl+D

The preceding table summarized all of the important tasks that you perform in the Code Editor. The next section describes the shortcut keys for the Form Designer.

Keyboard Shortcuts for the Form Designer

The Form Designer is used to design forms. Visual Studio .NET offers a number of default shortcut keys that can be used to align controls on the forms and change their properties. Some of the shortcut keys are listed in Table A.2.

Table A.2 Keyboard Shortcuts for the Form Designer

Task	Shortcut Key
Increase the indentation of a control	Ctrl+T
Decrease the indentation of a control	Ctrl+Shift+T
Invoke the Properties window for a control	F4
Open the Form Designer window	Shift+F7
Toggle between HTML and Design views	Ctrl+PageDown
Change to Full Screen view	Shift+Alt+Enter
Make text bold	Ctrl+B
Underline text	Ctrl+U
Italicize text	Ctrl+I

Keyboard Shortcuts for the Visual Studio .NET IDE

There are some shortcut keys that are applicable to the Visual Studio .NET IDE (*Integrated Development Environment*). These keys work irrespective of the component of Visual Studio .NET that you run. The shortcut keys are listed in Table A.3.

Table A.3 Keyboard Shortcuts for the Visual Studio .NET IDE

Task	Shortcut Key
Open the Server Explorer	Ctrl+Alt+S
Open the Toolbox	Ctrl+Alt+X
Open the Solution Explorer	Ctrl+Alt+L
Open the Resource view	Ctrl+Alt+E
Open the Class view	Ctrl+Alt+C
Open Dynamic Help	Ctrl+F1
Add a new item to the project	Ctrl+Shift+A
Add an existing item to the project	Shift+Alt+A
Save all project files	Ctrl+Shift+S
Create a new project	Ctrl+Shift+N
Debug an application	F5
Start an application without debugging	Shift+F5
Create a breakpoint (in the Code Editor)	Ctrl+B

Remembering Shortcuts

The easy way to remember keyboard shortcuts is not to learn them by heart. Instead, remember them as you use them. After going through the list of shortcuts given here, you might retain quite a few of them, especially for the tasks that you perform frequently.

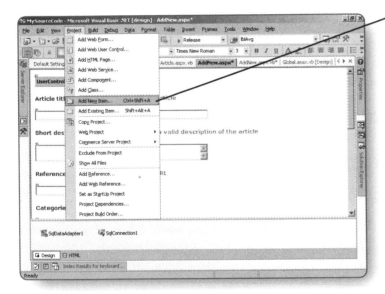

As you work in the Visual Studio .NET IDE, you will realize that the shortcut keys to each menu option are given next to the menu option itself. Thus, the Add New Item menu option in the Project menu reads Add New Item...Ctrl+Shift+A. As you use more menu options in the IDE, you will learn more about the shortcut keys.

B

Developing ASP.NET Applications in Visual C#

To code ASP.NET applications, you can use Visual Basic .NET or Visual C#. I have explained almost all of the code snippets in this book using Visual Basic .NET. However, Visual C# offers an equally easy and powerful programming approach by enabling you to perform the same tasks that you can perform in Visual Basic .NET. The pages that you created using Visual Basic .NET can be easily created in Visual C#. The purpose of this appendix is to introduce you to Visual C# and highlight the differences between programming in Visual Basic .NET and Visual C#. In this appendix, you'll learn how to:

- Program Visual C# applications in Visual Studio .NET
- Convert Visual Basic .NET code into Visual C# code

Programming Applications in Visual C#

The syntax of Visual C# is quite similar to the syntax of Visual C++. If you have programmed in Visual C++, you will have no problem creating applications in Visual C#. However, if you are making a transition from Visual Basic .NET to Visual C#, there are quite a few differences in the language syntax. You also need to get accustomed to the slightly different way of performing the same tasks in the two languages when you use Visual Studio .NET.

This section will provide you with adequate knowledge to start coding your applications in Visual C#. First, I will examine the differences in the syntax of Visual C# and Visual Basic .NET. Next, I will summarize how coding Visual C# applications in Visual Studio .NET is different than coding Visual Basic .NET applications.

Syntactical Differences in Visual C# and Visual Basic .NET

Syntactical differences make it easy for you to differentiate between Visual Basic .NET and Visual C#. One of the most basic differences is that each statement in Visual C# ends with a semicolon, which is not the case in Visual Basic .NET.

In this section, I will list differences in the programming syntax of Visual Basic .NET and Visual C#.

Using Semicolons

You need to place a semicolon at the end of each statement in Visual C#. Note that when I say statement, I do not mean that you need to place semicolons at the end of conditional clauses, such as if and while.

Thus, if you have a code snippet that changes the text displayed in a label to Hello World, the code in Visual Basic .NET is written as:

```
Label1.Text="Hello World!"
```

The same code in Visual C# would be written as:

```
Label1.Text="Hello World!";
```

Understanding Case Sensitivity

Visual C# is case sensitive. This is a marked difference from Visual Basic .NET, in which you can declare a variable as MyVariable and use it as myvariable. The following code snippet would work fine in Visual Basic .NET.

```
Dim intCounter as Integer
intcounter=intcounter+1
```

However, when written in the C# syntax, the same code will generate an error, such as "The name 'intcounter' does not exist in the class or namespace," because you have changed the case of the term intcounter.

```
int intCounter
intcounter=intcounter+1;
```

Using Braces

In Visual C#, you need to use braces for different blocks of code. This is not required in Visual Basic .NET. For example, the following code will work fine in Visual Basic .NET.

```
Namespace RatingArticle
    Public Class ClArticleRating
        Dim SelOption as Integer
        Public Sub GetSelection()
            If Opt1.Checked=True Then
                SelOption=1
            End If
        End Sub
    End Class
End Namespace
```

However, in Visual C#, you would need to write the same code as:

```
namespace RatingArticle
{
    public class ClArticleRating
    {
        int SelOption;
        public void GetSelection()
        {
```

```
        if (Opt1.Checked)==true
        {
            SelOption=1;
        }
    }
}
}
```

Notice that in the preceding code, I have enclosed the expression Opt1.Checked in parentheses. To learn more about why this is necessary, refer to the "Using Selection and Conditional Statements" section later in this appendix.

Declaring Variables

To declare variables in Visual Basic .NET, you need to use the Dim keyword. However, variables in Visual C# are declared without using the Dim keyword, and the data type of the variable is given before the name of the variable. The following code snippet illustrates variable and object initialization in Visual Basic .NET.

```
Dim intVar1 as Integer
Dim myCommand as SqlCommand
```

The equivalent C# code for declaring these variables is

```
int intVar1;
SqlCommand myCommand;
```

Declaring Functions

When you declare functions in Visual Basic .NET, you need to append the return type of the function to the end of the declaration. For example, if a function returns a Boolean value, the function is written as:

```
Public Function CheckNumber(Var1 as Integer) as Boolean
End Function
```

The same function is written in Visual C# as:

```
public bool CheckNumber(int Var1)
{
}
```

If a function returns a void in Visual Basic .NET, you use a subroutine.

```
Public Sub CheckNumber(Var1 as Integer, Var2 as Integer)
End Sub
```

For functions that do not return any values in Visual C#, you use the keyword void.

```
public void CheckNumber(int Var1, intVar2)
{
}
```

Importing Namespaces into an Application

Often, you need to import namespaces into your application to use the classes provided by the .NET Framework class library. For example, you need to import the System.Diagnostics namespace to use the debugging classes of the .NET Framework. The syntax for importing namespaces in Visual Basic .NET is

```
Imports System.Diagnostics
```

The equivalent syntax in Visual C# is

```
using System.Diagnostics;
```

Using Selection and Conditional Statements

There are two important differences in the syntax of selection statements in Visual Basic .NET and Visual C#. In Visual C#, the condition for which you want to check is placed in parentheses. Also, the comparison operator in Visual C# (= =) is different than the comparison operator in Visual Basic .NET (=).

I discussed the syntax of the if statement in the "Using Braces" section earlier in this appendix. The Visual Basic .NET syntax of the while loop is similar to the syntax of the if statement.

```
While counter<100
     AddNumbers()
End While
```

The equivalent syntax in Visual C# is

```
while (counter<100)
{
    AddNumbers()
}
```

One selection statement that differs significantly in Visual Basic .NET and Visual C# is the
Select Case statement (or the switch statement,
as it is called in Visual C#). The syntax of the
Select Case statement in Visual Basic .NET is

```
Select Case myReader.GetInt32(10)
    Case 0
        lblDiff.Text = "Beginner"
    Case 1
        lblDiff.Text = "Intermediate"
    Case 2
        lblDiff.Text = "Advanced"
End Select
```

The equivalent switch statement in Visual C# is

```
switch (myReader.GetInt32(10))
{
    case 0:
        lblDiff.Text="Beginner";
        break;
    case 1:
        lblDiff.Text="Intermediate";
        break;
    case 2:
        lblDiff.Text="Advanced";
        break;
}
```

> **TIP**
>
> Although I have used braces in the preceding statements, you can omit the braces if only one statement follows the condition.

Understanding Comment Entries

The comment entries in Visual Basic .NET begin with the ' (apostrophe) symbol, whereas the comment entries in Visual C# begin with the // symbol.

Visual C# also enables you to mark a block of code as a comment using the /* and */ block. An example of a multi-line comment is

```
/* This is a multiline comment in Visual C#.
For the same functionality in Visual Basic .NET,
you would have had to use the ' symbol in each line. */
```

Coding Visual C# Applications in Visual Studio .NET

Some of the tasks involved in creating a Visual C# application in ASP.NET are different than the tasks involved in creating a Visual Basic .NET application. In this section, I will list some of the tasks that you need to perform differently in Visual C#.

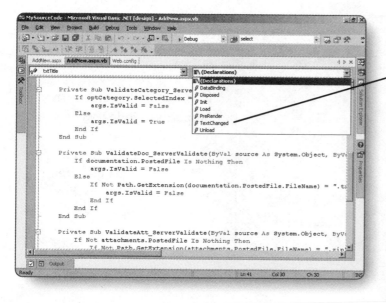

Adding Event Handlers

In Visual Basic .NET, you add event handlers directly in the Code Editor window. For example, if you want to add an event handler for the TextChanged event of a TextBox control, you select the control in the Code Editor and then select the event handler event from the second list, as shown here.

However, if you want to add an event handler in Visual C#, you need to use the Properties window. Keep reading to see how you can add an event handler in Visual C#.

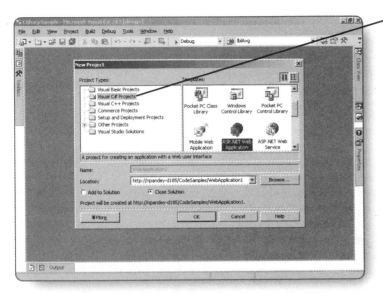

Create an ASP.NET Web Application in Visual C# the same way you would in Visual Basic .NET. The only difference is that you need to select the ASP.NET Web Application template from the Visual C# Projects project type instead of the Visual Basic Projects project type.

After you create a new project, add a TextBox control to its default form. Next, follow these steps to add an event handler for the TextChanged event of the form.

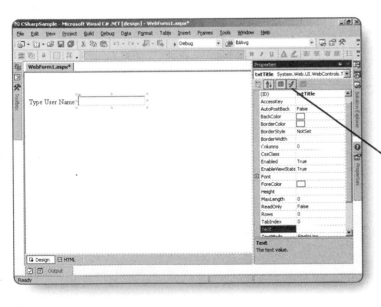

1. Right-click on the TextBox control. A shortcut menu will appear.

2. Click on Properties. The Properties window will appear.

3. Click on the Events button. The list of events that are supported by the TextBox control will appear.

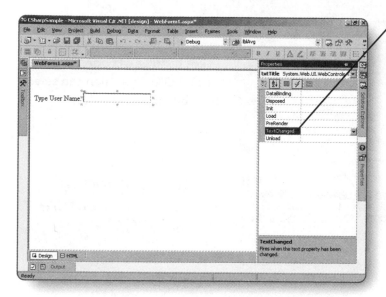

4. Double-click on TextChanged. An event handler will be added for the TextChanged event of the TextBox control.

After you add an event handler, the procedure to write the code for the event handler is the same in Visual C# and Visual Basic .NET.

Deleting Event Handlers

Just as the procedure for adding event handlers is different in Visual C#, so is the procedure for deleting event handlers. In Visual Basic .NET, you simply delete the definition of the event handler to remove it. In Visual C#, you also need to delete the declaration of the event handler.

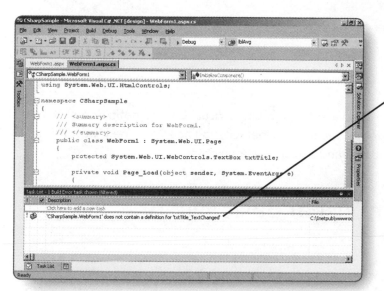

The easy way to find the declaration of an event handler is to delete the definition of the event handler and build the form. When you do so, an error message will appear, as shown here.

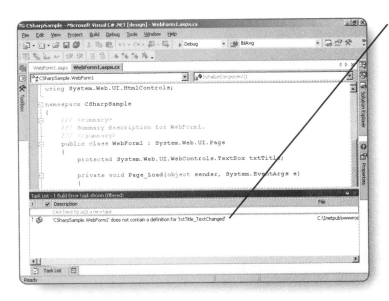

If you double-click on the build error, the declaration of the event handler will open in the Code Editor. You then can select the definition and delete it.

Understanding the IntelliSense Feature in Visual C#

The IntelliSense feature of Visual Studio .NET works slightly differently in Visual Basic .NET and Visual C#. If you type **Private Property SelOption() As Integer** and press Enter in Visual Basic .NET, the following code will be added to the form.

```
Private Property SelOption() As Integer
      Get

      End Get
      Set(ByVal Value As Integer)

      End Set
End Property
```

However, if you type the equivalent statement in Visual C#, the definition of the property will not be added to the form by default; you need to type it out. This is also the case with conditional and selection statements.

Moving from Visual Basic .NET to Visual C#

In the previous section, you learned about the syntactical differences between Visual C# and Visual Basic .NET. You also learned about the different programming practices in the two languages. In this section, I will show you a practical implementation of the C# code by writing the code for a user control in Visual C#.

The steps to create a control in Visual C# are exactly the same as the steps to create a control in Visual Basic .NET. The only difference is that you need to follow the Visual C# syntax. Therefore, in this section I will include the C#-equivalent code for the user control that was created in Chapter 12, "Creating a User Control in ASP.NET," using Visual Basic .NET.

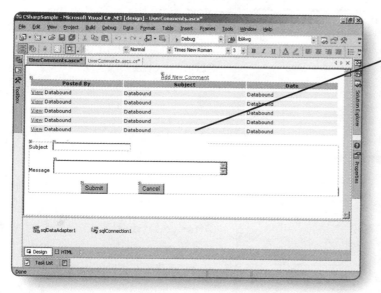

Designing a Control

The steps to design the form are exactly the same as the steps to design the form in Visual Basic .NET. You need to add the DataList, LinkButton, Panel, TextBox, Button, SqlConnection, and SqlCommand controls to the form.

The steps to add and configure these controls were discussed in Chapter 12. After you add these controls to the form, you need to write the C# code for the user control.

Writing the Code for a Control

After you design the form, switch to the Code Editor and type the C# code for the user control. The code snippets for the Load event of the form and the ItemCommand event of the DataList control are shown here.

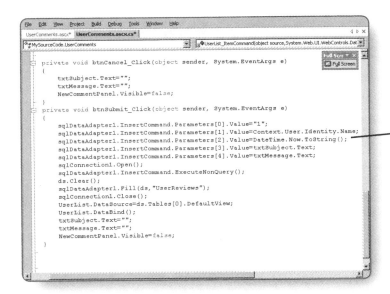

If you compare this code to the Visual Basic .NET code for the user control, you will realize that the code follows the same logic but uses the Visual C# syntax.

Next, type the code for the Click event of the Cancel button and the Click event of the Submit button.

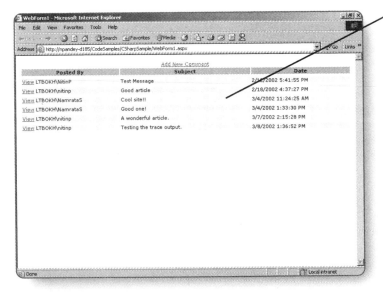

After you type the code, add the user control to a form and run the application. The output of the application will be exactly the same as the output of a Visual Basic .NET application.

C

Migrating from ASP 3.0 to ASP.NET

If you have been using ASP for a long time, you might have written some applications in ASP 3.0. You can migrate these applications to ASP.NET to benefit from the enhanced features of ASP.NET.

Although the actual steps for migrating the application will depend on the structure and the logic that you have used for your application, the basic steps to migrate an application to ASP.NET are common across all applications. This appendix will walk you through the steps to migrate an ASP 3.0 application to ASP.NET. In this appendix, you'll learn how to:

- Prepare a Web site for migration
- Migrate a site to ASP.NET

Preparing a Web Site for Migration

When you plan to migrate your Web site to ASP.NET, you should make a backup of your site and the site databases, so that if anything goes wrong during the migration of the site, you can revert to the ASP 3.0 Web site.

In this section, I will examine the steps to make a backup of a site and its databases.

Replicating the Virtual Directory

ASP 3.0 applications are deployed on IIS. Each application has a virtual directory associated with it. The virtual directory maps to a local directory on the hard disk in which the ASP 3.0 files for the application are stored.

When you decide to migrate your Web site, you should copy all of the ASP 3.0 files to a new folder and make a virtual directory for the folder, so you have two copies of the same Web site. You can then use either of the two copies to migrate your Web site to ASP.NET.

To make a new virtual directory for your Web site, copy all of the files that are in the root folder of your Web site to a new location and open Internet Services Manager. Internet Services Manager is the administration tool for IIS; it can be accessed from the administrative tools in Windows NT, 2000, and XP.

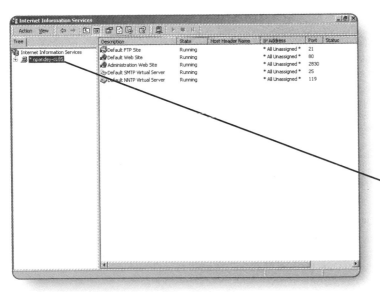

After you open Internet Services Manager, follow these steps to create a virtual directory.

1. Double-click on the name of the computer on which you want to create the virtual directory. The list of Web sites installed on the computer will appear.

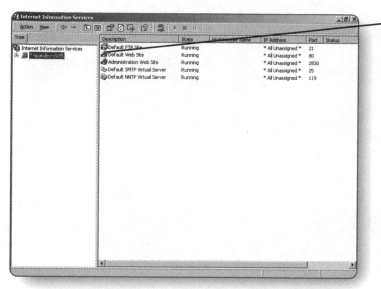

2. Right-click on the Default Web Site option. A shortcut menu will appear.

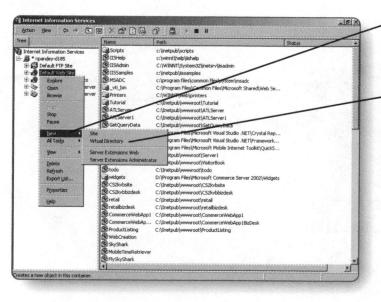

3. Move the mouse pointer to New. The New submenu will appear.

4. Click on the Virtual Directory option. The Virtual Directory Creation wizard will appear.

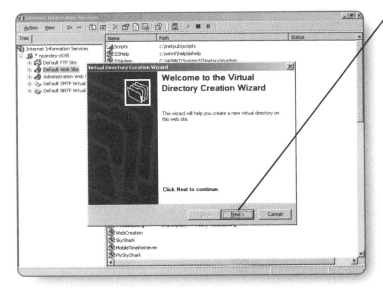

5. On the Welcome screen of the wizard, click on Next. The Virtual Directory Alias screen will appear.

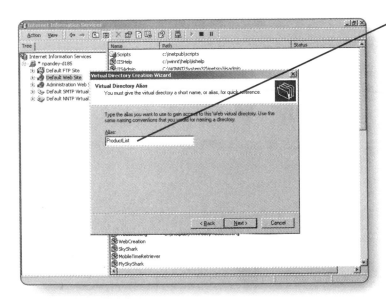

6. Type a name for the virtual directory that will be used to navigate to the application and click on Next. The Web Site Content Directory screen will appear.

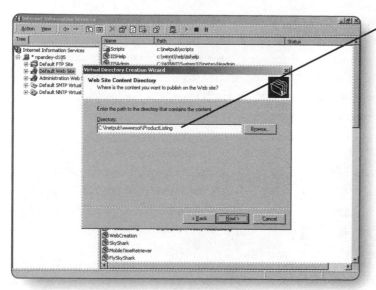

7. In the Directory text box, type the location of the directory in which the ASP pages of the application are stored and click on Next. The Access Permissions screen of the wizard will appear.

8. Retain the default access permissions for the virtual directory and click on Next. A screen will appear to notify you that you have successfully completed the wizard.

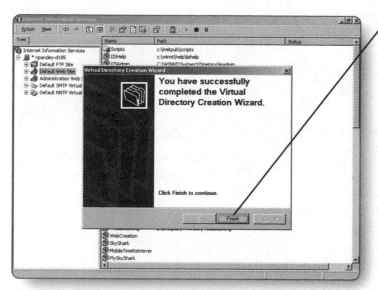

9. Click on Finish to complete the creation.

When the wizard has finished, a virtual directory with the alias name that you specified in Step 6 will be created. You can browse your Web applications by typing http://computername/aliasname, where *computername* is the name of the computer and *aliasname* is the name of the virtual directory.

Backing up the Database

Most ASP sites access databases for displaying information on the Web site. You should back up the database of your Web application to ensure that you can revert to it if the site does not migrate successfully. To back up a SQL Server database, you can use SQL Server Enterprise Manager.

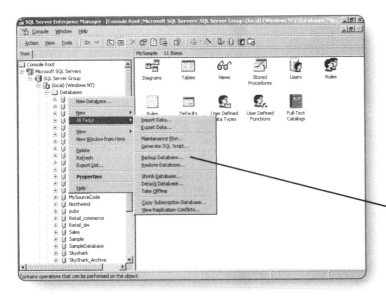

To back up your database, open SQL Server Enterprise Manager (from the Microsoft SQL Server submenu of the Programs menu) and follow these steps.

1. Right-click on the database that you want to back up. A shortcut menu will appear.

2. Move the mouse pointer to All Tasks and select the Backup Database option. The SQL Server Backup dialog box will open.

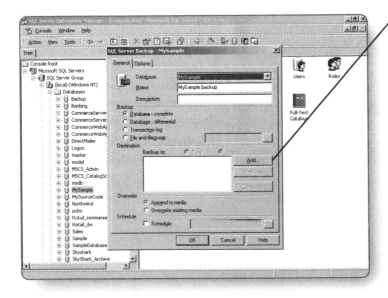

3. Click on Add to add a backup device. The Select Backup Destination dialog box will open.

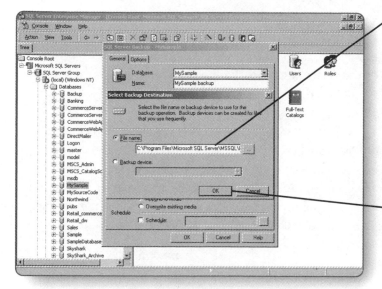

4. Append the name of the backup file in the File Name text box and click on OK to select the backup location. The Select Backup Destination dialog box will close and the location that you specified will be listed in the Backup To list in the SQL Server Backup dialog box.

5. Click on OK to back up the database. You will be notified when the backup is complete.

After you have backed up your database, you are ready to migrate your Web application to ASP.NET.

Migrating a Site to ASP.NET

ASP.NET applications can coexist with ASP 3.0 applications. Therefore, you don't need to install ASP 3.0 and ASP.NET applications on different Web servers. You can also continue to run your ASP.NET and ASP 3.0 applications on the same computer.

Migration of a Web application to ASP.NET is a three-step procedure. First, you need to change the extension of ASP 3.0 Web pages from .asp to .aspx. When you change the extension to .aspx, the page will be executed in the .NET Framework. Next, you need to change the application code to make it compatible with ASP.NET. Finally, you can optimize your application after you have migrated it. In this section, I will examine all three of these tasks.

Renaming ASP.NET Pages

You need to change the extension of ASP 3.0 pages from .asp to .aspx. To do this, navigate to the location of the ASP pages and change the file extensions the same way as you would rename any other file.

If you are using the global.asa file for managing application variables, you need to change the extension of the file from .asa to .asax. You should also note that you cannot share application and session state information, which is initialized in the global.asa or global.asax file, between ASP 3.0 and ASP.NET applications. Therefore, until the migration of your Web site is complete, you will have to rely on a third-party solution to share state data between your ASP 3.0 and ASP.NET applications.

Upgrading Application Code

After you rename your ASP files, you need to upgrade the code that is incompatible with ASP.NET. Depending on the level of incompatibility with ASP.NET, you might have to either tweak your code or completely revamp it.

In this section, I will list some of the tasks that you need to perform to upgrade your site to ASP.NET. You might need to perform one or more of these tasks, depending on the existing code in your Web application.

- **Use the @Page directive**. The @Language directive on Web pages needs to be changed to @Page. Thus, the directive <%@Language="VBScript"%> needs to be changed to <%@Page Language="VB".

- **Pass values by reference explicitly**. When calls to functions are made in Visual Basic .NET, parameters are, by default, passed by value. This is a deviation from Visual Basic 6.0, in which values are, by default, passed by reference. Therefore, if you need to pass parameters by value, use the ByRef keyword.

- **Enclose code in script blocks**. In ASP 3.0, you can use code delimiters (<% and %>) to code functions. However, in ASP.NET, all functions need to be enclosed in the <script> block. By using the <script> block, you can also increase the readability of your Web page by making it more organized.

- **Discard render functions**. In ASP.NET, you cannot use render functions to alternate ASP code with HTML tags. You need to enclose code to render text in a function and invoke the function when the text needs to be rendered.

As an example of the render function, consider the following ASP 3.0 code.

```
<B>Price:</B> $<%= g_rsProduct.Fields("cy_list_price").Value %>
<BR>
<B>ISBN:</B> <%= g_rsProduct.Fields("isbn").Value %>
<BR>
<BR><%= g_rsProduct.Fields("description") %>
```

This code is used to display the ISBN number and description of a product on a Web form; it will not work in ASP.NET. To make the code work in ASP.NET, you should write it in a function, as shown here.

```
<script language="vb" runat="server">
Sub DisplayDetails()
    Response.Write("<B>Price:</B> $" + _
        g_rsProduct.Fields("cy_list_price").Value)
    Response.Write("<BR><B>ISBN:</B> ")
    Response.Write(g_rsProduct.Fields("isbn").Value)
    Response.Write("<BR><BR>")
    Response.Write(g_rsProduct.Fields("description"))
End Sub
</script>
```

Although the preceding code snippet will work in ASP.NET, I would not recommend it because ASP.NET offers a number of data binding server controls that enable you to format and display data easily. In addition to data binding server controls, ASP.NET also includes other features to help you optimize your Web site. Some of these features are discussed in the next section.

Understanding Optimization Opportunities

There are several ways to optimize a Web application after you have migrated it from ASP 3.0 to ASP.NET. For example, you can use the Web.config file to configure your application. In this section, I will examine some of the aspects of a Web site that can be optimized after the site has been migrated to ASP.NET.

- **Use the Web.config file**. The Web.config file stores the configuration of an ASP.NET application. If you use the Web.config file to configure your application, you can implement directory-level configuration. Therefore, one subdirectory of your Web application might be using Windows authentication, and another directory might be using Forms authentication. Such a provision does not exist when you configure your application using IIS.

- **Use the concept of the code-behind file**. In ASP.NET, you can separate the application code from the HTML tags that are used to render the page. This feature not only simplifies the structure of a page, but also enables you to concentrate on the programming logic of your application.

- **Port your application to Visual Studio .NET**. When you upgrade your application, it is a good time to port it to Visual Studio .NET. All you need to do is create a blank solution and import each ASP.NET page into the solution. After you port your application to Visual Studio .NET, you will be able to perform all subsequent updates to the Web application using Visual Studio .NET.

- **Implement user controls**. You can implement the same functionality across Web pages by creating a user control and using it on multiple forms. By using the same control, you save yourself the effort of replicating the same functionality on all Web forms.

- **Implement caching**. ASP.NET includes extensive caching support. Caching frequently used data can improve the performance of your Web application considerably. See Chapter 18, "Caching in ASP.NET Applications," for more information on implementing caching in an ASP.NET application.

- **Create a multi-tiered Web application**. Although the code might be complicated, adding a data layer to your application can enable you to streamline data access in your application. Visual Basic .NET and Visual C# are object-oriented; therefore, you can implement code for database access in a class and create an object of the class on all of your Web forms that require database access.

I have listed the important aspects of optimization here. However, when you upgrade your Web application, you might be able to use other optimization features. For example, you might use datasets to reduce the load on your database server. You can continue to explore possibilities of optimization as you upgrade your Web site.

D

Online Resources for ASP.NET

There are more than 50 community and developer sites available for ASP.NET. If you consider the wide acceptance of ASP.NET, many more will undoubtedly come! Although it is not possible for me to list all of the sites, in this appendix I will provide you with a list of sites that I found useful and which provide comprehensive information about ASP.NET. You can refer to these sites while you continue learning about ASP.NET.

- **Microsoft ASP.NET (http://www.asp.net)**. This is the official Microsoft Web site for ASP.NET. Microsoft ASP.NET provides useful tutorials for getting started with ASP.NET. The Web site also includes a section that is dedicated to server controls, where you can find and download useful server controls free of cost. You can also read a number of articles by developers who have implemented ASP.NET.

- **GotDotNet (http://www.gotdotnet.com)**. GotDotNet is the Microsoft community Web site for Visual Studio .NET and ASP.NET. The site is well organized and provides excellent articles and news updates on .NET. You can browse this site frequently to get updated news on Visual Studio .NET and ASP.NET.

- **Microsoft Corporation Web Site (http://www.microsoft.com)**. The official Web site of the Microsoft Corporation provides extensive information on all Microsoft technologies. Information about the latest developments taking place at Microsoft can be found on this Web site.

- **Microsoft Developer Network (http://msdn.microsoft.com)**. The Microsoft Developer Network Web site is the best online resource for developers of Microsoft technologies. A favorite resource of developers, this site offers a section dedicated to ASP.NET (http://msdn.Microsoft.com/net/aspnet) and another section dedicated to Visual Studio .NET (http://msdn.microsoft.com/vstudio/default.asp).

- **Microsoft Newsgroups (http://msdn.microsoft.com/newsgroups)**. Microsoft Newsgroups enables you to participate in discussions with developers of ASP.NET and other Microsoft technologies. It is an excellent resource for resolving your queries with other developers.

- **Code Project (http://www.codeproject.com)**. A comprehensive resource on .NET technologies, Code Project offers articles and code downloads on .NET programming languages ranging from Visual C++ .NET to ASP.NET. The site presents an easy-to-navigate interface and is updated daily with a range of new articles and code snippets.

- **.netWire (http://www.dotnetwire.com)**. .netWire is a useful resource for news on Microsoft .NET. This site is updated daily and includes a newsletters section to help you catch up on events that you might have missed. The site includes extensive coverage of ASP.NET, ADO.NET, .NET Framework, SOAP, and Visual Studio .NET.

- **123 ASPX (http://www.123aspx.com).** 123 ASPX provides a listing of other resources on ASP.NET. The links on this site are frequently updated. Also, ASP.NET resources that have been frequently accessed on other ASP.NET Web sites are frequently updated, providing you with links to the best available resources on the Internet.

- **ASP 101 (http://www.asp101.com).** ASP 101 provides links to useful articles on ASP.NET. This site also provides links to other ASP.NET Web sites.

- **ASP Alliance (http://www.aspalliance.com).** ASP Alliance provides a number of useful articles on ASP.NET. The articles on the Web site are grouped by category, making it easy to search for a specific topic.

- **DotNetJunkies (http://www.dotnetjunkies.com).** DotNetJunkies includes the latest news and articles on ASP.NET. It also provides a useful listing of books available for programming in the .NET Framework. Apart from all this, the site provides a section on ASP.NET FAQs (*Frequently Asked Questions*), where you can resolve your queries about ASP.NET.

Index